D0546146

Revolving Culture

Revolving Culture

Notes from the Scottish Republic

Angus Calder

I.B.TAURIS PUBLISHERS
LONDON · NEW YORK

for Kate and Douglas

Published in 1994 by
I.B. Tauris & Co Ltd
45 Bloomsbury Square
London WC1A 2HY

175 Fifth Avenue
New York
NY 10010

In the United States of America
and Canada distributed by
St Martin's Press
175 Fifth Avenue
New York
NY 10010

Copyright © 1994 by Angus Calder

All rights reserved. Except for brief quotations in a review,
this book, or any part thereof, may not be reproduced in any form
without permission in writing from the publisher.

A full CIP record for this book is available from the British Library
Library of Congress Catalog card number: 94–60186
A full CIP record for this book is available from the Library of Congress

ISBN 1–85043–647–9

Typeset by Datix International Limited, Bungay, Suffolk
Printed and bound in Great Britain by
WBC Ltd, Bridgend, Mid Glamorgan

Contents

v

Contents

Four: Revolving Culture

Foreword

The two dozen pieces in this book have arisen as responses to the remarkable transformations of Scottish culture – both 'lived experience' and 'artistic production' – sensed in the 1980s. The earliest, on Grassic Gibbon, was in hand at the beginning of the decade: the latest date from days of doubt after the 1992 general election.

They represent a view of Scotland which is emphatically not 'Unionist', but isn't 'Nationalist' either: I call myself a 'socialist home ruler'. This position has involved me in many arguments with friends sceptical about the value of Scottish home rule and (more commonly, such has been the temper of the times) with colleagues and friends who take out-and-out Nationalist positions.

I am grateful to those editors, both in Edinburgh and outside Scotland, who, by pushing books in my way or accepting my own suggestions, have aided and abetted my Scottish obsessions. Much of this book first appeared in *Cencrastus*, a magazine founded by Edinburgh University students after the 1979 referendum débâcle, which in approaching 50 issues since has published articles on almost every aspect of Scottish culture as well as creative work by almost all the best Scottish writers. Among those involved in its successive editorial *équipes*, I particularly thank Cairns Craig, Sheila Lodge, Geoff Parker and the current team of Raymond J. Ross and Tom Nairn. The *London Review of Books* has also been generous with stimulus and forbearance: my thanks to Karl Miller, Mary Kay Willmers and Susannah Clapp. *Scotland on Sunday* outsells all its broadsheet rivals north of the Border, and I am very grateful to Alan Taylor for my frequent appearances in its review pages. Relations between editors and contributors extend to cutting, subbing and (sometimes) pained responses to both. In some cases here I have restored matter dropped (I vainly presume) for reasons of length. In others I have tacitly accepted sensible editorial action, and I have refrained, in these and other cases, from updating my judgements. One cannot, as the man said, jump in the same river twice.

I am also grateful for permission to reprint pieces which first appeared in *Chapman* ('Morganmania'); *Landfall*, New Zealand ('Jackie Kay's *Adoption Papers*') and *Circa*, Belfast ('Art for a New Scotland'). 'Scott and Goethe' began life as a paper requested by Douglas Gifford for a Strathclyde University conference; 'Burns, Scott and the French Revolution' was commissioned by Ian MacDougall as part of Midlothian's recognition of that notable Parisian bicentenary. 'A Mania for Self-Reliance' first appeared in *The Uses of Fiction*, a festschrift for Arnold Kettle edited by Graham Martin and Douglas Jefferson (Open University Press, 1982). The piece on Alasdair Gray's *Lanark* was originally an address given in presentation to the novel's author of the last Frederick Niven Award for Scottish Fiction in 1984; 'Workers' Culture – Popular Culture' was devised at Douglas Allen's invitation as a keynote address to the 1990 conference of the Scottish Labour History Society: and 'Thomas Campbell's Liberalism' as a paper for a Shelley bicentenary conference on *Romantic Discourses* hosted by Horst Höhne for the University of Rostock in 1992. In that year also my friend John Pilgrim asked me to rework a paper on Samuel Smiles for the excellent Anarchist quarterly, *Raven*.

I anticipate the objection that certain very important figures are not specifically discussed at length in these pages. I have two replies. One is that it is part of my general argument that Scottish culture has been a communal creation, not just a procession of one-off Great Men; from which it follows that the neglected Campbell and misunderstood Smiles are worth consideration, while Carlyle is securely in the hands of many other scholars. My second reply is that I have published on Scottish culture elsewhere: two short books on Byron; an essay on MacDiarmid's enormous effect on my life in *Chapman*'s centenary issue; one on MacCaig for an Edinburgh University Press book about the poet edited by Joy Hendry and Raymond Ross; an introduction to Hamish Henderson's collected essays, *Alias McAlias* (Polygon, 1992); and teaching material for the Open University on

David Lindsay, Alexander Montgomerie, James Boswell and Sorley MacLean. The piece on Spark included here is a spin-off from work on A319, *Literature and the Modern World*.

A great source of pride and pleasure over the whole period of this book's gestation has been my involvement in successive Open University courses on the Enlightenment (A204 and A206). These course teams have supplied one arena at least in England where my obsession with Scottish culture has not seemed egregious. I am very grateful for permission to include, at this book's outset, a modified version of an introduction to eighteenth-century Scotland written for A206.

I could list dozens of people whose friendship, conversation and ideas have markedly affected the contents of this book. But, not to be invidious, I will give my final very warm thanks to my editor, Emma Sinclair-Webb of I. B. Tauris, whose critical enthusiasm has brought *Revolving Culture* to life.

1

Introductory: Culture, Republic and Carnival

All culture derives from place. It may seem odd to state this at a Post-Modernist moment when satellites beam upon Bengali peasants the fictionalised lifestyle of affluent America and entrance a Serbian taxi driver – this actual example comes from the Dublin press – with the spectacle of Irish Football: the fastest, most beautiful sport, he says, on earth. (He may well be right: I shall come back to this.)

But however cosmopolitan an Erasmian scholar or Modernist artist may have tried to be, no one has ever lived everywhere. Most people even now pass most, if not all, of their lives in one region, if not one village – in one nation, if not one city. When English labourers trudging across the plain of their toil first saw York Minster towering, shimmering, vaster in her and his mind than any twentieth-century skyscraper has been for us, what the building was presumably intended to impress was a notion of Universal Catholic Church. What their descendants eventually made of it was 'Yorkshire' and 'England', cultural terms denoting difference.

Hugh MacDiarmid caused some supporters much pain when he asserted (I once heard him do this) that folk-songs were 'the ignorant droolings of swinish shepherds'. In relation to the extraordinary Scottish tradition of song, which through country and western music is one of the most potent influences on satellite culture, MacDiarmid was manifestly perverse. But I felt, and feel, that I know what he meant. Whatever the virtues (and we must always concede these) of the basic cultures of more or less isolated human groups, changing very little over centuries, complexity and the free play of mind are not among them. 'Authenticity' is a word to be howled down whenever used. We have seen what it means in practice when

1

wielded by Nazis or Afrikaner nationalists. Joyce, perhaps the greatest of all twentieth-century writers, celebrated after his fashion by MacDiarmid in the latter's longest poem, wondrously opposed the anarchically syncretic, lusciously unstable forms and processes of real language to the petty but dangerous – and closely allied – obsessions of grammarians and racist nationalists. ('Everyone should learn to write good English' means 'you tinks and keelies, you Paddies, Taffs and Jocks, you Nigs and Pakis, into line there!')

'Identity' is a less execrable word – so Protean that no Menelaus can bind it. It has acceptable, meaningful usages as well as those which make it, after 'Purity' the sixth Horseperson of the Apocalypse. My display of cultural referents so far will have suggested to you that I seek to express an 'identity' involved in Western cultural tradition, and suppose that you do too. We both know what oppressions and badness massifications of 'Western identities' have led to. On the other hand, we have to be something, and can hardly step entirely out of the particular stream which has borne us. And C. M. Grieve, when he invented the identity of 'MacDiarmid', was not attempting to make himself more 'authentic' or 'pure' – he was seeking a new kind of Scot in a new Scotland, in which Shuggie the Borderer merged with the Gaelic tradition. The search for 'identity' is valid, in persons and nations, I am suggesting, so long as we realise it's something made and examined, not 'rediscovered' and thereafter granite, inert, or iron, bladed.

I write this near Sligo, in the 'Yeats country', just after watching Telefis Eireann's sports roundup. I am inclined to agree with the Serbian taxi driver who gushed forth his rapture to an Irish journalist while taking him to belepered Belgrade. The only sport more beautiful, if skill at speed is what you mean by beauty, than Irish-rules football, is perhaps hurling, where stick and foot, hand and leap coordinate in ballet beyond Diaghilev because it cannot be choreographed. But a glance at the gaze of C. L. R. James, from the cover of his book on the table beside me, reminds me that nothing, inside or outside sport, has ever been more beautiful to witness than Sobers driving the ball on the up or to see Michael Holding glide at sprinter's pace to the wickets to hurl a ball at a hundred miles an hour. As James often told us, Barbados, an island with a population less than that of one medium-sized English or Indian city, has produced at least a dozen grand masters in a sport which packs stadia in Bombay or Calcutta and is somehow held to represent the authentic soul of the yeoman Englishman.

Revolving James and Yeats together is fascinating and brings me back to my opening assertion: 'All culture derives from place.' And I do not mean by this the truism that all culture happens wherever it happens to happen.

To visit Florence is to see at once how the productions of Dante and Machiavelli, Brunelleschi and Masaccio originate not from discrete, 'relatively autonomous' traditions, but simply from the same pattern of streets within a fertile landscape, the *contado*. The invention of perspective and the elaboration of ideals of civic, republican humanism derived from the street life vividly evoked in the fourteenth-century frescoes of Andrea da Firenze, as clearly as Sobers' batsmanship (James will tell you), the play of a boy from a poor home beginning with a piece of box or a coconut branch applied to a succession of sour oranges, was inspired by the coexistence in Barbados of the mighty 'three Ws'.

Why Florence, of all places? That is much harder to answer than questions about Bajun cricket (or, indeed, about Scottish cricket, a fairly large subject on which I have touched elsewhere). But cultural forms and practices, and ideas within and about culture, deriving from Florence, have gone everywhere with that city's mark on them. Just so the peculiar understanding of the predicaments of modern urban humanity which we derive from Gogol and Dostoevsky cannot be separated from the long straight streets and 'white nights' of St Petersburg; and the 'universal' aptness of Lorca's piercingly beautiful protest is fully understood only when, in Granada, we see a city whose bourgeois Fathers still refuse to acknowledge the gay spokesman for gypsy energies and for the repressed women of town and country. (Incredibly, in 1992 there was no plaque or other token to commemorate Lorca in the hotel made out of the house where friends last sheltered him before the Falangists caught and shot him.)

You might imagine that far from the Sligo he knew as a child, Yeats invented a fantasised north-western Ireland to suit, first, paying customers for Celtic Twilight, then, his own brand of élitist nationalism: that his child stolen by the faeries in Glencar Lake, his Innisfree isle in Lough Gill and his 'girls in silk kimonos, both beautiful, one a gazelle' remembered in Lissadell's light of evening – Eva Gore-Booth and Con Markiewicz – are as fictive as his admitted invention, Red Hanrahan: that is, he 'romanticised' them and with them his vision of 'indomitable' Irish peasantry and a unified Irish national culture. Post-structuralist criticism has been very leery, so to speak, of John O'Leary:

> Romantic Ireland's dead and gone,
> It's with O'Leary in the grave.

But to state the irrefutable truth that language and ideology exist together in their own system, arbitrary in relation to the 'real', which is itself a fabricated category, is to miss the equally important truth that if anything at all exists, Sligo does. So does Irish football. And it was not mere fantasy (if anything at all isn't) which led some of Yeats' nationalist contemporaries to promote Gaelic sports in pursuit of an Irish ideal of an ideal Ireland. Lissadell House is remarkably ugly, a point which Yeats' great poem disguises by speaking of light through its 'great windows'. But Con Markiewicz, beautiful or not, did struggle and suffer heroically for something like the values which Irish football was taken to represent.

Yeats vehemently rejected 'popular culture' in favour of a restored agrarian order – when Constance turned to the urban Irish, he wrote of 'Blind and the leader of the blind,/Drinking the foul ditch where they lie'. But when he also avowed that Synge and himself saw all culture as springing 'Antaeus-like' from 'the soil', he offered, without wishing to, a variant of a point not yet made by C. L. R. James.

All culture derives from place. All culture derives from the people.

Again, this is not a truism: 'Without people there is no culture.' I mean that the flagrant attempts of post-Restoration landed proprietors and nineteenth-centry bourgeois to rip culture away from 'the people' ('popular classes', 'swinish multitude', etc.), to use it as a shield against the people, or more benevolently, forsooth, to *teach* it to the people through repressive institutions such as British state schools, must now be exposed as the shifts and lies which Tolstoy knew them to be when he strove to put his incredible skills under service to the peasantry.

The mendacious separation of 'high' from 'popular' culture derives from three schisms in European society. First, between rulers and ruled. This created 'court' cultures in centres of strength and opulence. (In Florence, momentously, such physical separation did not obtain.) Second, there was the divide between literate and illiterate, expressed in the creation of universities where 'learned' men read till their spectacles become useless. ('Lord what would they say/Did their Catullus walk that way?') Third, in genealogical succession, via intermarriage of Mac Power and Ni Learning, the separation of intellectuals and masses.

Yet everything which the 'high' professed to value came from the 'popular' ... Start (as the 'high' have always tended to do) with Homer.

No one knows, nor can more than guess, about the processes which created the Homeric epics. E. S. Sharratt in a recent inspired speculation has suggested that the poems themselves are archaeologically stratified like the remaining artefacts and other material evidence to which we can relate them, and that the oral sources from which they must have derived (the Greeks having had no writing) concentrated attention on periods of crisis when ruling groups had sought to legitimise their rule.[1] The poems are, of course, about 'kings'. But what kings! As fastidious eighteenth-century taste noted with a shudder, these kings might be found herding sheep. Their 'noble' companions might be swineherds. Their daughters could act as washerwomen.

Recycled, revolved, through literate Athenian democracy and Virgil's Rome, the 'classics' educated European rulers. Lo and behold – in one of the best plays of the greatest dramatist acknowledged by the courts of Elizabeth and James, a Queen with a 'gypsy's lust' of which Lorca would have approved 'hops twenty paces down the public street', bewitches and ruins the master of Imperial Rome. Just as the Bible was always a dangerous text for rulers, so their Homer, and then their Shakespeare, were full of hazard.

In February 1959, C. L. R. James published a wonderful piece about 'Carnival' in the Trinidad *Nation* (this was before independent Trinidad was recognised as a 'nation'). Pointing to the hard but joyous labour which went into Carnival, James observed:

We have the extraordinary spectacle of entertainment, sport, free competition, and the practice of the arts to one degree or another, being carried on by a populace; in fact by all sections of the population, without any educational instruction, without any encouragement or stimulus by philosophically minded persons or persons who are interested in the arts as such. You have colour, line, individual and mass representation, elementary drama, music, popular ballads, such a mass of creative activity as staggers the observer who knows how hard educators work to try to inculcate these things.[2]

As James implies, such spontaneous dedication is what 'national' rulers all over the world *claim* they *want*. Into the courts of kings came Shakespeare and Lope and Molière with trophies from the equivalent of Carnival; into Enlightened Edinburgh Burns bore what the moderate literati and the hard-drinking lawyers saw they needed to cope with their sense of relationship with the unruly, singing city they lived in. The distance Burns had to cross was much less than Molière's, because Edinburgh, like Renaissance Florence, was republican, in spirit though not in form.

Another point about Carnival: West Indian cultures are, famously, mongrel. African, European, East Indian and, residually, native American elements combine yet retain distinct presence. Because most, though far from all, participants have been pinko-grey in pigmentation, the mongrel character of Scottish culture is less obvious to the naked eye. Yet when the kingdom of Scotland was established in the first millennium of the Christian era, there were four main linguistic groupings. Over this ground were laid later Norse and Anglo-Norman populations. Strong influences from France and The Netherlands affected language and mentality in the 'Early Modern' period. Heavy immigration from Ireland in the nineteenth century transformed what had been a monolithically Protestant lowland core. Among recent immigrant groups, Jewish, Italian and Asian communities have significantly affected both 'lived' culture and artistic production in recent Carnivalesque manifestations.

Thom Gunn has appended to his powerful sequence *The Man with Night Sweats*, about Californian friends dying of AIDS, a celebration of a street fair, *At the Barriers* in San Francisco in 1988. He expresses a vital aspect of Carnival; it permits the maximum expression of difference, yet dissolves differences into community:

6

Introductory: Culture, Republic and Carnival

We enter the alley's door
to the party, the music, the drift of laughter and conversation,
we mingle with the jeunesse dorée, we enter the Fair's embrace
of men attracted by men and of women attracted by women,
all together, though there are mixed couples too, all are welcome,
for it is an open place, once you have found the way in, like the field
where the poet and lover are active, an Arcady of tarmac;
but there must be complication and conflict, humans cannot get by
    without them,
black boots on the black street making a show, a play,
a play of strength, a show of power put on to be disarmed
through the lingering dénouement of an improvised masque
in which aggressiveness reveals its true face as love,
its body as love at play . . .

Each of us a sum of specifics, each an Arcadian
drawing attention to our difference, our queerness, our shared
    characteristics,
as if this were an Italian-American street fair, or Hispanic, or Irish,
but we include the several races and nations, we include the
    temperaments,
the professions, the trades and arts, some of us alcoholic bums,
our diverse loves subsumed within the general amity,
and 'returning to roots of first feeling'
we play, at the barriers, the Masque of Difference and Likeness.[3]

*

My subtitle for this book is '*from the* Scottish Republic', not '*towards
a* Scottish Republic' because it embodies my sense of two truths, one
learned through books, paintings and music, the other experienced,
as I thought, directly.

Scotland as a place has changed more than some people allow
since the days when Calgacus defied the Roman legions. Not only
have cities been built and rebuilt, bogs drained, roads blasted and
landscapes made and remade. But my sense of Scotland as an
abidingly distinctive place is reinforced at this moment by writing
under Ben Bulben. Genetically close (intermixed), culturally aligned,
as Scots and Irish are, difference persists. It cannot be separated from

geography: the stark Scottish mountains, the lush Irish green. Even Castle Rock in the centre of Edinburgh is craggier than Ben Bulben, where farmland climbs amazingly high. The land, as Grassic Gibbon insists at the end of his great *Quair*, endures.

Creeds, he likewise suggests, change like passing clouds. Catholic clannit Scotland gave way to the Land of Knox, which became Irn Bru country, the domain of dominantly heavy industry attuned to serving world-wide Empire. Scots, till 1745, were peculiarly addicted to kings, especially to monarchs homerically roaming the lanes as gaberlunzie men, so one song said, plotting to kill their wives' lovers, as another song suggested, or fleeing in disguise at the mercy of retainers and subjects, as happened in what we can call fact. This sat badly with the Presbyterian insistence that God's kingdom was paramount and the elders and ministers of the Kirk would know God and His ways better than fusionless men of high degree. The Scottish Enlightenment, on a practical level, reconciled this contradiction.

Mid- and late-eighteenth-century Edinburgh, even the Edinburgh of Walter Scott's heyday, functioned on republican terms. This will be emphasised several times in this book. Having no Parliament since 1707, Edinburgh had lost the periodical intrusions of regal pomp and state which the institution had represented. No ruling king visited Scotland between James VII of Scotland and II of England and George IV. In the city of Hume, Adam Smith and Ramsay literati dazzled spellbound lairds with wonderful ideas. The city of Scott and the *Edinburgh Review* dictated taste to England and the continent (a phenomenon already noted by Voltaire, no less, decades before). The ethos of civic humanism, in a genealogy including ancient Athens and Renaissance Florence, marched with a patriotic spirit of practical improvement. I will come clean and say that the Scotland of those early years of Union seems to me to have had much more real 'independence' than our 'Scotland in Europe' nationalists dream of demanding today. Who needs a Parliament when one has Hume and Scott? 'Identity' was a painful problem for these men. We look at what, in the place where they were, they made out of the pain, and we marvel.

Came the railway. Came the ascendancy of M'Choakumchild liberalism which found its prime expression in the perversion, through miniature Bastilles which beat Scots and Gaelic out of bairns, of the Knoxian educational tradition. Came Balmoralism, the ideology which sustained anglicised landowners and English interlopers as they shot grouse and hunted deer over the rugged lands so loved by Queen Victoria: the constitution of the Faithful Highland Gillie as ideal Scot. Came Clydesidism, the boast of prideful men, owners and workers alike, that the burly male Scot made best whatever heavy objects the world might require for large-scale slaughter: for example, battleships. Came all kinds of ideological deformities from which MacDiarmid and Gibbon strove to rescue their compatriots.

Came, in 1947, the Edinburgh Festival, initially an offspring of Balmoralism. ('*What* a pretty city! Do you think these nice people would mind if we bought Bruno Walter here? Oh, Tyrone, *what* a clever place to find for that *quaint* Scots play.') Came, partly forged in opposition to the EIF's cultural élitism, when Norman Buchan set up his People's Festival, the folk-song revival. And came, as the disintegration of Empire deprived Scots of the basis of their British identity, the first real electoral impact – ever – of Scottish Nationalism, in the late 1960s.

Note the moment: the end of Empire coincided with the notorious permissiveness of the Beatles epoch. Hence the early stirrings of MacDiarmidism, as the new phase of Scottish ideology might be called, coincided with restless and often reckless experiment: a good thing, in my humble opinion. It meant that the erratic drives of political nationalism, expressed through the Scottish National Party with its bewildering array of self-appointed leaders – naïve idealists, hairy racist curmudgeons, smart young men on the make and, to be fair, dedicated and principled constitutional reformers – were contained within a broader, bubbling stream of cultural self-assertion. The energies of Carnival were released. And the second Scottish republic arrived. Scots turned their backs on London, argued, and entertained each other.

The treaty of 1707 had left Scotland with certain national institutions intact. Its Established Kirk plumed itself with the notion that its annual General Assembly represented a kind of vestigial Scottish Parliament. As the drive towards Scottish autonomy developed, the Kirk, with its falling membership and genuine concern for the state of a disindustrialising society, seemed to lose faith progressively in the Union. Much of the best arguing in the new Scottish republic came from clergymen. The law, whereby Scottish specialists were secured by difference from English competition in their own sphere, provided less than might have been expected. Education, similarly safeguarded in 1707, progressively saw that its interests lay in maintaining difference and even increasing it – academics and teachers deployed professional eloquence on behalf of home rule.

Among institutions which the framers of Union could not have imagined, the media inevitably played an enormous role. Good journalists foreswore the well-beaten path to Fleet Street and stayed at home to fight. Locally produced TV and radio naturally reflected the rising dissatisfaction with Union among those whose ears and eyes they had to drag from London-based rivals. *Good Morning Scotland* and its chat-show sequels on BBC Radio became one forum in which the republicans talked to each other.

But overarching and pressing on all politicians, professionals and programme-makers was MacDiarmidism in the arts. MacDiarmid, *qua* Grieve, seems to have known little about music, high or low: he favoured ambitious composers whose works found little audience. Hence his admitted 'influence' on some of a brilliant generation of young avant-gardists (which includes Edward McGuire, William Sweeney and James Macmillan) is hardly surprising. But these people have also been affected by the unrepentant MacDiarmidism of Hamish Henderson. Whatever Grieve said about folk-song, Henderson was going to make it serve MacDiarmidian purposes if he possibly could, and the brilliantly varied and pungent results of the folk revival which Henderson above all led were often utterly counter to rural idiocy or inert sentimentalism. This had effects in another direction: by the 1980s Scotland was the home of vastly popular rock bands, whose output, influenced by 'folk' difference (this was extreme in the cases of Run Rig and Capercaillie which sang in Gaelic) saturated airwaves with republican accents.

The Gaelic revival was not exceptional, in a Europe where Basques and Sardinians were asserting their linguistic peculiarity and in an island where the Welsh language made great political gains. But the stature of Sorley MacLean, the Gaelic poet, MacDiarmid's friend, became quite extraordinary, as Lowlanders, taking note of his international fame, honoured the major living exponent of a dying tongue which they had often been brought up to despise.

10

Again, Russian and Romanian poets used to reading in football stadiums would not have been awed by the audiences collected for public readings of verse in Scotland. By British standards, though, they could be remarkable, as was the atmosphere of entertainment (Carnival) which they roused. A generation of immense poets moved past the landmarks of senectude – 60, 70, 75, 80 – saluted by packed laughing halls: MacLean, MacCaig, Morgan, Henderson, Crichton Smith. The musicians were there to pay tribute, as were the lexicographers who had completed the compendious *Scottish National Dictionary*, and the younger writers among whom Liz Lochhead, a great all-round entertainer, represented one new face of republican Scottish woman: liberated, candid and very funny.

Lochhead also created notable plays. John McGrath's 7:84 Scotland from the early 1970s had pioneered an attitude to drama which became widespread. Touring community halls or storming big proscenium arch stages, travelling theatre companies mixed pantomime and politics, music and sentiment, laughter and rage. A sublimation (as it were) of this was seen in John Byrne's television saga *Tutti Frutti*, about the progress of an ageing rock band round Scotland. This danced away from TV naturalism towards Carnival. Still closer to Carnival was the effect of Gerry Mulgrew's Communicado Theatre Company, exploiting with small resources music, movement and language to tell great stories. You couldn't exactly explain how it was political, in the republican spirit, yet it was.

I write at the end of this book about two young artists, Ken Currie and Keith McIntyre, whose work and attitudes epitomised what was going on. It would be tedious to inventory all the Carnivalesque activities of the 1980s which Scots improvised to defy the Thatcherite threat to their country: let me just mention the West of Scotland novelists – McIlvanney, Gray, Kelman and others, whose biting and witty work dealt with the grimness of daily life which Carnival subsumes but cannot by itself remedy.

Between 1974 and 1990 Scotland got into five World Cup finals. Each time, the team exited after the first round. This was nevertheless an amazing achievement for a small country: beyond those of such noted nations as France. Likewise, with a tenth of the populations of England or France, the Scottish Rugby team twice (1983, 1990) accomplished Grand Slams in the Five Nations

11

championship, beating teams from both as well as from Wales and Ireland.

I remember running into Joyce McMillan in Bennet's Bar, Edinburgh, not long after the 1980s ended. She is a well-known, acutely penetrating theatre critic, columnist and constitutional reformer. The immediate company consisted of politicians who had been debating before students at Napier College. Labour, Nat and Tory quaffed together. But I said to Joyce, 'I'm starting to feel nostalgic for the eighties already.' She agreed. We felt that the Carnival was ending.

At that point victory seemed a racing certainty. By 1987, unable to cope with Carnivalesque tactical voting, the Tories, who alone among Scottish parties opposed the re-establishment of a Scottish Parliament, had been reduced to 10 out of 72 Westminster seats. One more heave . . . But it didn't happen. In 1992 they got all of 11, and the expected 'hung Parliament' which would have ensured a Scottish assembly on lines already devised by the prospective coalition partners, Labour and Liberal Democrats, through the Scottish Constitutional Convention, did not materialise. John Major, bucking the opinion polls, got his majority.

Well, James couldn't pull off his West Indian Federation. Nor was the Ireland of Eamon de Valera exactly what Yeats had had in mind. Staying in Ireland, watching TV and buying newspapers, I am aware of two somewhat contradictory feelings. One is that the life of this patchily thriving country, notably efficient and friendly compared to most of the United Kingdom, is very quiet after the rages and tempests of 1980s Scotland. The other is that Yeats, James and those of us who still want Scottish independence, are vindicated in faith and pride in small nations. This is a decent republic, where politics, however inept and at times corrupt, are conducted in a republican spirit of rational debate, and issues affecting everyday life come under closely detailed journalistic scrutiny.

As between a decaying imperial state lumbered with anachronistic institutions, infested with byzantine class distinctions and still possessed with delusions of grandeur, and a small country which prides itself on its wholesome agricultural produce and its wicked writers, what person in their senses would choose the former? 'Scotland small,' I hear MacDiarmid growling, 'Our infinite Scotland small?'

Well, yes, the land itself is bigger than St Lucia, beside which Trinidad bulks like Texas. See Derek Walcott? See him? See Homer? . . .

Lissadell, July 1993
Edinburgh, September 1993

One

The Scottish Republic

2

Scotland in the Eighteenth Century

In the eighteenth century, as now, the term 'Scotland' denoted a very large proportion of the land of the north-west European archipelago. Its borders, unchanged since the late fifteenth century, lay exactly where they do today. As with Sweden and Norway (and it is often helpful to compare Scotland with Scandinavian countries) there was a 'far north' of difficult terrain, and population was quite small relative to geographical area.

How did a country which apparently stood on the periphery of European culture contribute so much to Europe's Enlightenment (and to the diffusion of it to America)? Hume was a key figure in the philosophical awakening of the period. His profound influence was acknowledged widely and most gracefully in this compliment of Kant's: 'It was David Hume's remark that . . . interrupted my dogmatic slumber and gave a completely different direction to my enquiries in the field of speculative philosophy.' Burns was not the first Scottish poet of the century to gain international fame. Robert Adam's Neo-Classical architecture left an enduring mark on the surface of Britain. An Edinburgh lawyer, Boswell, wrote a biography of his friend, Johnson, on an unprecedented scale, using 'novel' methods in both senses of that word. The pioneering excellence of medical studies at Edinburgh University was represented, for instance, by James Lind's pioneering *Treatise of the Scurvy* (1753) and by the vast international success of William Buchan's *Domestic Medicine* (1769). To Scotland in an earlier century can be traced the origins of freemasonry, that favourite cult among 'enlightened' men, integral to Mozart's *Magic Flute*. Historians of ideas find in eighteenth-century Scotland the onset of modern approaches to 'economics', 'social science' and 'history'.

In 1755, Scotland produced one of the very earliest examples of the scientific 'census'. Dr Alexander Webster computed the country's population at rather over 1 265 000. The grander all-British census of 1801 gave a figure of 1 608 000. Such an expansion is wholly plausible: the rise of population all over Europe was a feature of the period, with important economic and social consequences. In Scotland's case, it accompanied a significant shift in north–south balance.

In 1755 just over half the people had lived north of a line from the Firth of Tay to the Firth of Clyde: by 1820 this proportion had dropped to two-fifths, and almost half the Scots now occupied the central belt where only twenty-seven per cent had lived before. Edinburgh, Glasgow, and their satellite towns and villages had swollen. The population of Glasgow, soaring from 31 700 to 83 700, had rapidly outstripped that of Edinburgh (81 600 in 1801).[1]

Such figures explain why we talk about an 'industrial revolution', since Glasgow was a centre of expanding industries, especially in textiles.

In his *Annals of the Parish* (1821), the novelist John Galt presented the history of a village in south-west Scotland over the half century following 1760, through the eyes of its Church of Scotland minister. The book remains an ideal introduction to the material and social life of that period. At the end of it, the old man speaks of 'the great spread that has been in our national prosperity'. Commerce and industry, within one lifetime, had transformed a country which traditionally regarded itself, and had been regarded by natives of others, as 'poor'. Along with pride in advancing prosperity – seen as a result of native enterprise and hard work – came a sense of loss: distinctively Scottish ways, it seemed, were being dissolved into the international culture of commerce and Enlightenment. No one felt this so clearly as Walter Scott, author of the epoch-making best-seller *Waverley* (1814), set in the period of the 1745 rebellion. The vision of Scottish history projected by Scott in his Waverley novels was an astonishing achievement, based on saturation in relevant sources. But it had the effect of presenting 1745 as a watershed. Before it, there was Old Scotland, an arena of endemic violence, poverty, religious bigotry and fatalistic attachment to doomed causes. After it, a country of 'enlightened' thought, 'improved' agriculture, peace and general thriving. This over-simplification obscures the deep roots of 'enlightenment' and 'improvement' in Scottish culture.

Scotland in the fifteenth century had been a much more peaceful place than England, France or Italy. It had produced magnificent poets and internationally acclaimed philosophers. Two developments, within a few generations, obscured the effulgence of this 'Scottish Renaissance'.

Scotland became a factor in the rivalry between England and France, with phases of English and French occupation of the Scottish Lowlands. The Scottish Reformation of 1559 emerged under English protection, and its proponents adopted the English translation of the Bible. The young King James VI developed, nevertheless, a promising court culture of music, architecture and Scots poetry. But in 1603 he inherited the crown of England. His departure south with his courtiers robbed Edinburgh of cultural eminence. For over half a century, from the late 1630s, religious disputation inspired Lowland Scottish life at every level.

By 1689, it was, up to a point, settled: the defeat of James VII of Scotland and II of England at the hands of William of Orange, his daughter's husband, was the prelude to the establishment of a Presbyterian Church of Scotland, without bishops. But Episcopalians remained disaffected, and 'Jacobite' insurgency on behalf of the exiled King's son, 'James VIII', 'the Old Pretender', continued inter-mittently for more than half a century, till the 'Young Pretender', Charles Edward Stewart, leading a largely Highland army, was defeated at Culloden in 1746.

Meanwhile, by the Treaty of Union with England in 1707, Scotland lost its own ancient parliament in return for the right to send MPs to Westminster. In the 1690s, Scottish leaders had tried to bring their nation into the thriving world of 'commercial revolution'. England now led Europe in commerce; England had colonies: Scotland should have a colony. The Scottish attempt to found a trading colony on the isthmus of Panama, open to both Atlantic and Pacific commerce, wasn't daft but it didn't work. An enormous proportion of the nation's liquid capital was destroyed in the Darien colony's failure. English parliamentarians wanted to ensure that when childless Queen Anne, last of the Stewarts, died, her crown passed to the House of Hanover, not to the Catholic 'pretender' in exile, and wished to bind

Scotland to such a settlement. Prudence persuaded Scots leaders to enter Union, which at least gave their people licit access for the first time to England's possessions and trading posts overseas.

Sentiment ensured that few of the many Scots who backed the abortive Jacobite rebellion of 1715 suffered for their commitment. But by 1745, advantages from Union seemed plain to many more. Charles Edward led a minority of Gaelic-speaking Highlanders (the great Campbell clan, among others, fought against him), allied with disaffected Episcopalian elements in the Lowlands. English-speaking, Presbyterian Scotland triumphed at Culloden in 1746, though it was convenient to attribute the brutalities against Gaels which followed to the 'English' leadership of the Hanoverian army. The outcome was richly noted by Johnson and Boswell on their tour of the Highlands in 1773.

The feudal powers of clan chiefs were taken away. Tartan and weapons were (ineffectually) forbidden to Gaels unless they served in the king's Highland regiments. For a time, many clan chiefs tried to harmonise their traditional position as fathers of their clans, conceived as families, with the need to make money. Finding a cash crop in kelp (seaweed yielding potash, used in bleaching cloth), they resisted for some decades the drive to emigrate among their followers – who were often spurred to do so by raised rents. Meanwhile, many Highlanders washed up in the cotton mills of Glasgow or the richly cultivated fields of Lothian rather than the wastes of Canada.

However, going to Canada might be no bad thing. A Scot with views in that direction, Samuel Veitch, had revived, immediately after the 1707 union, the term '*British* Empire' first used by a Welshman in the sixteenth century, and for the same reason – it meant that Celts were in on the act. England's richest colony was Jamaica: Scots soon supplied a disproportionate number of planters in, and governors of, that prime sugar-producing island. Glasgow rose to greatness by trading in Virginian tobacco. From the 1720s, Scots secured a remarkable quantity of patronage at the disposal of the East Indian Company. Money from trade in India, together with fortunes amassed by soldiers in the EIC service, helped to transform the physical appearance of Scotland, with stately homes and 'improved' fields. Scots – Highlanders – dominated the fur trade of Canada after Wolfe's conquest and made an indelible mark on its vast area.

After 1707, Scotland remained an independent country, as much as Denmark, say, is independent in the present European Community. In return for delivering Scottish votes at Westminster, the managers of the country and their allies were allowed a free hand. Plenty of Scots sat for English parliamentary seats: no Englishman became a Scottish MP. Many Scots, including the Murray who became Lord Mansfield, did well as lawyers in England. But Scotland retained its own law, closer to continental models than to the English one. First the Campbell Dukes of Argyll, then from the 1700s, Henry Dundas, a Lothian lawyer of lairdly stock, 'managed' Scotland masterfully. Though Dundas was nicknamed 'King Harry the Ninth' he was more like the president-for-life of a comfortably corrupt republic: first among equals with his fellow Edinburgh lawyers; a commoner (till he got a peerage himself as Viscount Melville) with no need to defer to the progressive aristocrats who went along with his way of doing things. It was a great convenience to him that the electoral base in Scotland – some 3000 – was even smaller and more open to bribery than in most parts of England.

Scottish society gravitated towards the middle. Great hereditary landowners – Campbells in the Highlands, Gordons in the north-east, Scotts in the Borders, for instance – retained enormous territorial influence buttressed by the 'clannishness' which characterised Lowland as well as Highland society. But in return for loyalty, they often gave it, furthering the 'improvement' of their domains and assisting the careers of fellow countrymen.

In Edinburgh, where parliament still served as a law court, landed magnates had less to do with setting the social tone than did the legal profession. The Lords of Session, judges who took non-hereditary titles on appointment, formed Scotland's supreme court in criminal causes. Fourteen in number, they were presided over in the Court of Session by a fifteenth, the Lord President. These were men of learning, and some of them made important intellectual contributions: Hailes, Kames, Monboddo, for instance (*alias* Dalrymple, Home and Burnet).

So did many ministers of the established Church of Scotland. Aristocrats and lairds retained rights of patronage in many parishes. But ideally the Presbyterian minister was installed with the favour of his congregation. Regional synods held some sway, but the Church's governing body was the annual General Assembly in Edinburgh, with a Moderator appointed, or reappointed, annually. Calvinist bigotry was far from dead, as the young Robert Burns found growing up in Ayrshire. But the generally diffused 'Puritanism' of the 'grave livers' (Wordworth's phrase) in the Kirk of Scotland now quite commonly consorted with intellectual open-mindedness. Dr William Robertson, a pioneering historian with an international reputation, served both as Moderator of the Church and as Principal of Edinburgh University. The 'moderate' element dominant in the Church in the later eighteenth century was socially conservative (deferential to patrons) but could be intellectually innovative.[2]

The Edinburgh which Johnson visited for the first time in 1773 had long been possessed by the spirit of 'improvement'. Physically it was a very strange city: two rows of immensely tall houses facing each other across the spine of the volcanic rock which ran from the Castle down to Holyrood Palace. Aristocrats lived in flats in these tenements above and below commoners – not merchants and clerks merely but also plebeian dregs. The English were astonished by this. It wouldn't do. James Craig's plan for a 'New Town' across the festering swamp of the Nor'Loch was approved in 1765. Slowly it rose until in the new century the vastly expanded Edinburgh middle class was installed in a handsome pattern of regular 'Georgian' stone streets, crescents and 'circusses'. But the social *apartheid* which this entailed, with the prosperous settled in the New Town and the Old becoming one of Europe's worst slums, did not prevail in the day of David Hume (though he was an early New Town resident).

Gravitating towards the middle, alumni of the University (often from modest backgrounds) could mingle in all kinds of clubs and debating societies with 'improving' aristocrats and famous intellectuals. There seems to have been a sense of cooperative mission infusing this great centre of 'enlightenment', giving scope for 'genius' large and small. Beside the towering achievements of Hume in philosophy, Adam Smith in economics, Adam Ferguson in sociology, we should set those of lesser figures such as George Wallace. In 1760, Wallace produced a *System of the Principles of the Law of Scotland* which attacked the legal basis of the slavery from which so many of his compatriots profited in the New World. Plagiarised by the French *Encyclopédie*, his arguments attained comprehensive influence. As

21

for encyclopaedias, the Scots were not backward: *Britannica* was launched by obscure young men in Edinburgh in 1771.

'North *Britain*': surprising numbers of Scots accepted that term. This helps to explain why some historians (and not only English ones) have assumed that Enlightenment followed Union as effect from cause. Their view may be simplistically stated thus: after centuries of poverty-stricken barbarism, the Reformation brought Scotland a new basis for violence – religious bigotry. Whether mouthing biblical texts or hunting down those who did so sword-in-hand, the Scots were helplessly immersed in internecine fighting until first the Union, then Culloden, brought peace. Striving to 'emulate' their English fellow-citizens, the Scots civilised themselves very quickly. Result: instant Enlightenment.

Dr Johnson believed something like that: Walter Scott after him produced a more sympathetic account on the same broad lines. But the 'North British' view of Scottish Enlightenment now seems extremely suspect.

Take the case which favours it most – 'agricultural improvement'. Certainly the creation by John Cockburn MP of a famous 'model' village on his property at Ormiston in Lothian was inspired by the desire to drag Scotland up to the level of southern England. The zeal for improvement of the countryside which flavoured so much high talk in Edinburgh did have an anglophile tone. But advanced English methods in agriculture had come, in the seventeenth century, from Holland. Through Calvinist religion and the similarity of the Dutch 'Roman' law to Scottish law, independent contact between Scotland and The Netherlands was incessant long before the Union. The opportunities of Empire depended on Union and largely helped to supply cash for 'improvement'. It does not follow from this that England was the necessary source of new ideas.

Some Jacobite landlords were keen improvers. Those devoted to the Stewarts had their own links with the Continent – with France, where the exiled family sojourned, and with Italy. While the influence of such English thinkers as Newton and Locke, and of English literature of all kinds, was powerful in the 'Scottish Enlightenment', this could easily have happened without Union. David Hume cannot be explained as leaping fully formed from the Union like Minerva from the brow of Jupiter.

Scotland had four universities to England's two. Boys entered
them before what we would now consider 'sixth form' age. Buildings
were not fine as at Oxford and Cambridge. But the breadth of the
Scottish curriculum was such that it attracted away from Oxbridge
not only religious Dissenters, who were debarred from English universities, but even, by the end of the eighteenth century, such English
aristocrats as the future Prime Ministers Melbourne, Palmerston, and
Russell.

The Scottish curriculum, like the English, heavily featured the
study of Latin. But it combined, rather momentously, two further
features: an acute commitment to discussing all subjects to and from
first principles (i.e. a strong 'philosophical' bias), and a strong
'improving' bias toward the practical, which favoured the development of natural and social science. The two emphases can be seen
together in Adam Smith's great *Wealth of Nations* (1776), the work
of a man who had made his first reputation as a moral philosopher,
but now proceeded to set economics on a systematic 'scientific' basis.
Smith had lectured at the University of Glasgow. That institution,
and Aberdeen's colleges, provided centres of Enlightenment to rival
Edinburgh. Thomas Reid, professor first in Aberdeen, then in Glasgow, produced the subtlest riposte to the dangerously anti-Christian
views of David Hume, and his philosophy had vast international
influence.

John Millar, author of *The Origin of Distinction of Ranks* (1771),
was a long-serving Glasgow professor. Together with Adam Smith,
his one-time teacher, he crystallised an immensely influential conception: human society, it was thought, had progressed in sequence
through four 'stages'. First people had lived by hunting, then by
'pasturage' (keeping cattle), then by settled agriculture. Finally, commerce became dominant, with the middle-classes in the driving seat.
Scotland had entered the 'commercial' phase. Belief, as with Smith
and Millar, in a conception of 'progress' related easily to the remarkable innovations of Scottish businessmen, helped by scientists and
technologists.

The great chemist, Joseph Black, moved from Glasgow to Edinburgh in 1766. Like his friend, the pioneering geologist James Hutton,
he had been a medical student. In this area, Scotland's pre-Union
connections with Holland were decisive. The inspiration of the

Edinburgh 'medical school' undoubtedly came from Leyden. Between 1705 and 1807, nine chairs associated with medicine were founded at Edinburgh University. (Glasgow acquired ten between 1713 and 1818). By the late-eighteenth century, Scotland was supplying the world with doctors. Of students enrolled under James Gregory, Professor of Physic at Edinburgh, between 1785 and 1790, an average of well under half came from Scotland, almost exactly matched by numbers from England and Ireland: the remainder came from America and Europe.[3] The practical need for doctors provided an academic basis for wide-ranging scientific enquiry which in turn had practical results. Black continued to work as a doctor while teaching chemistry and acting as an industrial consultant, advising textile manufacturers on bleaching processes, brewers on beer, sugar-refiners, tar-makers and so on. One of his earlier associates, a Glasgow instrument-maker named Watt, owed something to Black's science when he perfected his world-transforming steam engine. As for Hutton, the author of the *Theory of the Earth* (1795) employed his geological skills on the cutting of the Forth–Clyde Canal, opened in 1790 to link the North Sea with the Atlantic.

The strong practical emphasis on the great figures (and small ones) of Scottish Enlightenment has been linked with the relatively democratic character of education in Scotland. The touching notion that the country's universities were crammed with the sons of ploughmen and stonemasons, 'lads o'pairts', released into light and fame by devoted dominies in village schools, does not bear sceptical examination. But it retains imaginative force, if only because a ploughman, Robert Burns, showed what intellectual stuff the Scottish rural proletariat was made of.

Scottish Calvinism (not least thanks to Burns) has had a very bad press as prudish, life-denying, bigoted, and hypocritical. Hume reacted profoundly against it. Yet the dominance of a disputacious creed which emphasised the need for literacy (so that the Bible could be endlessly jawed over) was probably the most important precondition of Scottish Enlightenment. Presbyterianism laid down that every parish should have a school open to all. Calvinism is a pre-eminently logical creed, and its hard line with superstition and ceremony clears the way for cold, clear thought about nature and society. Furthermore, Calvinism can be seen as a bridge between Hume and the philosophers of mediaeval Scotland, from Duns Scotus (*c.* 1266–1308), through to John Mair (or 'Major') who taught John Knox theology at St Andrews. Alexander Broadie points out that by Hume's day Scotland 'had acquired a rich philosophical tradition, and it is past belief that in the absence of that tradition the philosophy of the Scottish Enlightenment could have been written.'[4] David Allan has shown how the writing of history – a preoccupation of intellectuals from Mair to Hume – in a practical way transmitted that tradition.[5]

Though Scottish Presbyterianism eschewed vain and frivolous things, like pictures on church walls and profane stage plays, the achievements of Robert Adam in architecture were not merely utilitarian. Scottish painting, by the latter part of the eighteenth century, produced what has been called its 'Golden Age', with outstanding portraitists, Allan Ramsay and Raeburn, whose informal warmth conveys the benevolent good feeling towards which Enlightenment Edinburgh aspired. No Scot excelled in musical composition of the kind we now call 'classical', but native traditions of folk-song (including Gaelic song) and fiddle-playing were strongly developed.

Did Enlightenment, as Scots practised it, stunt 'literature'? Dedication to dry, systematic thought might seem likely to inhibit creative expression. It is sometimes suggested that the polished English prose style cultivated by Hume and others was inimical to the maintenance of Scottish tradition in the vernacular; that a gulf opened up between head (English) and heart (Scots or Gaelic). Yet the century of Enlightenment saw a revival in published Scottish literature which carried forward into the early nineteenth century heyday of Walter Scott. Many important collections and editions of old poems and songs in Scots appeared. The fame of James Thomson, author of *The Seasons* (1730) – a long poem acclaimed throughout Europe which eventually inspired a choral work by Haydn – might be discounted because he emigrated to London. But before his early death Robert Fergusson wrote in Edinburgh the most vivid poetry in Scots to appear for nearly two centuries, and it made a profound impression on Robert Burns.

Both anglicising and nationalistic tendencies flourished not merely within the one Scottish intellectual community, but within its individual members. Hume earnestly tried to rid his English prose of 'Scotticisms', yet sneered at 'barbarians who live on the banks of the

Thames' and was active for a time (though he did cool off) in encouraging James Macpherson in his 'translation' of 'epic' poetry from Gaelic. Macpherson attended Aberdeen University in the 1750s. Professor Thomas Blackwell there was an enthusiast for the epic Greek poetry of Homer. His contention was that Homer was so powerful because he wrote directly from experience of a violent society. Unfortunately, great art, as Blackwell had to conclude, was self-defeating. Poetry helped to civilise savage peoples: civilised people couldn't produce great poetry.

This dilemma was at the heart of the Scottish Enlightenment. Its great thinkers tended to yearn for the nobler attitudes and values of the past which 'improvements' were designed to erase: see, for instance, the *Essay on the History of Civil Society* (1767) by Adam Ferguson. As his editor Duncan Forbes remarks, Ferguson 'is typical of the Scottish enlightenment, in his emphasis on sympathy, humanity, fellow-feeling, social solidarity'.[6] But modern commerce and statecraft tend to destroy solidarity, along with the heroic virtues: men became self-centred and partisan. People, in fact, don't become more 'civilised' with the progress of civil society. Among the Iroquois Indians of North America, for instance, 'the titles of *magistrate* and *subject*, or *noble* and *mean*, are as little known as those of *rich* and *poor* ... While the community acts with an appearance of order, there is no sense of disparity in the breast of any of its members.'[7]

Dangerous stuff. Such views help to explain why Ferguson, too, encouraged Macpherson. This young man rose on a tide of sentimental interest, after Culloden, in the culture of the Gaels. Out of old manuscripts and texts transcribed from current Gaelic singing he assembled materials for an 'epic', *Fingal* (1762), which conquered Europe completely. Instead of the ponderous measures (couplets, etc.) of fashionable English verse, he offered incantatory prose. The blind bard Ossian was supposed to have composed this epic in the third century AD after the mighty Fenian warriors of whom he sang had gone down into death, like the heroes of Culloden Moor. The plangent, elegiac tone connected specifically with the widespread sense of loss among Macpherson's fellow-Gaels, but more generally with fears in intellectual circles, not only in Scotland but in Rousseau's France and throughout Europe, that luxury and over-improvement were destroying essential human virtues:

Often have I fought and often won in battles of the spear. But blind, and tearful, and forlorn, I now walk with little men. O Fingal, with thy race of battle I now behold thee not. The wild roes feed upon the green tomb of the mighty King of Morvern.[8]

Jefferson loved this. Goethe loved it. Napoleon loved it. The major British 'romantic' poets, from Burns and Blake onwards were all deeply affected by Ossian. However, Macpherson did not bring adequate reinforcement to the egos of quasi-nationalist Scottish professors because spoilsports, mostly English, objected that Macpherson wasn't *really* 'translating' *ancient* epic.

So if Burns hadn't surfaced with the publication of a volume of poems in Kilmarnock in 1786, someone would have had to invent him. There was nothing inauthentic about Burns. He could write polished couplets when he chose, he could also perform in certain fiendishly tricky metres peculiar to the tradition of writing in Scots and he had a touching way with 'pastoral' song. He was well-read, he knew how Reid had answered Hume and he carried his plebeian person into aristocratic *salons* and 'enlightened' clubs with sturdy dignity. He was something the English didn't have, and the English also loved and admired him.

How could Scotland's flourishing commercial civilisation be 'decadent' if it produced a man like this? And now that he had given the vernacular language such memorable new life in literature, surely the old Scotland of heartfelt sentiment, true solidarity and heroic gallantry must (somehow) be destined to live forever?

(1993)

3

Scotch Myths: The Patriot, the Manager and the Rebel

Some details from the pageant of Scotland's past. In March 1708 a French fleet set sail for Scotland in support of the exiled Jacobite King. The weather frustrated it. But meanwhile, a large number of Scots had been arrested. They included Andrew Fletcher of Saltoun, a vehement anti-Jacobite who had, however, opposed the Union of Parliaments the previous year. Lesson: the state, in panic, does not discriminate rationally between its opponents.

After the Napoleonic Wars had ended and economic hard times had set in, Whitehall and the Scottish landed élite grew worried about the growth of 'physical force' radicalism in the west of Scotland. The Scottish Lord Advocate alarmed the House of Commons by reading out a secret oath which radicals were said to be taking in Glasgow, pledging the establishment of democracy by violence if need be. The House at once gave him new powers of repression. Maconochie was probably drawing on material given him by one Alexander Richmond, formerly a leader of the Pollokshaws weavers in their strike of 1812, latterly a small businessman and spy. When he brought four radicals to trial, the evidence was so shooglie that the jury was obviously reluctant to convict and none got 'more' than six months' imprisonment. The Lord Advocate looked like the fool he was. Lesson: our rulers are no cleverer than we are. However, their folly rarely lands them in jail, even for six months.

On 30 June 1917 the Marxist educator John Maclean, who had been in prison since his sentence to three years penal servitude in

April 1916 on charges which included actively trying to discourage recruitment to the armed forces in wartime, was released on 'ticket of leave'. Alarmed by the response of the British labour movement to the February Revolution in Russia and by mass demonstrations demanding the release of Maclean and other political prisoners, the Government had decided to be conciliatory. But the military top brass in Scotland kept an eye on him, and badgered the Lord Advocate to arrest him again. As one wrote: 'The form of revolutionary propaganda indulged in by Maclean and his associates is viewed by the Commander-in-Chief as constituting a danger in an area such as Glasgow where indications of unrest continually prevail.' By May 1918, Maclean was back in jail. The authorities put it about that he was mad, suffering from weird delusions that he was an important and influential person. Some of his rivals on the Marxist left were happy thereafter to echo the story that Maclean had gone mad in prison. Lessons: (1) only mad people, army generals and cabinet-ministers ever believe that the Left has any influence. (2) Imprisonment in humiliating conditions might just drive you mad. (3) On the left, as so famously in the Tory Party, your worst personal enemies are the guys on your own side.

The British state is certainly, on 'mainland' United Kingdom, less ruthless towards the organised Left than it was in Maclean's day. During the Second World War, it handled peace campaigners gently and Marxist opponents with restraint. A generation of Establishment figures seems to have recoiled in shame from the moral horrors of the 'war to end all wars' and the hysteria which was whipped up at home. COs in 1939–45 suffered incidental discomforts but were in no risk of their lives. But the recent record of the state *vis à vis* non-whites living in Britain and people who might just harbour IRA sympathies shows that the leopard has not outworn its spots or lost its claws.

Beatrice Webb once suggested that people in the labour movement could be divided between 'As' – 'anarchists' – and 'Bs' – 'bureaucrats'. It is tempting to suppose that historians might also be divided between those 'Bs' for whom preservers of the continuity of institutions of law and order, hierarchy and deference, are the heroes, and, 'As' who are agin all governments past, present and perhaps future and idolise intransigents like Fletcher and Maclean. However, life

29

isn't as tidy as that. Historians tend, like everyone else, to justify means such as coercion and chicanery where these achieve ends which they desire, and to criticise similar methods practised by others whose ends they don't like. They take sides. They can't help it. Is it therefore bourgeois delusion which lures us to seek 'truth' about history in their writings?

*

It is often suggested, in defence of the teaching of history, that without a sense of their past, people cannot know who they are. This makes much less sense than the counter-proposition, that 'history', as a subject, and as a discipline, can exist only because peoples always, everywhere, have had a sense of their pasts. This will consist of a mish-mash of myths and legends, of petrified gossip, of ancient propaganda and slanders, together with relatively reliable oral history. As the rational spirit of the Enlightened eighteenth century scrutinised all human affairs, it was bound to turn its attention to this element in life and to begin to develop procedures for studying it 'scientifically'. Any sane person can now appreciate the difference in principle between a genuine 'historical' statement founded on documentation and a merely superstitious or propagandist assertion. Not that all documents yield unambiguous truth – far from it. But a statement based on material available for inspection by other scholars is, to use the Popperian term, 'falsifiable' and therefore 'scientific.'

However, the Kuhnian term, 'paradigm', also applies. Historians, like others claiming scientific authority, cannot escape as a rule from the 'mental sets' of their generations, classes, communities. Many are 'set' as apologists for a *status quo*, seeking 'Whiggishly' in the past for the foundations of a present society deemed to be virtuously progressive. Others seek to destroy Whiggish paradigms. In recent years, labour history, black history, women's history have mounted such challenges to British Whiggery and its very similar adversary, British Tory historiography.

We cannot, whatever paradigms we think in or challenge (and in practice all genuine historical scholars feel obliged to modify, if not shatter, paradigms), seriously claim permanent authority even for our 'facts', let alone for our judgements. Statistics which look safe turn out to be delusions. Periodisations once confidently accepted crumble into dust. The Seven Years' War becomes 'in fact' a war of nine years. George III's 'madness' turns out to be something else. It will never, I think, be shown that Boswell didn't know Johnson, but brilliant scholarship may yet transform our sense of that relationship and the literary documents from which we have constructed it.

Nevertheless, the project of honest historians must surely be to reveal what 'really happened'. Deconstructionists, who cannot deny that shells have fallen on Sarajevo and that if one had hit Jacques Derrida, he would have died, may nevertheless help us realise the extent to which that siege has been 'manufactured' as a 'media event' on Western TV. In that case, however grudgingly, they serve the quasi-scientific project of history which aims to distinguish truth from falsehood.

People who don't respect the need for documentary evidence, and for stringent analyses of such evidence, can't claim to be historians. The task of historians, recognising their own fallibility, is to look with special care for evidence counter to their own hypotheses – formed, as these must be, *a priori*, from prejudice. The arts can do with historical events and personages whatever they like. Journalists may be forgiven for rhetorical use of folk history. Politicians are entitled to play around with the past in their perorations. But I hope we can agree that it is important that there should be scholars around who started, in childhood, with folk history and media history like everyone else, but have gone on to seek a sounder grasp of what past eras, or the bits of them they have time to study, 'were actually like'.

This said, history without a modicum of 'artistic' flair and 'journalistic' persuasiveness is unreadable except by ultra-specialists. Historians who have no strong convictions of any political or religious variety will be thereby stunted as human beings. The imagination which grasps the past must be nurtured by engagement in the present. No one indifferent to feminist issues, for instance, is likely to seek and recover important new sources of understanding of women's history.

The authors of the latest studies of 'the Patriot' Fletcher of Saltoun, of Henry Dundas ('King Harry the Ninth', Boswell called him) and John Maclean (Sorley MacLean's 'battlepost of the poor') have all, to their credit, engaged vigorously in recent political debate. Paul Scott is a leading figure in the Scottish National Party. James D. Young was a member of Jim Sillars' Scottish Labour Party and later helped found the Scottish Socialist Party: that is, he has operated, like Maclean himself in his last days, on the Nationalist edge of the labour movement. Michael Fry is one of the handful of people who might be called 'intellectuals' associated with the Scottish Conservative and Unionist Party. Though he was once a parliamentary candidate, his devolutionist views (in some respects considerably more radical than those favoured by the Constitutional Convention) have sidelined him politically, except as a newspaper columnist particularly severe on what he sees as the encouragement by lefties and SNP-ers of a mentality in Scotland dependent on state jobs, state ownership and state patronage. Like Young, he is more of an 'A' than a 'B'. Paul Scott, on the other hand, sometimes gives the impression that his heart's desire is a Scottish state much like a miniaturised version of the Whitehall one, as when he leads the call for a 'National Theatre' to match, presumably, that grisly Bastille on London's South Bank.

Men not without public salience themselves (Young has been a charismatic teacher at Stirling University), these historians are well aware of the role of historical mythology in present day politics. They do not want to present history in ways that will prejudice causes dear to themselves. But all three fully realise that they cannot persuade other scholars to see things as they do without gathering evidence from primary sources and presenting it with the usual apparatus of scholarly reference. This encourages me, in my turn, to try to assess their contributions dispassionately. I find that while my own prescriptions for society are closest to Young's (I am a libertarian, democratic socialist), I have to conclude that Fry's book is not only the longest of the three, but probably the most impressive, thought-provoking and useful.

To explain why I think this, I must invoke a fourth historian, John Mackenzie of Lancaster University, who chose to give his inaugural lecture as Professor of Imperial History on 13 May 1992 on 'Scotland and the Empire'.[1] 'Imperial history' is a highly unfashionable term of dubious political correctness. Edinburgh University settled decades ago for the mealy mouthed 'Commonwealth' alternative. As for 'Scotland and the Empire', doesn't every week see a letter or two in the *Scotsperson*'s 'Points of View' columns denouncing the ongoing rape of our autochthonous blood and soil by the vile, denatured

English Imperialists and their unaccountably fiendish, native hirelings in the Labour and Conservative parties? Is there any more to be said about Scotland's relationships with Empire than that we have been enslaved like Africans, hounded down and shot like Australian aborigines, acculturated and debauched with ardent spirits like native Americans and now, as the dreaded white settlers and their tanks move forward daily, ethnically cleansed like Bosnian Muslims? Well, Mackenzie thinks there is. Bear with me, and him.

*

Mackenzie discusses 'both Scotland and the Empire and the Empire and Scotland. What is intriguing [he goes on] about this reciprocal formulation is that the effects of Scotland on the Empire have generally been viewed in positive ways while the influence of imperial rule upon Scotland, certainly in modern times, have been viewed almost entirely negatively.'

There has been a great deal of exclamation and outright boasting over the extent to which Scots, from the eighteenth century onwards, overran, instructed and administered the 'British' Empire. Whether we research Jamaican sugar, Virginian tobacco, Canadian furs, the staff lists of the East India Company, the leading edge of 'exploration', trade and missionary activity in Africa, jute in Bengal, opium, etc. in China, the Scottish surnames pour out at one. Of the first six governors of New South Wales, three were Scots. From Calgary and Banff to Perth and Dunedin, the colonies were littered with Scots place-names. As Mackenzie notes, 'Although Scots stood to English in Great Britain, in the ratio of 1:7, it has been calculated that the Scots' contribution to Canada in terms of emigrant numbers was almost equal. In the case of New Zealand it was roughly 1:2; South Africa 1:3; and in Australia 1:3.5. It has been commented recently that there are some 10 million descendants of Glaswegians in the Commonwealth, an awesome thought.' Unlike Irish emigrants, Scots tended to rise rapidly and stamp their names and their money on new societies. The Disruption of 1843 ensured duplicated efforts in the missionary field, so that both Established and Free churches conspired to make what is now Malawi a distinctly Scottish colony. Meanwhile, kilted hirelings marched hither and thither terrifying the fuzzy-wuzzies with their bagpipes, though 'Scots constituted a lower proportion of the British army than their population warranted'.

But what, asks Mackenzie, did all this expense of spirit overseas do to Mother Scotland herself? Much recent historiography has presented a dismal vista: the Union of 1707, which made Scots imperial derring-do possible, rendered Scotland stateless, open to Anglicising processes which affected even those spheres left independent – Church, law, education and banking. After the cultural achievements of the Enlightenment Scottish talent drained south – Carlyle, the Mills, Macaulay, Ruskin, Gladstone – while the tartan culture of the Highlands was recreated and appropriated by Anglicised and English landlords, Queen Victoria to the fore. Business enterprises founded and capitalised in Scotland moved south. The heavy industries of Scotland, based on iron and coal, which dominated imperial markets, also depended on them: they crashed to their doom in the twentieth century.

But Mackenzie rejects the notions that Scots were merely 'collaborators' or always 'victims'. Present-day historians stress 'the extraordinary capacity of popular culture to maintain a hidden integrity, to resist in subtle and not always obvious ways'. While complacent or guilt-stricken metropolitans assume that West Indian slaves, African 'tribesmen' or Scottish labourers are enthralled by the culture of their economic masters, such tinks and keelies retain their own world-views. Mackenzie, further, embraces G. E. Davie's formulation that post-Union Scotland saw 'unification in politics, separation in ethics'. And he argues – I believe this to be original – that Scottish ethics infused arenas of Empire. 'Even if the law and administrative systems, the language and outward show, of empire were essentially English, the Scots succeeded in transferring aspects of their civil society.' Besides, as he concedes, joining in all the thuggery and exploitation, Scots at key moments in key places enforced their different 'ethics'. In north India, English viceroys supported the great landholder zemindars. 'In the south and west . . . Sir Thomas Munro and Sir John Malcolm set about establishing a direct relationship with the superior peasants, who would effectively enjoy a measure of private tenure as a quasi-yeomanry.' In New Zealand a century later, a Scottish Minister of Lands, also John McKenzie, born in the Highlands, 'set about breaking the power of the large and often absentee landowner'. In early nineteenth-century South Africa, Thomas Pringle struggled for press freedom, John Philip for black rights. 'But above all it was the reputation of David Livingstone that most helped to define and disseminate this notion of an independent social ethic in relation to empire and home.' Supreme example of working-class self-help, self-educated polymath, this man of mixed Highland and Lowland ancestry was idolised by monarch, élite and public throughout the United Kingdom. His alleged empathy with Africans was held by biographer after biographer to derive from Scotland – 'He understood their oral traditions, their historic and didactic tales, their concern with ancestors and heroic exploits. Above all, he understood the bond between Africans and their chiefs, supposedly so similar to the Scottish clan system.' He was thus 'both nationalist and internationalist, a major world figure by virtue of his very Scottishness'. And for Scots he was not a sell-out. Never denying his own Scottishness, he represented to the custodians of the kailyard* 'a moral superiority in effectively heading an English concern ... The social ethic represented by Livingstone not only influenced England and the Empire, but looped back to Scotland in the founding of missions, societies and memorials to his name. In the national context he became the reconciler of Highlander and Low-lander, the central problem of Scottish nationalism.'

Scots, Mackenzie argues, used Empire as 'a means of enhancing rather than destroying Scottish institutions'. John Buchan, pre-eminently, was an arch imperialist who believed that Scotland should have a Parliament again, as part of the imperial family. 'The most influential parts of Scottish nationalism between the 1880s and the 1940s at any rate placed their nationalism within an imperial frame.'

So the Empire, 'far from being a source of Scots servitude, was actually a means whereby Scotland asserted her distinctiveness in relation to England'. And now that Empire is gone, Europe fulfils the same role in Scottish consciousness, as the larger entity in which the Scottish social ethic can find echoes and scope. The bizarre spectacle of our football supporters transforming themselves when abroad from the plunderers of Pittodrie and Parkhead, the Huns and bigots of Ibrox and terrors of Easter and Gorgie Roads into 'the friendliest

---

* The Scots word for 'cabbage garden' is applied to a school of sentimental fiction about rural life originating in the late nineteenth century and by extension to the vanishing of an imaginary Scottish way of life which it projected.

fans in Europe' is completely relevant to Mackenzie's argument. The point is to establish our moral superiority to the thuggish, chauvinist English. In Europe, as Mackenzie notes it is 'the English whose institutions and attitudes are anomalous'. The electoral revulsion of Scots against Thatcherism involves a reassertion of the 'moral sentiment' with which Adam Smith, unlike his latter-day London eulogists, combined his *laissez faire* theories. Mackenzie pleasantly concludes, 'Perhaps it can be said of the Union of 1707, "It cam wi' an empire and it'll gang wi' an empire."'

*

Because the issues of independence, devolution and 'Scotland in Europe' have often dominated political debate in Scotland since the 1960s, the correspondence columns of the better newspapers have rarely been without historical wrangling. Not much of this has been over those 'romantic' figures foregrounded by the tourist industry, Mary Queen of Scots and Prince Charles Edward Stewart. Nor, sadly to my mind, have the issues in Church history which once vexed every serious Scot had proportionate attention. Economic and cultural history, both implicated in the 1707 Union, have bulked largest, with the nineteenth-century Highland Clearances and the historical fate of the Gaelic language generating most heat. Alongside this war of prejudices, an historiographical explosion – in part a product of the post-Robbins expansion in higher education and the consequent proliferation of PhDs, more importantly a reflection of the local political agenda and the ways that has directed new scholarship – has transformed our understanding of every recent Scottish century. The new studies mentioned above, all published in Scotland, represent this afflatus and draw on its results.

Paul Scott, in one of the essays reprinted in his Polygon 'Determinations' volume, *Towards Independence*, takes a sturdily traditional view of the relations between Scotland, England and Europe. In 'the longest war in European history' English king after English king sought to take over the well-established nation to the north. This provoked the classic expressions of Scottish 'national consciousness' – the Declaration of Arbroath of 1320, Barbour's *Brus* and Hary's *Wallace*.

One of the consequences of the long war of resistance against England was that Scotland was encouraged to seek markets, allies and cultural and intellectual exchange with continental Europe. Above all we had a close alliance with France for over 300 years ... We were actively and consciously European centuries before the European Community. This Scottish involvement with the rest of Europe was so different from the much more insular and self-sufficient attitude of England that it alone accounts for many of the radical differences between the Scottish and English traditions.[2]

Alas, the brutish insular English, not content with pillage, rape, massacre, etc. resorted to bribery – 'seeking out disaffected, greedy or ambitious Scots'. This reached its climax in 1707, when bribed Scots consented, in their Parliament, to an 'incorporating Union' which transferred legislative power to Westminster, whither the Crown had fled in 1603. This event, and the subsequent *débâcle* at Culloden were, Scott suggests, 'so painful' that they explain the tendencies of the thinkers of the Scottish Enlightenment towards abstraction. 'If their ideas evolved from their Scottish experience, there is remarkably little sign of it in their writing.' Numbed by their nation's destruction 'they had to disguise their thought in generalities' and usually 'moved in a disembodied world of pure intellect'. However, things got worse with the wholesale Anglicisation which set in towards the middle of the nineteenth century. 'It is puzzling,' Scott remarks, 'that the country succumbed so easily when it had such solid achievement behind it and such a history of determined resistance.' Here he concurs with Mackenzie that Empire and its opportunities were crucial, but views this influence as baleful. Scottish candidates for imperial service had to take exams based on the English educational system and 'the Scottish schools and universities had to adjust accordingly ... This helped to establish a habit of concentration on English history and literature to the exclusion of the Scottish.' Meanwhile 'the energy which Scots expended' in the Empire was 'lost to Scotland'. It brought benefit only 'to individuals, not to Scotland as a whole'. There was no Scottish Parliament to discuss the 'massive haemorrhage of talent, energy and skill', threatening the 'very survival of Scotland' represented by the 'wholesale clearance of the Highlands and the emigration compelled by the neglect of Scotland'.[3]

At the basis of all Paul Scott's arguments is the notion of an ideal Scotland which, without English interference, would have been prosperous, creative, 'European', democratic, educated and just. Un-fortunately, this Scotland never existed and we cannot separate the Scotland which actually exists from centuries of interaction and symbiosis with the larger English cultural area – not necessarily, always, thuggish and philistine nor, latterly, 'dominant'. Insofar as, after the Union, Scots played a major role in UK as well as in Empire, affairs. 'UKanian' culture was largely a Scottish production. English patriots in the 1760s, yelled on by John Wilkes, denounced the intrusion of ravenous, cunning Scots spearheaded, they said, by Prime Minister Bute. The English loved being patronised by Thomas Carlyle who told them they were very fine doers of deeds because they were typically incapable of thought. They embraced other stereotypes of themselves created by Walter Scott, R. L. Stevenson, Conan Doyle, John Buchan, Kenneth Grahame – Scotsmen all – and latterly identified with the James Bond invented by an Anglo-Scot and personified on screen by our charismatic Edinburgh milkman. Now *Taggart* beats even *Morse* in the UK ratings. But elements in the Scottish cultural tradition which has so profoundly influenced England were themselves English in origin, from the fertile influence of Chaucer on Henryson and Dunbar, through the magnificent language of the English Bible named after Scottish King James, the effects of Addison and Pope on Hume and Burns, of Shakespeare on Scott, of Hogarth on Wilkie. We are, to state an obvious fact, not only 'part of Europe', but also inhabitants of the north-west European Archipelago, implicated every which way with the English, Irish and Welsh, in and out of the Empire which these peoples created with us. (And let us not forget those doughty Orcadians who provided the Hudson's Bay Company with a preponderance of its early servants.)

Hence the big problem presented by Scott, the question that he cannot answer – 'Why did the leaders of this delightful, patriotic, distinctive nation sell it out in 1707? How could the Land of Heart's Content nurture such viperous miscreants?' – is falsely posed. There is no doubt whatever that largish sums of money, besides titles, offices, etc., were distributed to Scots legislators from English sources and that these men then voted for 'incorporating' Union. It does not follow that they saw such Union as entailing loss of Scottish identity, nor that they would have voted against it indefinitely had they not been bribed.

Scotch Myths: The Patriot, the Manager and the Rebel

What were the alternatives? The Scottish élite classes had lost a huge proportion of their capital in the attempt to set up a trading house in Central America – not a 'Scottish Empire' exactly, but a bridgehead for Scots in the intercontinental trade which had made London, suddenly, momentously, rich, so shifting the balance of economic power within the island massively in England's favour. The English élite wanted to secure a Protestant succession to the childless Queen Anne: its aim initially was merely to get the Scottish Parliament to vote for Hanover. When the Scots refused, the idea of incorporating Union gradually emerged as the answer to the perennial problem that an independent nation to the north, traditionally allied to France, posed to England's security. But most Scots were Protestant. Only a minority wanted a Jacobite successor to Anne, and only a fool could believe that the English, faced with a hostile Scotland under its own King and Parliament, would not sweep both away and occupy the country again as Cromwell had done in the 1650s.

The Scottish Parliament was an institution without much tradition. Its only famous meeting before 1703 was the one which Lindsay imagined in his great *Satire*: you will recall that the Three Estates entered this backwards, and it took Divine Correction to sort out their base affairs. Whereas the English Parliament, to some extent 'representative', had played a decisive and perhaps heroic part in the 1640s, the Scottish Parliament was dominated by peers and otherwise composed of land-owners elected by land-owners and burgesses put forward by little cliques. The surprising thing, really, is not that this assemblage of the very people who had most to lose from English trade boycott and English invasion decided to incorporate their Parliament with Westminster, but that for several years it made patriotic and provocative noises. Reading, in his new biography of Andrew Fletcher, Paul Scott's admirably clear and well-documented account of its proceedings, we can only marvel at the earnest public spirit and, no doubt, Kirk-schooled disputatiousness, which kept elderly men debating, without dinner, late into the night amid the stench of their own flatulence, sour wine fumes and guttering candles.

Scott's new biography supersedes previous accounts of Fletcher.[4] Documentation about the man is sadly scarce – it seems that the mass of relevant papers may, in the 1760s, have been consigned to

Jean Jacques Rousseau, who said he wanted to write a biography, but presumably mislaid them. Perhaps they may yet turn up in some Swiss or French archive where they have mouldered forgotten. Meanwhile, Scott has made exhaustive use of what is available. Fletcher's early continental travels remain obscure, his sexual predilections, if any, are irretrievable, but a consistent image of the public man emerges. His contemporaries noted his fiery temper. (More than once, he went up to and beyond the point of provoking duels in the famous parliamentary debates. He had no sooner landed in southwest England with Monmouth to launch the latter's rebellion of 1684 than he shot a prominent local man in a quarrel over a horse, and had to go back to the Continent. Luckily for him, as the rising was smashed.) But he was generally praised, even by opponents, for the strength of his oratory and the purity of his patriotism. The word 'patriot' indissolubly attached itself to his name.

Let us consider what 'patriot' meant in those days. It was a word later claimed by the rebellious American colonists of the 1760s and 1770s. While it had the general meaning 'lover of country', it was attached to a particular political tradition: that of property-owning 'republicanism'. Fletcher didn't say there should be no kings. But his contemporaries, when they called him 'republican', responded to his basic conviction that society should be controlled not by monarchs but by land-owners, appropriately assembled in a Parliament. His notorious suggestion that unemployed people in Scotland should be made 'slaves' fits into this tradition – though we might note in passing that all he advocated was a benign form of the familial 'servitude' then generally accepted in the English-speaking countries, not plantation slavery as in the Caribbean, which deprived its victims of all rights.

There was nothing essentially 'Scottish' about Fletcher's patriotism, though it did have special features, as we shall see. H. T. Dickinson in his authoritative study *Liberty and Property: Political Ideology in Eighteenth-Century Britain* mentions Fletcher, in the English context of the 1690s, as a member of 'a small, closely knit group of Real Whigs or Commonwealthmen' waging a pamphlet war against the British Court: that is, as a representative 'Country Whig'.[5] This tradition was in a sense 'revolutionary' and Fletcher could make it sound 'democratic' to our ears, as when, in October

1706, he told Parliament that the anti-union mob in the streets outside were 'the true spirit of this country, for the Reformation and Revolution were both brought about by them.' But as a well-to-do land-owner Fletcher never questioned the system through which Parliament was dominated by land-owners.

In his thorough discussion of Fletcher's relationship to 'country' tradition, Paul Scott notes his affinities with such English predecessors as Harrington and his Irish contemporary Molyneux. Suspicion of centralised power, London rule, was integral to 'Country' thinking. Where Fletcher went beyond his precursors was in prefiguring typical concerns of the Scottish Enlightenment. He took a special, albeit-paternalist interest in the plight of the poor (like the Tory, Jonathan Swift, who despised him) and offered a general account of European history when arguing in the late 1690s against mercenary standing armies and in favour of a voluntary militia. In the upshot his diagnosis was that liberty and virtue were barely if at all compatible with 'luxury' – the increasing wealth which was flooding into London. While he favoured active promotion by virtuous legislators of economic development in Scotland, his attitude to incorporating Union – a noble one – was that whatever wealth it might bring to some was not worth having if it entailed loss of liberty. In so far as his opponents were branded by Burns, adapting tradition, as a 'parcel of rogues' who sold out the nation for 'English gold', Fletcher's theorising, as well as his passion, have powerfully conditioned the ways in which later generations have viewed the exchange of independence for opportunity in 1707.

But there was never any chance that a highly individualistic person like Fletcher, secure in the income of his substantial East Lothian estate but unable to offer patronage on his own account, could determine the outcome of the debates in which his oratory was so admired. Paul Scott attempts to present him as what we would call a 'party leader' – leader, that is, of the 'Country Party'. This 'party' was, to adapt Robert Frost, a thing 'next most diffuse to cloud'. The weight of the great territorial peers was always going to decide how Parliament acted. The 'Country Party' looked to one of these, the Duke of Hamilton. For reasons which Scott, like others before him, cannot fully elucidate, this imposing man postured as the arch-patriot, yet at more than one decisive juncture assisted, by manoeuvre or default, the progress of Union. He had estates in England. He had a claim on the British Crown. His contradictory interests, rather than 'English gold', seem to explain his behaviour.

The paradox that Fletcher was ineffectual, was outvoted, yet was admired then and thereafter for his stand must relate to the saturation in the classics which education for the élite then entailed. However sore they were about Darien losses, however fearful of English anger, however temptable by Court patronage, his fellow-parliamentarians had imbibed noble conceptions direct from the Latin. They wished their confused and sometimes sordid deliberations to have dignity. As 'Cicero' of the Country Party, delivering fine speeches in immaculate English – Scott observes that he was a master of that tongue before Addison's *Spectator* set the eighteenth-century standard – Fletcher, though no good at impromptu cut and thrust (unless perhaps with an actual weapon in hand) suited them admirably: he may be compared in this respect with Henry Grattan in the Dublin Parliament later in the century, before that, too, was 'incorporated'. It is also worth remembering that Don Quixote, that besotted bibliophile, was a favourite fictional character of the period. Fletcher was a great book-collector, very learned, and contemporaries dismissive of his ideal political conceptions may have been delighted both by his learning and his Quixotry.

He remains a deeply appealing figure. In what is described by Scott as 'the most remarkable passage in all his work', Fletcher (this is 1703) suggests that the interests of all countries are interdependent. 'No people ever did injustice to a neighbouring nation, except by mistaking their own interest.' War could be abolished, 'as far as may be possible', if Europe were divided into ten sections each with 'ten or twelve sovereign cities well fortified'. Such territories would be well-equipped to defend themselves, but 'unfit' to make conquests. A system of 'divers small sovereignties' would help preserve mankind not only from war but from 'corruption of manners' and would be 'most proper to give to every part of the world that just share in the government of themselves which is due to them'. Such sovereign cities would not necessarily be republics. A prince might preserve peace among several such polities. Fletcher says that, 'The island of Britain and that of Ireland' seem conveniently situated to become one of the large sections of Europe, like Iberia, for instance, and the area from Albania south to Greece. The 'three kingdoms' of England, Scotland and Ireland, as things stand, are exposed 'to the fate of a single battle, if a great army of enemies could be landed near London'. But suppose there were twelve well-fortified cities, and a strong (presumably combined) naval force – conquest would be impossible. Fletcher envisages, quite explicitly, 'city states' centred on London, Bristol, Exeter, Chester, Norwich, York, Stirling, Inverness, Dublin, Cork, Galway and Londonderry, leagued with each other under one monarch, with a common navy.[6]

The good news for Fletcher's admirers in the Scottish National Party is that he can be regarded without doubt as a prophet of 'Scotland in Europe'. The rather more awkward news is that he imagined several Scottish city states as part of a British confederation. As an 'A' to the core myself, I enjoy the thought of the republic of Inverness treating on equal terms with the republics of Barcelona and Ljubljana while continuing to acknowledge the House of Windsor. But I don't think that's quite what Jim Sillars and Alex Salmond have had in mind.

Fletcher admitted that his list of the major British cities was not final. But he clearly did not anticipate the extent to which economic developments would swiftly make it seem quaint, with the rise of Liverpool and Glasgow, Birmingham, Manchester and Belfast. His aversion to all overseas conquest implicitly ruled out such operations as those which gave Britain imperial pre-eminence and made these cities wealthy. The distinction of Henry Dundas, Michael Fry's book suggests, is that, while remaining an intensely patriotic Scot, he got for a time, as it were, into the driving-seat over the horses of industrial revolution, agrarian change and imperialist venturing which were hauling his native land forward whether he (or we) liked it or not.[7]

*

Fry's study covers a century and more of Scottish history. It is immensely detailed, based on research in many archives as well as extensive reading in published sources. Fry writes very well, so it's lively, too.

Between 1715, when Robert Dundas, later Lord Arniston, became Solicitor General for Scotland, and the great reform of the 1830s, a relatively obscure landed family from Lothian acquired and

43

maintained an astonishing position in Scottish affairs. This was not due to any gathering of vast wealth. For all his reputation as a monster of corruption, and his ennoblement as Viscount Melville, the great Henry Dundas himself died in debt. But he worked immensely hard to master the Scottish electorate, less than 3000, which returned 45 MPs to Westminster. His family, generation after generation, produced shrewd lawyers and able politicians, intelligent enough to cope with, even to manipulate, such great peers as Argyll and Buccleuch and Sutherland, who still dominated vast Scottish lands.

In this society where power still came from ownership of land, the Dundasses, themselves land-owners, were hardly 'bourgeois'. Yet the term 'middle class' perhaps applies. Theirs was not an 'aristocratic oligarchy' on the European model. As a Westminster politician, Henry's distinction was his grasp of, and insistence on, the crucial importance of intercontinental trade. Reorganising the affairs of the British in India, the hottest political issue when he rose to the top in the 1780s, certainly gave Dundas scope to reward Scottish clients with lucrative jobs. But he didn't use it without regard to merit. In the wars with France from 1793, Dundas (who never set foot outside Britain) thought destruction of the overseas trade of the French and their allies was the key, not comparatively footling engagements of the British army in Europe. South Africa, Ceylon, Malaya were wrested into the British imperial embrace. The most positive assessment of Dundas before Fry's came, not surprisingly, from the imperial historian Vincent Harlow, in his massive, now almost unread study of the *Founding of the Second British Empire* (1952). Dundas secured Britain, for a period, a virtual monopoly of overseas colonies.

Yet Dundas, born in 1742, was a child of the heyday of Scottish Enlightenment. Fry's book persuades me that an old puzzle is easily solved. Why did such incisive, radical thinkers as Adam Smith and Adam Ferguson, such exploring scientists as Black, such sensitive writers as Scott, go along cheerfully with 'Dundas despotism'? Answer: they saw in Dundas something of a fellow spirit. His schemes for Indian government or for rebuilding the navy sent 'Enlightened' ideas into action. Dundas was both disciple and patron of Adam Smith. He became the most active and significant associate of Pitt the Younger, a fellow Smith-ite, who set about modernising British government in the 1780s. In the spring of 1787, Dundas invited Smith to stay at his villa in Wimbledon, where he could 'discuss all his books' with him 'every evening'. When Smith arrived, Pitt was there. At the Prime Minister's insistence, the company stood till the Sage of Kirkcaldy was seated, since, as Pitt said, they were all his pupils. Historians during this century have generally presented Dundas as a cynical fixer standing for no ideas, let alone principles. Fry will persuade others, beside myself, that this view is plain wrong.

Dundas was a good lawyer whose strong brain triumphed, in the Westminster Parliament, over a strong Scottish accent which made people laugh. Solicitor General for Scotland from 1766, then Lord Advocate from 1775 to 1783, by the time he came to Pitt's aid he had built up a Scottish power-base which gave him great weight in the chaotic factional politics of the era. Parties, as we now know them, did not exist, still less effective party whips. Anyone who could reliably produce 20, 30, 40 docile Scottish votes for the Government of the day had, accordingly, huge clout.

In 1784 Dundas' nephew Robert became Solicitor General, then, in 1789, Lord Advocate. Meanwhile, Dundas himself held key offices – Home Secretary, President of the Board of Control for India, Secretary of State for War. He fell, with Pitt, in 1801, was ennobled as Viscount Melville, and took over the Admiralty when Pitt came back in 1804. A kind of tragedy ensued. The following year, Melville was impeached in Parliament for allegedly corrupt use of public funds back in the 1780s. He became a victim of the higher standards in public administration which he and Pitt had set out to promote. He was acquitted, but, shown up as a creature of Old Corruption, was able to secure no further high office and died embittered in 1811.

However, his son, another Robert, an MP since 1794, and a more scrupulous, less ebullient politician, continued the 'Despotism', managing Scottish elections with great success, if less flair. President of the Board of Control in 1807, head of the Admiralty in 1812, Robert remained a key figure in British politics until he retired, in 1830, just before the Reform Acts swept away the system which had made the Dundasses seem almost omnipotent in Scotland.

Fry carefully inspects the elections they 'managed' and revises earlier estimates of their exact degrees of success. But success it always was, give or take a seat or two. In 1796, when Parliament dissolved, Henry Dundas made it his ambition to 'prevent the return of any one member for Scotland hostile to the government'. And 'he very nearly succeeded'. He won forty-three Commons seats 'and failed only by a fluke in the other two'. Furthermore, several Scots who were also his followers took English seats, 'either purchased by themselves or supplied by him'.

Fry sets out to portray 'Harry' Dundas 'warts and all' and the adjectives under 'character' in his index display his subject's contradictions. He was 'ambitious' but 'clannish' – family and friends rose with him, as, indeed, did any Scot prepared to play things his way. He was 'coarse'. His lechery was legendary. His drinking was prodigious. But he was also 'conciliatory', surprisingly well-liked by many opponents, 'kind', especially to old ladies, 'conservative', 'efficient', 'tough', and above all 'realistic'. Like Adam Smith he wanted to break the East India Company monopoly. But he ca'd canny, and free trade with India came only two years after his death.

We can argue with many of Fry's judgements and emphases. He is over-generous to 'Harry' on the matter of the abolition of the slave trade, which, significantly, followed his fall from high office. He is still more lenient with him regarding the persecution of democratic radicals in the 1790s which more than anything else has damaged his recent reputation. However, he has a fair point that it was Dundas' Whig opponents, not he, who were set on Anglicising Scottish institutions in the name of reform, who would favour, as he didn't, Anglicising policies overriding native cultures in India, and who tended towards a grimly utilitarian, rationalistic view of the agricultural and industrial poor, typified by Loch's role in the Sutherland Clearances. Above all, I think he make the case that, so far from being a tool of Westminster 'managing' Scotland to please English masters, Dundas set out to 'manage' British affairs in such a way that distinctive Scottish institutions were safeguarded. While plenty of Scots in his day sat for English seats, Englishmen penetrated Scottish representation only after the 'reform' of the 1830s. He exemplifies perfectly Mackenzie's point that Scots typically sought an enlarged *Scottish* identity through the British Empire. Over nearly two decades, when he was Pitt's strong right arm, he was the first Scottish politician to exercise huge influence in English and imperial matters. No wonder Walter Scott thought he was a Good Thing.

*

The railways as well as reform ensured that the tenaciously autochthonous Scotland of Dundas was melted and mixter-maxtered in the UKanian stewpot. So did the growth of an industrial working class, of which skilled members, 'self-helping', sought 'independence' in North America, Australia, England or organised trade unions in solidarity with fellow tradesmen south of the border. Dundas would have boggled at the football and music-hall culture which had emerged by the end of the nineteenth century (though his conviviality and talents would certainly have made him a successful 'manager' in either sphere).

John Maclean and his generation of 'Red Clydesiders' had little or no time for popular culture. It has been alleged, somewhat quaintly, that Maclean used to go to watch Queen's Park because it was the only non-professional club left in the big league. (But another account has him supporting Third Lanark.) It is asserted, perhaps more credibly, that while a schoolteacher he was a demonic card-player. But someone joked that his brain must have been addled by all the gaseous soft drinks he consumed for company's sake, and there is general agreement that his personality was formed by a fiercely puritanical Calvinist background. The Original Secession body to which his parents adhered eschewed even the use of an organ in their churches: the Free Church Training College in which he qualified as a teacher was by comparison vastly broadminded. He was heir to the Covenanting tradition and in letters he wrote near the end of a life curtailed to forty-four years by the toll that campaigns for socialism took of his slight frame, something very like the Cameronian* combination of belief in the imminent millennium, alternating with grim dedication to martyrdom, can clearly be descried.

Maclean died on 30 November 1923. He had written to a comrade, James Clunie, a few weeks before: 'Capitalism has lost its balance and is staggering and plunging to its well-merited doom . . . Should a crisis arise I feel sure the people will come to me for guidance.' But he informed his wife sixteen days before he died, 'If I go down, I must go down with my flag at the top mast. Nothing on earth will shift me from that. Now, there's a tragedy for you.' A week later he

---

* This term applies to the extremist followers of Richard Cameron, leader of a rump of armed Covenanters in the 1680s.

told the voters of Gorbals, 'The Social Revolution is possible sooner in Scotland than in England' and predicted, as was by this time his wont, imminent war between the British Empire and the United States, his secular equivalent of Armageddon. At this stage he had fallen out with many former comrades and was struggling for the cause of his own tiny Scottish Workers Republican Party. The former Soviet Consul in Glasgow now seemed to most people in politics a sad failure.[8]

Yet his martyr's death swiftly made his memory indispensable to the Glasgow left of all sects and parties. He entered the very same popular culture from which he had stood aloof. In a city of sleaze, he stood for incorruptibility. In an arena of sectarian gangs he represented the unity of the workers of the world.

By 1939, when James Barke published his novel *The Land of the Leal*, Maclean's image as the great street-corner preacher was fixed:

The fingers bunched into a fist and the arm rose and fell, beating out a burning crescendo of denunciation. The crowd roared its approval: there was a tumultuous storm of applause ... He was determined, authoritative and yet there was a burning pleading urgency about his words. His voice was not pleasant ... There was a harshness, a roughness about it that repelled. Repelled and yet fascinated. There was a forthright integrity, a downright basic honesty about it ... But above all there was a violence about it, an uncompromising violence that seemed to storm the heights of all vacillation and hesitancy ... For surely this was not only a man of words but a man of deeds.[9]

Davey Kirkwood MP, the trade unionist turned MP (eventually 'Lord') who represented precisely the kind of compromise with the system which Maclean abhorred, had called him in his autobiography (1935) 'as sincere as sunlight and as passionate as a typhoon'.[10] This suggests the type of the great Christian preacher. Others who knew Maclean emphasised his personal kindness and even humour. But Barke's image of a Scottish Lenin had more force, not least for the poets, MacDiarmid and Sorley MacLean, who elevated him to a majestic symbol. And of course, very straightforwardly, he did represent in Scotland that generation of tragic Socialists – Connolly, shot, Liebknecht, shot, Luxemburg, shot – whose fate was to call for insurrection and die by violence. (I myself cannot think of them, or of him, for long, without tears.)

When he fought the 1922 election in Gorbals he described himself as a 'Bolshevik, alias a Communist'. This presents a problem for James D. Young, who wants to dissociate Maclean from Leninism and identify him as a prophet of peace, of feminism and of Young's own brand of libertarianism.[11] Young has done a lot of research on Maclean and has assembled materials which place him in wider context than is customary, finding them in such widely dispersed places as Wisconsin, Moscow, Dublin and Stockholm. Advanced students will note much in his references which will be worth following up. For beginners, for general readers, and even for well-informed socialists, his book, I'm afraid, is useless. It pitches them into the arcane left-sectarian wrangles of the first quarter of this century without providing the straightforward chronology of Maclean's career, and history of the sects and parties themselves, which are needed to make them comprehensible.

And Young's rambling, repetitious, unchronologised methods are not faulty only because they make for confused reading. Inherently, they falsify their subject. As we know very well, yesterday's (unionist) Militant may be today's (republican) Scottish Socialist. To understand Maclean's succession of views and their relationship to contemporary movements such as syndicalism and Bolshevism, we need a clear chronological patterning including precise local, national and international context. What we get is remarks like this:

In the light of the way the communists inflated William Gallacher's role in the revolt in the Clyde later on, it will be a useful corrective to their propaganda to quote the De Leonists' criticisms of the omissions in the Glasgow *Forward*'s report on the shop stewards meeting with Lloyd George.[12]

Here, the statements, as Huck Finn would put it, is tough.

Let us try to clarify what Maclean did achieve. He was a major propagandist. When he spoke for genuinely popular causes, as he often did during the war, this gave force to his Marxist propaganda. Whether the Clyde was really 'Red' in 1914–22 is a question already much debated by demythologisers. It certainly wasn't the powerhouse of world revolution which Maclean wanted it to be. But Maclean became (in no pejorative sense) a 'mythical' figure because he came to represent a notion of what Glaswegians should be: disrespectful of authority, uncompromisingly on the side of the workers, committed to communal rather than individualistic values. He extended, to adapt Mackenzie's thesis, the distinctive Scottish social ethic. To *prove* that a teacher and propagandist, which is what Maclean incessantly was, has influenced subsequent events and to show *how*, are impossible tasks. But it can be said without contradiction that his incorporation into Clydeside legend shows that something politically potent had entered, in his day, west of Scotland working-class culture, and that he came to represent this potency.

*

The images on the covers of these three biographical studies repay thought. Fletcher's image, from the Scottish National Portrait Gallery, is that of a self-consciously honest man. He could have asked the artist to make him look more handsome. With his big nose, small challenging eyes, mouth which could be half-smiling or might be about to burst into angry comment, he is blunt Country Patriotism personified.

Raeburn's portrait of the first Viscount Melville standing in his robes, left hand fingering papers bound in red tape (affairs of state), retains a touch of the informal humanity characteristic of the artist's best work. The big nose (again) is there. The smile is friendly as well as triumphant. The eyes twinkle. But we have here, no doubt at all, an imperial statesman, not the cheerful customer of Edinburgh howffs which Harry Dundas had once been.

Finally, Ken Currie's image of Maclean from his Glasgow People's Palace sequence of murals. The characteristic homburg hat shadows his face. Lit from behind, the teacher (book open in front of him) is darkly impressive. Around him sit representative workers of the world. At bottom left, a placard reads 'We Want Justice'. Currie's thoughtful, worried faces suggest that we might not get that, but that if we ever do, such a process of learning will be necessary.

(1993)

4

Rewriting Scottish History: The Arnold History of Scotland

Contrary to what *Scotland's Story* on STV suggested, Calgacus, the leader whom Tacitus had defying the Roman legions, was not a Glaswegian of Catholic Irish descent (i.e. Billy Connolly). Nor was he a 'Scot', though he lived in Scotland. His Pictish people were one ingredient in the stockpot or Scotpot which produced, by the early modern period, a population of mixed Celtic, Norse and Anglian blood overlaid by lords largely of 'Norman French' origins. We might tell the earlier parts of the story triumphally: up to 1650, a territory never wholly conquered by an army from outside sustained a slowly matured, but at last fully achieved, national identity which led Covenanting ideologues to compare Presbyterian Scotland with ancient Israel – two sworn nations of the Lord.

But Episcopalians and Catholics rejected that identity. In any case, English occupation under Cromwell brought in English genes and a persistent inferiority complex. In the nineteenth century vast numbers left Scotland to populate the United States and the Empire, and large-scale Irish Catholic immigration disrupted cultural continuity, much more directly than the Disruption itself.

Is language, then, the surviving basis of Scottish distinctness? Incomers, adopting ways of speech developed from the Middle Ages, could be held to have incorporated themselves thereby into Scottish community. But alas, leaving aside those reared to elocute 'pure' English, there are two competing Standards of Scottish speech – the lightly-Scotticised English of our TV presenters and thought-for-the-day clerics and an indeterminate Standard Scots synthesised for literary purposes, and often rejected as incomprehensible by born-

and-bred Scots who adhere to the other, diluted Standard (which is more a matter of accent than lexicon). Such people can often use the *patois* of Glasgow, Fife or Aberdeen, but none of these helps to unify the 'nation'. The survival of Gaelic merely embarrasses, even annoys, most Lowlanders.

So I offer these definitions – they're not facetious. A Scot is someone living in the area which comes under Scots law, so long as that person also supports Scottish athletes against those of other countries or identifies strongly with some other aspect of Scottish culture – our folk-music say. A Scot abroad is anyone who still fulfils the latter condition. The Scottish 'nation' exists insofar as many Scots believe that it exists. Its basis cannot be ethnic, linguistic or religious, though its character, as perceived by believers in it, is modified by such things as 'being Celtic' and 'speaking the Doric'. Its basis is territorial and legal. Its existence within exactly its present boundaries dates back to 1482. If, like Wales, it had no separate legal and educational systems it could not credibly subsist, because, unlike Wales, it cannot attach itself to a single cultural tradition. But for 500 years Scotland's boundaries have remained unchanged. The history of Scotland, therefore, is the record of what has happened since time immemorial within those boundaries. Scottish 'race' is a nonsensical idea, 'Scottish culture' a deeply problematical one. 'But Sark rins o'er the Solway Sands, and Tweed rins to the ocean, to mark where England's province stands' – that line creates a 'nation'.

How did the line come to be there – not between Forth and Clyde defining a Celtic heartland never conquered by Romans or English till Cromwell, not flung further south to include areas of Cumbria and Northumbria which at times were ruled by kings based within present-Scotland? And why is that line, without custom posts or forts, so potent that travellers either way across the border are sharply conscious of moving from one country into another, despite a common standard language and so much common history? The task of historians is to answer such questions. One chief test to be applied to a new multi-volume history of Scotland is whether it does so in such a way as to convince the intellect and compel the imagination. A second is whether it might help the inhabitants of Scotland to confront the future with better heart.

Rewriting Scottish History

The Edward Arnold 'new History',* is modelled on the successful *Gill History of Ireland*, except that the latter ran to eleven paperback volumes.[1] This one has only eight textbooks, but, like the Gills, they are in a format useful both to beginners and to advanced scholars; the author surveys major events and developments over a given period, then supplies a full and up-to-date bibliography Comparison with the 'standard' four-volume *Edinburgh History*[2] reveals the advantage of the new venture. Each Arnold book slips comfortably into a handbag or pocket. Revision and replacement as need arises will be easier. Nine brains (volume 7 is co-authored) by their different perspectives, suggest the real complexity of history better than Edinburgh's four authorities, of whom William Ferguson had to cope alone with all the vast changes between 1689 and the present day.

Jenny Wormald, Arnold's general editor, deserves our gratitude for her labours; it is no mean feat to get nine academics into a posture to publish eight volumes within four years. And each volume in turn is highly serviceable. The delineation of sections is in itself a challenge to thought; '1603 and all that' is implicitly demoted by Wormald's own boundary dates, 1470–1625, and 1746–1832 is an inspired periodisation.

That said, the series is, of course, uneven. Christopher Harvie's *No Gods and Precious Few Heroes, Scotland 1914–1980* is already established as the best introduction to twentieth-century Scotland. Its structure is highly original and works very well: detailed studies of Scottish society 'in action' from the periods 1911–22 and 1964–80 flank four analytical chapters, each of which surveys an aspect of history over the entire intervening period. This permits narrative of the impact of the First World War and the 'Red Clyde', and again of the politics of Nationalism, Oil and Referendum, and thus emphasises such high drama as can be found north of the line during the period. Harvie writes (just after the 1979 *débâcle*) as a rather pessimistic but thoroughly *parti-pris* Neo-Nationalist, chastising in turn native industrialists for taking their capital from Scotland after 1918, getting out

* This 'review article' published in 1985 seems worth reproducing because the 'Arnolds' – now reprinted in revised editions by Edinburgh University Press – have been much used (not least by me). They represent the first 'popular' impact, so far as most periods are concerned, of the upsurge in revisionist historiography noted in the last chapter.

'while the going was good, vaulting on the post-war boom to the head of a British consortium', then Labour for its fickleness over home rule and uncharismatic local leadership, and even the intelligentsia of the 'Renaissance' and after, for setting themselves apart from the industrial working class. His insights into economics, the arts and politics are all equally stimulating. With its topical, polemical thrust, this book is of a different kind from the others.

Among the other volumes, two seem to be outstandingly good. Bruce Lenman's *Integration, Enlightenment and Industrialisation, Scotland 1746–1832* divides this crucial phase into eight sub-periods and manages brilliantly to bring the rich cultural history of the times into relation with state affairs and economic change: his 'placing' of vast problematic figures like Dundas, Adam Smith and Scott is uncannily fine. Alexander Grant's *Independence and Nationhood, Scotland 1306–1469* is organised thematically in three blocks – 'Wars of Independence', 'The People of Scotland' and 'Government and Politics'. The disemphasis on narrative which this entails is something I would normally object to – but it consorts very well with Grant's contention that the violent affrays over which previous historical accounts have lingered, the apparently disastrous effects of rule by royal 'minors', mask a 'success story'.

Scotland became a smallish but compact and estimable European nation, with its own kind of orderly society, during a period when England was riven by peasant rebellion, swept by the Wars of the Roses, and, we might add, bereft of any writer of the stature of Henryson:

... Late-mediaeval Scotland never suffered conflicts between crown and parliament on the scale found in England ... because the general nature of Scottish government and society limited the areas of potential conflict so much. The use of unpaid armies, the strength of 'popular' justice, the normal ability of the kings to live within their regular revenue, and the extensive but not uncontrolled delegation of local administrative responsibilities, all meant that late-mediaeval Scotland could be governed without heavy pressure being placed on the people.[3]

Concentration on kings – only one part of the political system – has led to one-sided, 'gloomy' narrative such as may still be found in John Prebble's popular *Lion in the North*:

Conflict was a cancer from which it seemed Scotland must bleed and its people fought among themselves ... The King's brawling brothers were a microcosm of the kingdom ... The people breathed an air that was for a while free from the stench of blood.[4]

Thus Prebble, opened almost at random.

Against Lenman and Grant must be offset disappointments. Understandably, the senior historians involved in the series seem to bring less zest to their work than those who are still making reputations. G. W. S. Barrow's *Kingship and Unity, Scotland 1000–1306* is as we could expect a magisterial textbook, not without nationalistic flourishes:

It would be foolish [he says] to judge Scottish achievement of the earlier Middle Ages, a time of confidence and nation-building, by the sterility of our own day.[5]

But it says little to provoke fresh thought. More seriously, two later periods crucial to any positive restructuring of our sense of Scottish history are handled without any revisionist verve.

The later nineteenth century was the period when Scotland assumed its modern character, with Presbyterianism losing its ground to a Roman Catholicism reinforced by Irish immigrants who greatly affected the new working-class urban culture; with a shift of cultural predominance from Edinburgh to Glasgow which three weeks of Festival a year haven't fully reversed; and with the apogee of Scotland's impact, destructive and creative, on foreign peoples, especially within the Empire. Associated enigmatically with all this was the emergence of the mythologies of 'tartanry', 'kailyard' and 'Clydesidism' which workers in literary and media studies now see as central to their concerns.

Sydney and Olive Checkland have at their fingertips as much of the relevant information bearing on these fascinating matters as any two scholars alive. In places, their book, *Industry and Ethos: Scotland 1832–1914*, achieves uplift. Some sixteen succinct and lively pages, for instance, contrast and compare Scotland's four major cities. They would be just the thing to show an outsider inquisitive as to why Edinburgh and Glasgow, less than hour apart by modern transport, stand facing rather than angrily away from each other, and why Aberdeen, with its diversified economic base, is so utterly different in ambience from Dundee, where jute created a kind of industrial monoculture. But the volume overall is efficient, comprehensive, and tedious. 'Industry' and 'Ethos' are themselves too broad and vague to have intellectual bite or imaginative impact. Information is chopped up into sections – the astonishing story of Scottish involvement with Canada is implicitly diminished when dutifully accorded one not entirely accurate page, as it would not have been by half a dozen scattered, flamboyant, impressionistic paragraphs.

But what *can* be done with Victorian Scotland? Its politics, surely, might be made as interesting as those of the eighteenth-century 'reigns' of Islay and Dundas; but the latter would not, I suppose, compel our interest did they not emerge in paradoxical symbiosis with Scotland's vast contributions to 'Enlightenment' and 'Romanticism'. A narrowly practical politics of self-interest somehow satisfied the incomparable intellect of Hume, and was acceptable to the fecund imagination of Scott – and Bruce Lenman exploits these strange conjunctures. We need organising concepts of the same kind as 'Enlightenment' and 'Romanticism' to create a gestalt of the next period, in which Scots sustained an intense religious life which reinforced, rather than interfered with, capitalist individualism; when no novelist could project an adequate image of Glasgow yet that city vied with Milan and Chicago, even with Paris and New York, as a frontier of social and aesthetic experimentation.

It must be possible to dramatise the exploits of mid- and late-nineteenth-century Scottish capitalism at home and abroad while accounting for Scotland's literature, architecture and painting (native 'art' music, alas, will never make much showing). Glasgow was not only the capital of world shipbuilding, and the major centre in the British Empire of practical teaching and research in science and engineering, but also the place which adapted German philosophy for use throughout the English-speaking world. It lacked its Cockburn. We have no vivid mental picture of the atmosphere of debate in Kelvin's Glasgow. But surely modern scholarship can construct one? And surely while doing so it can take account of the age's dominant religious concerns?

The best 'story line' or 'organising concept' with which to vivify the period is probably to be found in the history of religion. As musty backrooms in second-hand bookshops testify, the concentrated ideological expression of Victorian Scottishness has been physically discarded from our libraries. Even the event-packed tales of 'missionary heroism' await survey, synthesis and decoding. We need for nineteenth-century Scotland a man like Perry Miller, whose books on the *New England Mind* took the rebarbative literature of seventeenth-century Massachusetts and wrested from its jargon moving human content – we need someone, that is, with the patience to 'reconstruct' ideological expression in relation to socioeconomic forces.[6] 'Mind' and 'Edinburgh' fuse in the concept of 'Scottish Enlightenment'. 'Mind', 'Glasgow', and also overseas doings, might be fused in 'Missionary Scotland'. It is bizarre that Canadians, Malawians, Japanese, New Zealanders and anti-racist South Africans, to name only a few, should be aware of the determination of aspects of their own cultures by a Victorian Scottish nexus of ideas and attitudes about which most native nationalists and literati are content to remain essentially ignorant.

But we must also 'Miller-ise' our own seventeenth century. From the Glorious Revolution till the First World War, controversy over the Scottish Revolution of the 1630s and later genesis of an Established Presbyterian church was a recurrent incitement to partisan history. Reaction against those fervours inspired Hume's scepticism, at a time when Church splinter groups vied as jealously for possession of the covenanting heritage as Trotskyite factions have done over the Russian Revolution. In the disturbed aftermath of the Napoleonic Wars, Scott was moved to write *Old Mortality*, one of his very best novels, a blatant effort to pre-empt recycling of the seventeenth-century tradition by artisan radicals. This enraged into refutation the Reverend Doctor Thomas McCrie, biographer of Knox and Melville and leader of the Secession Church, though he was himself ultra-conservative. As Bruce Lenman points out, McCrie and Scott,

the two greatest Scottish men of letters of their day ... held radically antagonistic views as to precisely what kind of heritage needed to be preserved.[7]

Another great man, James Hogg, no Jacobin, wrote a counter-fiction to Scott's, *The Brownie of Bodsbeck*, defending the Border peasant traditions of heroic Covenanters pitted against a diabolical Claverhouse.

Quite suddenly, early in our own century, the steam of this controversy gave its last mighty hisses and expired. The union of the Free Church and United Presbyterian Church in 1900, then that body's reunion with the Established Kirk in 1929, presumably help to explain a general shuddering away from the Covenanters, though Grassic Gibbon in the early 1930s was still prepared to acknowledge them as crucial in Scotland's otherwise rather scant heritage of radical resistance to class rule. Only in very recent years has historical scholarship returned to them, and the absence of controversy resulting, such as any book on the Clearances is liable to arouse, suggest that Montrose rules OK. Victory, in the minds of common reader and intellectual alike, has been conceded to Charles I's champion, a super-fit subject for romantic fiction.

Rosalind Mitchison has many well-known virtues as a historian. Her narrative *History of Scotland* is a very good example of how to move swiftly over tricky terrain, debatable though some of her judgements and emphases are.[8] Her work as a social and economic historian has been wide-ranging, and very important in the revival of Scottish historiography within the last couple of decades. But she is diametrically different from Perry Miller. She is not crassly Whiggish or overbearingly Unionist. However, she cannot conceal, in her *Lordship to Patronage, Scotland 1603–1745,*[9] her disgust at the temper of that Covenanting Calvinism which in the seventeenth century expressed for many ordinary people Scotland's true national consciousness. As a senior scholar, she is trammeled by Unionist assumptions which until very recently were challenged hardly at all save by romantics sustained more by rhetoric than by scholarship.

Mitchison handles some themes admirably. For instance, she manages in a couple of paragraphs to expound with pellucid clarity the distinction in the 1640s between 'Presbyterianism' in Scotland, where it implied the superiority of Church over State, and in England, where it referred rather loosely to puritanical persons committed to a new 'Erastian' church settlement made by Parliament, and came to apply still more loosely to the moderate party which allied with Presbyterian Scots when the latter favoured peace with Charles I; this business has worried me for years, but now I think I understand it. Her discussion of witchcraft is unique in the whole series as a vigorous argument from a feminist perspective. Four out of five accusations of witchcraft in seventeenth-century Scotland were directed against women. As Mitchison shows, women at this time were not always subservient. Some in the lower orders engaged in trade. Many gentry in the 1670s complained that they could not prevent their wives from attending Covenanting coventicles. The fact that deviant women – 'witches' – incurred criminal charges paradoxically marked a new status for women, whose husbands would formerly have been held responsible for illegal or anti-social behaviour by them.

But Mitchison's moralisings and asides elsewhere belong in the implicitly Unionist tradition of historiography which produced those 'gloomy accounts' of the fifteenth century that Alexander Grant has now challenged. She tells us that James VI on his death in 1625 left 'a country more prosperous and more at peace than it ever had been before'. Preceding volumes in the series make this statement seem entirely implausible. Reflection on the state of England and of Europe in general at this time suggests that, if she is right, Scotland (a country only twelve years away from revolution) must have been uniquely adept or fortunate, for reasons which Mitchison does not explain, in coping with a hard economic climate. Her view seems to depend on the assumption that Scotland was *bound* to be better off now its crown was united with England's. A few pages further on she finds it needful to explain that Napier's logarithms were 'for two generations, an intellectual cul-de-sac' because no one including Napier, understood the concepts he had stumbled upon; this is about as helpful as pointing out that Isaac Newton wasn't a deist and didn't anticipate Einstein.

Mitchison's remark that the 'benefits' of Cromwell's imposed incorporation of Scotland with England in 1651 were 'held back for a while' by the Glencairn rising of 1653–4 likewise betrays a Unionist reflex. She goes on to admit that Scotland was governed in the economic interests in England, that is, like a colony, then (apparently) to regret that 'the period of conquest was too short for major political developments to be achieved'. Benefits? Under colonial rule? In six years of political unsettlement? The kindest way of interpreting this is to recognise that Mitchison's secular, commonsensical temperament finds English rule maintained by brute force in the interest of economic and political power more congenial than the attempt at theocracy which had preceded it, governed by non-economic and extra-rational considerations.

She goes on to compare the Covenanting remnants whose resistance and brutal repression marked the whole Restoration period with the Marxist, Nationalist and Fascist extremists of our own time, much in the spirit of those who in effect blamed 'Scargill's miners' for being beaten up by the police. She is not interested in the sympathies of plain country people who cherished and protected outlawed preachers. She is not detained by the paradox, which her own book exposes, that Galloway, the Covenanting heartland, was also used as a fattening-place in the burgeoning cattle trade to England, nor by the fact (which Walter Scott recognised) that diehard Covenanters fathered merchant sons who helped Glasgow to flourish. And of course she wouldn't dream of 'Millerising' the tracts and martyrologies which represented the Covenanters' intellectual and psychic life – of cracking that specialised, now unappealing, code.

However, she is not disgusted by the messages which were exchanged, literally in code, by aristocratic politicians in the period preceding the Union of 1707:

Since in all ages a week is a long time in politics one should not be surprised that this correspondence tends to support the belief that all that mattered to these men was what could personally be secured in the next few days.[10]

As it happens, though, I agree with her that these men were not more 'corrupt' or 'rogueish' than counterparts elsewhere, and that Union was a rational solution to very dangerous economic and political problems. Furthermore, it gave Scots a chance – instantly seized by many – to redress the Darien disaster with legal venturing within the English overseas empire. Mitchison might have made more of this; to say that Scotland in the 1740s 'had not yet obtained much of a position in the East Indian Company' is to underrate the substantial flow of EIC patronage from the 1720s on. But otherwise her account of the early eighteenth-century transition from 'lordship' by great territorial magnates to 'patronage' administered by influential politicians looks durably convincing. Her statement that 'the filaments of patronage went through all levels of society like the mycelium of dry rot through old woodwork'[11] uses an image more striking than appropriate. It would perhaps be juster to compare it to the bubbles in soda water, since, sordid and immoral as it may seem now, the system permitted the Enlightenment and industrial revolution.

Regarding the post-'Forty-Five Scotland into which Burns and Scott were born, we could repeat Grant's formula; Scotland was peaceful and well-organised while England was in violent crisis. The Established Kirk had nothing to contend with comparable to the challenge of old Dissent and new 'Methodism' south of the line. While Wilkes' rioters terrorised respectable London, Scotland stayed quiet. Colonists revolted in America, the Protestant Irish gentry demanded and got legislative freedom for their Parliament, Yorkshire landowners clamoured for Parliamentary reform – and Scotland, as Lenman puts it, remained 'the most undemanding and subservient of British provinces'.[12] Was this where the 'auld sang' of nationhood really ended, to be sustained only in spurious fictional afterlife by literary men and opportunist politicians?

Of course not. This was not the first, and nor was it the last, crisis in which the inhabitants of Scotland seemed to accept English dominance while in fact maintaining a strong sense of separate identity. Leaving aside complex mediaeval instances, the sixteenth-century Reformation was achieved through English support, yet its heritage made for the most dramatic contrast between the two countries after 1689. The arrival of railways towards the mid-nineteenth century might have been crucial in drawing the Scottish cities into London's net: yet in fact it did not even prevent rivalry and distinction between themselves. Unionist dominance in Scottish politics in the 1950s proved merely a prelude to a Nationalist upsurge in the late 1960s. Every national culture in Europe has been subjected to the same processes of state-building, modernisation, 'Americanisation', as Scotland's, which surely remains in as good a defensive posture as any; and if the Val d'Aosta can make its voice heard in the European Parliament, the prospects for Scottish Gaeldom are not so bad.

In reconstructing Scottish history, it is important to maintain that pan-European perspective which Fletcher of Saltoun enunciated, and the still wider internationalist vision which animated 'Darien' Paterson. Such vistas permit us to see that Scotland was never a naturally rich country somehow cheated of its birthright by England. Nor is it naturally a poor relation, of violent and hard-drinking disposition, which should be grateful for sensible Westminster nannying. It is a nation which has done very well with mediocre resources, which has made intellectual and cultural contributions disproportionate to its small size, and which has a strong, if distorted presence in the minds of foreigners all over the world. Against every American speaking of 'Glasgow, England' we can offset a Nigerian who believes that the Scots are an oppressed colonial people or a Canadian proud to claim one-sixteenth Scottish descent.

It is easy and indeed necessary to jeer at the nineteenth-century exploitation or invention of such symbols as the tartan, the kilt, the Burns cult, the lad o' pairts: yet perhaps we should be furtively grateful that the Victorian Scottish bourgeoisie felt that it needed a distinctive mythology and provided us with a national 'image' which we can debunk for intelligent foreigners. Meanwhile Tom Nairn's 'great tartan monster' (see pp. 229–30) is really no more, if no less, repulsive than similar phenomena such as the 'Spain' of the package-holiday industry or the cult of the outback in Australia, which happens to be one of the most urbanised countries on earth. We have no Grieg or Ibsen, but Norway has no Burns. We have no Strindberg or Bergmann but has Swedish painting been better than ours? Our pretensions at soccer doubtless exceed our capacity – but the latter has taken the national team into three successive World Cup finals. We may even nurse a kind of perverse pride in the fact that North Americans and Europeans now usually beat us in two major sports, golf and curling, which we invented. We can go backwards into the past and forward into the international future recognising that Scottish life has had features which still need extirpation, but also good ones which deserve conservation and development.

In regard to Scottish nationality, geography has been limitation, foundation and challenge. Alfred P. Smyth's *Warlords and Holy Men, Scotland AD 80–1000* shows how the Roman Empire set up a system based on two walls, Hadrian's and the Antonine, designed not to box in the Picts but to defend southerly settlements against tribes over the whole turbulent area from the base of the Pennines in the Peak District to the Central Lowlands of Caledonia. Hence the *vallum* or ditch 'behind' Hadrian's Wall was actually designed to seal it off from enemies to the south. That wall did not mark the northern border of Roman *imperium*, nor, later, did the Antonine, which provided alternative forward bases against the barbarians whose movements the Latin soldiery monitored. This is one of Dr Smyth's controversial judgements: another is his insistence that the Picts were not a sharply different people from the 'Strathclyde Britons': the whole Pictish region was already Celtic-speaking 'and perhaps Gallo-Brittonic' by the first century. Later Pictish artists 'welded' together constituents from cultures all over Britain, hence the affinities of their patterns with both Irish and Anglo-Saxon art. Smyth further contends against scholars who have devised support from Pictish king-lists for the theory that this people were matrilinear. I cannot evaluate his arguments, but it seems to me inherently plausible to suppose that the Picts were a not un-typical Celtic people. What their heartland north of the Forth and Tay gave them, however, was a base almost impregnable to outright assault from the south over which the 'Scots' from Ireland gradually gained ascendancy. Kenneth McAlpin, about 840, was not the first warlord to govern both Picts and Scots, but he founded a new dynasty 'whose sustained success over many centuries gave added posthumous glory to Kenneth'.[13] In the early tenth century the King of Scots held the 'balance of power' between York and Wessex. Thereafter while Scandinavian York foundered and the Anglo-Saxon monarchy declined, the kingdom inherited by Malcolm II in 1005 exhibited 'security and vitality' – a fact systematically obscured by later Anglo-Norman historiography, which pretended that the Scottish realm had been a client of Wessex.

Smyth's book makes absorbing if rather heavy reading and establishes a firm basis for the optimistic view of mediaeval Scotland taken by Barrow and Grant. Scotland was not conquered by Normans. A refined version of feudalism arrived with David I (1124–53) whereas in England earlier a cruder version had been brutally imposed. English power was formidable enough to render the defence of Berwick and Lothian not always practical. But Scots, despite their weaker military technology, maintained an excellent home record in the long series of intrusions across the line from both directions, by avoiding battle and using scorched earth tactics. 'After 1347 English armies never stayed more than three weeks in Scotland.'[14]

Arnold's general editor, Jenny Wormald, has courageously tackled, in *Court, Kirk, and Community*, the period from 1470 to 1625 which includes the apparent apogee of the Scottish kingdom in James IV's and James V's 'Renaissance', the Anglo-Scottish crisis of the 1540s, the subsequent Reformation and the Union of the Crowns. In relation to all this, what might be called Grant's 'Merrie Scotland' model becomes somewhat problematic. Wormald begins by carrying it forward in a very convincing treatment over seventy pages of 'Renaissance Scotland'. Despite Flodden, the Stewart dynasty can be see as successfully ruthless. James V was probably just as nasty as Henry VIII. But the Stewarts were originally 'Stewards', as they themselves emphasised – loyal servants of the realm, 'Kings of Scots' not of 'Scotland', keeping the peace by active peripatetic rule, and able to do so without regular taxation because Scotland was so rarely at war.

The Scottish peerage had been remarkably stable since the mid-fifteenth century. Its magnates exerted power not through land but through kinship and personal lordship. The institution of blood-feud has been misrepresented – by this stage it was a legal device, a 'force for peace', because of the widespread acceptance of compensation after arbitration as the best way of dealing with crimes and disputes. Penalties were enforced swiftly, locally, by local lords, supported in the last resort by kings who accepted 'the justice of the feud'.

But if everything was going along so well, how do we explain the Reformation? There clearly was a social crisis of some kind in mid-sixteenth-century Scotland. Feus, not feuds, may be the key to it. James IV was the first king to give feu fermes to any extent. James V's massive taxation of the Church in the 1530s (contemporary with Henry VIII's Reformation) panicked ecclesiastical landlords into widespread feuing. Feuing looked much like leasing or renting – it involved a down-payment and an annual duty – but, crucially, it was hereditary. The superior got a quick profit, but in the long term, as the value of money fell, feus became excellent bargains for their holders. A whole new group of landed proprietors was created from those lucky enough to get feus; other sitting tenants suffered much like victims of enclosure in England, forced to leave or beg. Do we see the Reformation as merely a case of Scots following Continental and English fashion, as a product of social tensions created by feuing, or both? Wormald gives weight to the aspirations of an increasingly literate laity contemptuous of a Church which had made itself unpopular by dispossessing a third of its tenants.

But after the upheaval of 1559–60, some aspects of 'Merrie Scotland' could be descried again. The new church suited the middling classes – lairds, burgesses, and Reformed ministers – very well. The Catholics who remained were weak and regionalised; personal, 'clannish' ties stayed strong across religious divisions, and there was no persecution. However, Reformation on the basis of an English bible produced what Wormald calls 'a three-tier system' in language. English was at the top. Scots would soon fall out of fashion as a medium for literary expression. Gaelic was at the bottom. Lowlanders who could use English growingly shared James VI's racialist contempt for the Gaels; it was at this juncture that the Highland–Lowland divide opened momentously in what had formerly been, it seems, a cheerfully multi-lingual country. God's word was now heard in English, not in the Latin which had overridden linguistic differences under the old Church, and which still provided a medium for Scotland's great political theorist and pioneer of Celtic studies, George Buchanan.

The paradox of Scottish history with which we must live is that a durable nation erected on the bases of a Celtic heartland came, through the efforts of Knox and his successors, to express its peculiar sensibility in a version of Anglo-Norman speech. Church history – I repeat – must be revived if we are to understand satisfactorily key phases in Scotland's 'story', in the seventeenth and nineteenth centuries. It will not do to presume that Calvinism was an unfortunate temporary aberration, that the 'real' Scot has always been a jolly fellow much like an agnostic French aesthete. Scottish national feeling was at its peak in the 1630s when Charles I moved against the distinctive Scottish mode of Protestantism. In view of the key role of Earls of Argyll in the Covenanting period, that feeling did not wholly exclude Gaeldom – and in the nineteenth century Gaels took to Calvinism with the ferocity of new converts. Dialectically, our religious heritage accounts for all distinctiveness in our culture; Hume and Burns, reacting thoroughly against Calvinism, may tower over orthodox contemporaries, but who can read Byron or Carlyle or Stevenson or MacDiarmid or Grassic Gibbon without perceiving their various assaults on orthodoxy as fresh modulations within Knox's tradition?

It is a kind of superstition which makes the present-day intelligentsia fearful of taking church matters seriously. Only children, romance-readers and lumpen-Marxists can honestly believe that you go to history looking for people and movements *wholly* admirable in present-day terms. Persons prepared to swallow John Maclean's and MacDiarmid's outrageous self-contradictions in return for the energy of their expression can surely cope with Andrew Melville and David Livingstone. Historians of England have to comprehend 'gentry' and the Victorian 'gentleman'. Historians of Scotland have to understand Covenanting Calvinism, 'missionary Scotland' and the extraordinary native cult of inner-directed 'independence' and 'self-help' to which both the Checklands and Harvie point.

OK, so we're really quite different *now*? Secularised, Americanised, in tune with new Western morality? Sidney Devine and R. D. Laing are our prophets? In that case we had better stop trying to use our history, forget it and build a new nation from scratch. The Line is still there. Perhaps we could start with Scotland's reinvention of football, with the founding of Glasgow Queen's Park club in 1867, which the Checklands ignore? An English historian, James Walvin, shows that Queen's Park created a system of teamwork with the emphasis on passing rather than 'brilliant dribbling by individual players'. By 1876 'most clubs had begun to follow the Scottish passing pattern' and this tactical innovation 'paved the way for the transformation of football from a middle- to a working-class game'.[15] Division of labour prevailed as in factory life. Solidarity exerted itself over individualism. Dominance passed from English public-school amateurs to northern and Scottish professionals. I might end with what I hope is an uplifting image of 'independent' working men co-operatively at play, and await the fury of outraged feminists.

But seriously, we can deplore anti-Catholic bigotry without wholly losing touch with that Protestant of tragic open-mindedness, David Livingstone. And in any profound discussion of Victorian spirituality, the role of such women as W. E. Gladstone's Evangelical mother will emerge as fascinating and crucial. Reconstructing Scotland's religious heritage, we can set the pious mother beside, or over against, the heavy father. Some women found in 'Missions' of various kinds spheres of independent momentous action. 'Mary Slessor of Calabar', duly acknowledged by the Checklands, has never been forgotten. We should now disinter such counterparts as 'Cristina Forsyth of

Fingoland' (1844–1918) who lived for thirty years as the sole white woman in a remote part of South Africa, and we should try to understand the part played by a strict Presbyterian upbringing and marriage to a minister in the life of Helen Crawford (1877–1954) – militant suffragette, 'Christian Socialist', leader in the 1915 Glasgow Rent Strikes, then activist in the Communist Party of Great Britain. The point would not be to distract attention from the material conditions of life, or from class, gender and power; it would be to know how, here, all these were affected by a specific religious tradition.

(1985)

5

Burns, Scott and the French Revolution

Robert Burns was a young man when Britain's North American colonies revolted. Walter Scott was about the same age when the Bastille fell. While Burns died in the early stages of the long war between Britain and France, Scott's life from youth through middle age was dominated by news of it. The works of both Burns and Scott belong to what has been called the 'Age of Revolutions', and both men can be seen as revolutionaries in literature, producing ideas and sentiments which connected with the advancing spirit of democracy. Yet the Scotland which joyously responded to their writings and hailed both men as national heroes was overwhelmed by political conservatism. The poet of liberty and equality, Burns, and the novelist, Scott, who momentously created Jeanie Deans – woman of the people with heroic stature – were captives of Scotland's *ancien régime* – and Scott was that régime's eloquent defender.

Our understanding of that régime is, I believe, improving year by year and even month by month. The Whig version of history made it seem so ridiculous and contemptible that it was hard, even impossible, to understand how the great David Hume had accepted it and the sensitive Walter Scott had warmly supported it. It is good that we now see more clearly where its strengths lay.

In the first place, Scotland under the management of Henry Dundas enjoyed much the same degree of independence as seems to be envisaged by the SNP when it talks now about 'Scotland in Europe'. The nation's loss of independence – pace Burns' 'Parcel of Rogues' – didn't come in 1707 or 1746, it coincided with the triumph of Whiggery in the second quarter of the nineteenth century. Scotland's political institutions were then homogenised with those of England. The monolith of Presbyterianism was eroded by Catholic immigration, and cracked by the Disruption of 1843. The new railways cut travel time to London and made it perfectly convenient for English Liberals to sit in Parliament for Scottish constituencies.

In the eighteenth century, on the contrary, plenty of Scots had 'represented' English rotten boroughs and not a single Englishman was voted in by any of the amazingly rotten Scottish constituencies. It was possible for Walter Scott to be both a devoted Scottish patriot and a loyal Unionist because Union, so far, had not entailed any serious loss of Scottish distinctiveness imposed by England. If middle-class Scots took elocution lessons to polish and Anglicise their accents, they did so by choice not compulsion.

By the standards of the era of Gladstone, Henry Dundas, 'King Henry the Ninth', was an octopus of corruption whose tentacles strangled liberty. By the standards prevailing in British public life in 1789, this close associate of Mr Clean, the younger Pitt, was a very kind man who did lots of favours for people of all classes whose families accordingly gave him and his loyal supporters in Parliament their sympathy and, if they possessed them, votes. After something of an interregum Dundas had picked up where Lord Islay, dying in 1760, had left off. A solid block of Scottish votes, in an era when party machines and three-line whips didn't exist, gave its controller enormous influence at Westminster. Dundas accordingly was able to command in Indian and imperial affairs, and in the process increase his own resources of patronage. In a period when the English, especially Londoners, were particularly turbulent – the period of the Wilkesite riots, the Gordon riot and, after the French Revolution, the London Corresponding Society – Scotland was as usual peaceful, always easy to bring to order. There was no great popular upsurge with which Burns could have identified himself.

As Bruce Lenman puts it succinctly in his admirable study of Scotland in this period,

even Burns represented no real threat to the social order or Dundas ascendancy. Security for Burns and for the large legitimate and illegitimate brood he loved was his job as an Excise Officer in Dumfries, a job which he openly acknowledged he owed to the benign patronage of James, Earl of Glencairn and patron of Kilmarnock parish. Before he died in 1796 he recanted his pro-Revolutionary views to keep his Excise job. After 1793 he penned patriotic anti-French verse.[1]

Mention of Glencairn leads me towards a crucial point about the political atmosphere in Scotland in the 1790s which conditioned, indeed determined, the responses of Burns and Scott to the French Revolution. Glencairn's brother, the Revd. John Cunningham, married, in 1785, Lady Isabella Erskine, sister of the Earl of Buchan, a nobleman whose enthusiasm for the French Revolution was, later, quite extreme. One of Buchan's brothers was Thomas Erskine, who joined the Society of the Friends of the People in 1792, and defended Tom Paine when he was tried for publishing the second part of *The Rights of Man*. Six years before that, the Glencairn–Erskine circle had given Burns a warm reception when he came to Edinburgh. The poet had been introduced to Glencairn by James Dalrymple of Ayr. There is a fascinating Scottish link with India here which I cannot resist mentioning. The father of the Earl of Glencairn had saved his noble line from poverty by marrying in 1744 a young lady of a family which had been adopted by the remarkable Governor Macrae – an Ayrshire seaman who had become Governor of the East India Company settlement at Madras, and had made a vast fortune there. Her younger sister, who inherited the Governor's house, married Charles Dalrymple of Ayr in 1750, so that their son James – freemason and would-be poet – was the Earl of Glencairn's cousin. We have here a striking example of the role played by East Indian gains, often ill-gotten, in eighteenth-century Scotland. Long before Dundas got his hands on the India Office in the 1780s, East India patronage secured through Scottish directors of the East Indian Company was an important element in the management of Scotland.

So Burns enjoyed the admiration and patronage of powerful people. Another of Glencairn's brothers-in-law was Henry Erskine, a glittering ornament of the Scottish bar, elected Dean of the Faculty of Advocates in 1785. He was a leading proponent of reform of the Scottish burghs, but Burns' letters to him ooze with undemocratic servility – this despite the fact that both were masons and Erskine had introduced Burns to the Canongate Kilwinning Lodge in Edinburgh.

Burns writes of his 'humble muse' and professes himself to be Erskine's 'devoted humble servant'.[2]

Not only was Burns cautiously respectful in his dealings with this great man – Henry Erskine himself was first cowed, then humiliated, in the phase of horrified reaction against the French Revolution and its principles which swept aristocratic Britain in the 1790s. The Americans were attached to principles of English Liberty. Edmund Burke, close to the heart of Britain's *ancien régime*, was able to speak and write memorably on their behalf. Nor were the political classes in Britain alarmed when the Bastille fell. The French were at last showing sense, moving towards the constitutional model supposed to have been established in England by the so-called 'Glorious Revolution' of 1688. But events rapidly made clear that something new was at work in France, with the assertion of the Rights of Man. By August 1792, when the French royal family was imprisoned and feudal dues were abolished without indemnity it was clear that the French example was highly dangerous to Britain's *ancien régime*.

Tom Paine's tract *The Rights of Man* was finding avid readers, not least in Scotland. He called for government by election and representation, based on the principle of Reason. Monarchical sovereignty – 'the enemy of mankind and the source of misery' – should be abolished and sovereignty given to the people, the nation. The origin of kingship lay in robbery. 'What at first was plunder, assumed the softer name of revenue'.

It could be said that the blistering radicalism of Paine's assault of Britain's supposedly glorious 'mixed constitution' gave the privileged a shock so profound that we still observe its effects today. What could not, or so Paine argued, be defended rationally, had to be preserved by mystification. When Roy Hattersley pours scorn on Charter 88 or when Mrs Thatcher talks opaquely about Britain's gift of 'liberty' to Europe, it is clear that perfectly intelligent politicians still feel at the thought of constitutional change twinges of the fear which gripped Burke and many others in 1792, before the terror in Paris gave them an excuse for claiming that Paineite principles led to murder and anarchy.

Let anyone who thinks Burns a coward for not sticking to his principles, or Scott a time-server for cleaving to the *ancien régime*, consider the atmosphere in Edinburgh in 1792. The first General Convention of the Friends of the People in Scotland meets in the city. It makes what is by this time a stock demand, much canvassed in recent years by perfectly respectable people, for equal representation in frequent parliaments. Thomas Muir, one of its leaders, is tried for sedition and sentenced to 14 years transportation. In the three decades which follow, such trials continue intermittently, sufficiently often to remind anyone with democratic impulses that the Scottish courts will be ruthless with them if they voice their feelings openly. Though Scotland, as I remarked earlier, had shown no signs in recent years of developing any great radical movement, Dundas and the judges talked and behaved as if guillotines would spring up in every town unless democratical notions were stamped on.

A glance at memoirs referring to Edinburgh in this period shows that the capital of Enlightenment was an area of extreme intolerance. Pryse Lockhart Gordon, soldier in the Gordon Fencibles, recalled in 1830 that in the winter of 1794 it was dangerous for gentlemen of the army to be seen in company with Whigs or reformers. 'I was cautioned by the Lord Provost that certain persons, whose names it would be improper to name even at this distant period, though they are both judges, with whom I was in the habit of dining, were dangerous acquaintances.'[3]

Henry Cockburn devotes some of the most eloquent pages of his *Memorials* to this *grande peur*:

Everything rung, and was connected with, the Revolution in France; which, for above 20 years, was, or was made, the all in all. Everything, not this or that, but literally everything, was soaked in this one event ... Scotch Jacobinism did not exist. But Scotch Toryism did, and with a vengeance ... This party engrossed almost the whole wealth, and rank, and public office, of the country and at least three-fourths of the population ... Jacobinism was a term denoting everything alarming and hateful, and every political objector was a Jacobin.

Cockburn says of the Whigs: 'Self interest had converted some and terror more'. Most of those who held on to their principles were lawyers and 'they were constantly and insolently reminded that the case of their brother Thomas Muir ... was intended for their special edification ... In general, Whigs had to associate solely with Whigs. Very dear friendships were in many instances broken.'[4]

Archibald Fletcher was an Edinburgh lawyer who had striven for burgh reform and admired French Revolutionary principles. When Thomas Muir asked him in 1792 to join the Friends of the People, he refused, telling his wife, 'These violent reformers will create such an alarm in the country as must strengthen the government'. Nevertheless, people in Edinburgh honestly believed that his wife Eliza had provided herself with a small guillotine, and 'exercised the same in beheading poultry, or perhaps "rats and mice and such small deer", in order to be expert when "French principles" and practice in accordance, should prevail in our land . . .'[5] Fletcher did indeed stick to his Whig principles – and suffered for it in his profession because it was widely believed that the judges would not decide in favour of anyone employing a Whig lawyer. His co-thinker John Craig Millar, son of the great professor, left for America in 1796 having lost his professional employment as an advocate.

And even Burns' mighty friend, Henry Erskine, at last came to grief. He held back, in the current climate of opinion, from advocating constitutional reform in Britain: he feared it would further excite the lower orders with 'ideas on the subject of Government highly hostile to our happy Constitution . . .'[6] In November 1795 he nevertheless attended a meeting of protest against repressive new sedition and treason bills. Early next year he was voted out of his position as Dean of the Faculty of Advocates, by 123 to 38. Even that decided young Whig, Francis Jeffrey, felt unable to vote for him, and stayed away out of respect for the feelings of his father and his patron Lord Glenlee.

I have covered a great deal of perhaps over-familiar ground in order to establish clearly the context in which Burns and Scott reacted to the French Revolution. To Scott, an aspiring lawyer, support for Dundas was the obvious option, even if his infatuation with the feudal past had not predisposed him to Burkeian conservatism. Burns, even more dependent on patronage, had three choices – to conform, to emigrate, or to starve. In any case, the declaration of war against Britain by France on 1 February 1793 aroused British patriotism. For a hundred years, after all, Britain had been struggling with France for trade and empire. And in the situation of effectual independence which Scotland enjoyed, Scottish as well as British feeling expressed itself against the enemy.

Burns' main literary work in the revolutionary years was on his Scottish songs. In 1790, for instance, he provided for the *Scots Musical Museum* words for 'Johnnie Cope'. 'The White Cockade', 'Killiecrankie' and 'The Campbells are Coming'. In 1793 he gave Thomson 'Scots, wha hae . . .' In 1796, the *Musical Museum* published Burns' 'Charlie is My Darling'. These were, and of course still are, rousing ditties.

In 1797 Walter Scott joined the Royal Edinburgh Volunteer Light Dragoons, at a time when fears of invasion ran high. These young patriots loved to bellow out 'Hey Johnnie Cope'. In 1804, when Napoleon had assembled barges to invade Britain, and volunteers, as Scott reported, rendezvoused at Kelso, the Liddesdale men swept in to the tune of:

> O wha dare meddle wi' me
> And wha dare meddle wi' me?
> My name is little Jock Elliot.
> And wha dare meddle wi' me?!

The sentiment of this song expresses the egalitarian feeling inherent in Scottish lowland tradition, which Burns had recently released so powerfully in 'For a' that and a' that'. France under Napoleon was again despotic. There was no contradiction in setting British libertarianism against French tyranny, nor in the fact that the labour of collecting and shaping the great body of Scottish popular song, in which Scott had now followed Burns, proceeded apace in a period of inflamed Great British patriotism.

Let us probe the apparent inconsistency of Burns, who in 1795 contributes to the *Scots Musical Museum* his most intense expression of nationalistic feeling, 'Such a parcel of rogues in a nation . . .' yet a few weeks later writes for the Dumfries Volunteers fervid verses which not only evoke British patriotism but actually echo lines in the earlier song.

> Now Sark rins o'er the Solway sands,
> And Tweed runs to the ocean,
> To mark where England's province stands,
> Such a parcel of rogues in a nation.

clearly prefigures:

> The *Nith* shall run to *Corsincon*,
> And *Criffell* sink in *Solway*
> E'er we permit a Foreign Foe
> On British ground to rally.

James Kinsley in his monumental edition of Burns' poetry speculates that he left 'Such a parcel of rogues' unsigned in the *Scots Musical*

Museum because theme and refrain were not his own. He had no inhibitions about identifying himself as the author of the 'Dumfries Volunteers', written when he was helping to organise them in the spring of 1795. It appeared in several newspapers in May of that year.

It is worth considering all the words of 'The Dumfries Volunteers':

> Does haughty Gaul invasion threat,
> Then let the louns bewaure, Sir,
> There's Wooden Walls upon our seas,
> And Volunteers on shore, Sir:
> The *Nith* shall run to *Corsincon*,
> And *Criffell* sink in *Solway*,
> E'er we permit a Foreign Foe
> On British ground to rally.
>
> O, let us not, like snarling tykes,
> In wrangling be divided,
> Till, slap! come in an *unco loun*,
> And wi' a rung decide it!
> Be Britain still to Britain true,
> Amang oursels united;
> For never but by British hands
> Must British wrongs be righted.
>
> The *kettle* o' the Kirk and state,
> Perhaps a clout may fail in 't
> But deil a foreign tinkler-loun
> Shall ever ca' a nail in 't.
> Our Fathers Blude the *kettle* bought,
> And wha wad dare to spoil it,
> By heavens, the sacreligious dog
> Shall fuel be to boil it!
>
> The wretch that would a *Tyrant* own,
> And the wretch, his true-sworn brother,
> Who'd set the *Mob* above the *Throne*;
> May they be damn'd together!
> Who will not sing, God Save The King,
> Shall hang as high 's the steeple;

But while we sing, God Save The King,
We'll ne'er forget The People!

We note that Gaul is described as 'haughty' – associated, therefore, with despotic arrogance rather than 'mob rule'. The reference to 'British wrongs' which must be righted only by 'British hands' hints at the admission that much is wrong with British society. This is not contradicted by the jocular stanza which follows. A patch has failed in the cauldron of Church and State: cauldrons with holes in them leak and are useless. But it is not up to foreigners to hammer nails into the British cauldron.

The fourth stanza indicates that Burns did not share Tom Paine's contempt for royalty. Tyranny – depotism – is bad, but so is mob rule. Burns seems to be conferring approval on the mixed British constitution. And, as we have seen, his famous reforming friend Henry Erskine was a devout admirer of the constitution. If one is dismayed to think that Burns might have called for the knavish tricks of the Jacobites to be confounded, and rebellious Scots to be crushed, as he sang 'God Save the King', one must be reassured by the fact that his poem ends by pledging support for 'the people'.

At this time, citizens of the United States were appropriating the tune of 'God Save the King' and setting to it such sentiments as 'God Save America', 'God Save the Thirteen States' and 'God Save George Washington'. In 1794 Burns wrote an ode for General Washington's birthday. He sent a draft to his friend Mrs Dunlop with a letter informing her: 'The Subject is, Liberty: you know . . . how dear the theme is to me'. This poem was not published at the time. It is not, to tell the sad truth, very good as verse:

> 'Tis Liberty's bold note I swell,
> Thy harp, Columbia, let me take . . .

and so on, represents Burns' English at its weakest.

But, ideologically speaking, the ode is rich. It identifies 'Columbia's offspring' with 'The Royalty of Man'. It then, most interestingly, evokes King Alfred, associated in English radical tradition with the Saxon freedom overridden by the Norman yoke:

> Alfred, on thy starry throne,

76

> Surrounded by the tuneful choir,
> The bards that erst have struck the patriot lyre
> And roused the freeborn Briton's soul of fire,
> No more thy England own . . .

England in its dealings with the Americans had identified with 'The Tyrant's cause' and the 'generous English name' is now linked with 'damned deeds of everlasting shame'.

Caledonia is now invoked, 'Famed for the martial deed':

> To thee, I turn with swimming eyes –
> Where is that soul of Freedom fled?
> Immingled with the mighty Dead!
> Beneath that hallowed turf where Wallace lies!

What follows is rather obscure, as if Burns was unable to clarify his point or perhaps hesitant about making his political views clear, agitated by the thought that Caledonian traditions of liberty have been compromised:

> Is this the ancient Caledonian form.
> Firm as her rock, resistless as her storm?
> Shew me that eye which shot immortal hate,
> Blasting the Despot's proudest bearing:
> Shew me that arm which, nerved with thundering fate,
> Braved Usurpation's boldest daring!
> Dark-quenched as yonder sinking star
> No more that glance lightens afar;
> That palsied arm no more whirls on the waste of war.

It could be that Thomas Crawford's ingenious explanation is right – that this poem was originally preceded by a prologue found separately in Burns' collected works, beginning 'As I stood by yon roofless tower'. In this a lassie is represented as 'lamenting our lads beyond the sea' (for instance, those who had fallen fighting against Washington?) and a ghostly minstrel appears before her and plays on his harp such strains as might rouse the slumbering dead. In this case, the final stanza of the Washington ode refers to the 'glance' and 'palsied arm' of the minstrel, and the final stanza of 'I stood by yon roofless tower' applies to Burns' own situation in a time of political repression:

He sang wi' joy his former day,
He, weeping, wail'd his latter times:
But what he said – it was nae play!
I winna venture't in my rhymes.

But Crawford's hypothesis is only that: an hypothesis, apparently impossible to falsify or prove.[7] I can accept Crawford's case that in the 1790s Burns shared the outlook of the reforming Whigs. We have seen how cautious they became. By the end of 1792 Burns had been informed on as unpatriotic, and his loyalty had been the subject of an enquiry by the Excise Board. In view of the climate of repression which that represented, I think it is easy enough to understand why he could not articulate, even for private consumption, what it was he wanted to say in honour of Washington (who himself, of course, was a conservative slave-owner, by no means a friend of Jacobinism).

Another unpublished poem was 'The Dean of Faculty – A new Ballad', written after Henry Erskine's defeat. This is a jocular poem, jeering rather merrily at Robert Dundas, Erskine's successful opponent, a mediocrity with good connections. Burns addresses the 'Sublime majority' against Erskine:

With your Honours and a certain King
In your servants this is striking –
The more incapacity they bring,
The more they're to your liking.

It seems to be significant that even in a poem intended, presumably to be seen only by friends and allies of Erskine, Burns cannot specify whether he refers to the King of England, or some other monarch. Scott, of course, was in no danger of having his loyalty impugned. One of his most attractive traits was the friendly relations which he maintained with such 'dangerous' Whigs as Jeffrey and Cockburn. Towards the end of his life, when he was deeply perturbed by the movement for constitutional reform which they hotly supported, he confided to his journal 'I do not know how it is but when I am with a party of my opposition friends, the day is often merrier than with our own set. Is it because they are cleverer?'[8] The aim of the series of long narrative poems which were Scott's first substantial independent productions can be seen as national reconciliation – of Catholic with

Protestant in the *Lay of the Last Minstrel* (and so of British with
Catholic Irish), of English with Scots in *Marmion*, of Highlands with
Lowlands in *The Lady of the Lake*. All people and classes in the
British Isles must be inspired to unite in battle against Napoleon. In a
passage in the Introduction to *Marmion*'s first canto which used to
be commonly seen in anthologies, Scott eulogises Nelson and Pitt,
but also pays generous tribute to the arch-Whig Charles James Fox,
who had before his death reversed his opposition to war with France
and served in the 'Ministry of All the Talents'. Scott urges that
though his admirable qualities – genius, learning, reasoning powers,
keen feelings,

> . . . could not save
> From error him who owns this grave,
> Be every harsher thought suppress'd
> And sacred be the last long rest.

Scott had no doubts about where 'error' and 'truth' had been
found in the 1790s. Perhaps the strength of his anti-Jacobin patriotism
made it easy for him to be generous later to those who had fallen
into Whiggish error. In any case, his side had been very much on top,
even after Dundas, now Viscount Melville, had been impeached, but
acquitted for misuse of public funds in 1805 and the death of Pitt in
1806 had finished his active political career. The brief period, 1806–
7, when Tory rule lapsed (and Henry and Thomas Erskine became
respectively Lord Advocate for Scotland and Lord Chancellor of
Great Britain) did not shake the Dundas tradition of management,
which was continued by his son, the 2nd Viscount Melville.

Scott devoted the entire first volume – 375 pages in the edition
which I own – of his life of Napoleon, published in 1827, to a history
of the French Revolution. His view of its causation is wonderfully
characteristic:

The first and most effective cause of the Revolution was the change which
had taken place in the feelings of the French towards their government, and
the monarch who was its head. The devoted loyalty of the people to their
king had been for several ages the most marked characteristic of the nation;
it was their honour in their own eyes ... That very excess of loyalty,
however, was founded not on a servile but upon a generous principle. France
is ambitious, fond of military glory, and willingly identifies herself with the

fame acquired by her soldiers. Down to the reign of Louis XV, the French Monarch was, in the eyes of his subjects, a general, and the whole people an army. An army must be under severe discipline, and a general must possess absolute power; but the soldier feels no degradation from the restraint which is necessary to his profession, and without which he cannot be led to conquest . . . The King, according to this system, was regarded less as an individual than as the representative of the concentrated honour of the kingdom; and in this sentiment, however extravagant and Quixotic, there mingled much that was generous, patriotic and disinterested. The same feeling was awakened after all the changes of the Revolution, by the wonderful successes of the Individual of whom the future volumes are to treat . . .

French victories on the battlefield, and glorious royal palaces, according to Scott, compensated the poorer French for unequal and undue taxation: 'The people were like men inconveniently placed in a crowded theatre, who think little of the personal inconveniences they are subjected to by the heat and pressure, while their mind is engrossed by the splendours of the representation.'

In the eighteenth century, however, 'luxury and vanity . . . totally ruined the great part of the French nobility', who lost touch with traditions of chivalry. The nobility were too numerous and were divided among themselves. Only in the Vendée had

the nobles united their interest and their fortune with those of the peasants who cultivated their estates, and there alone were they found in their proper and honourable character of proprietors residing on their own domains, and discharging the duties which are inalienably attached to the owner of landed property. And – mark-worthy circumstance! – in the Vendée alone was any stand made in behalf of the ancient proprietors, constitution and religion of France; for there alone the nobles and the cultivators of the soil held towards each other their natural and proper relations of patron and client, faithful dependants, and generous and affectionate superiors.

The growth in wealth and numbers of the Third Estate led to greater and greater pressure of resentment against the privileges of nobility and clergy. Meanwhile, aristocrats foolishly patronised and encouraged the thinkers of the Enlightenment who, being nevertheless jealous of the privileges enjoyed by their patrons, made 'frequent and close inquiry into the origins of ranks' and 'ingenious argument, and eloquent tirades in favour of primitive and even savage independence'. Not only were Enlightened writers directly subversive, they were also licentious. 'Streams of impurity disgraced France' in the reign of Louis XV and continued to 'infect' society under his successor. Scott did not deny that the French constitution had needed some adjustment. But he argued that 'licence and infidelity' had made the French unable to resist the arguments of vain extremists.

It was to such men . . . that Heaven, in punishment of the sins of France and of Europe, and perhaps to teach mankind a dreadful lesson, abandoned the management of the French Revolution, the original movements of which, so far as they went to secure to the people the restoration of their natural liberty . . . had become not only desirable through the change of times, and by the influence of public opinion, but peremptorily necessary and inevitable.

War in alliance with American rebels not only gave respectability to the idea of 'defending the claims of the people against the rights of a established government', but also meant that French 'patriotism' detached itself from the King and adhered to an army whose officer corps had been infiltrated with plebeians, while high-spirited aristocratic commanders identified themselves with the popular cause. And the American war brought about the financial crisis which precipitated the Revolution.

Not all of Scott's analysis is nonsensical by any means. But some parts of it relate to elements widely found in his fictions, both poetry and prose, and in his public actions, which contribute to the diminished esteem which most people, sadly in my view, now accord him. His delight in feudal traditions did not prevent him from taking a fairly critical look at them in his best novels: he saw historic inevitability at work in the rise of the bourgeoisie and of capitalist values. But he clearly imagined that, in Scotland as in the Vendée, the land-owning classes were bound together with the cultivators of the soil in relationships based on affection and respect – that the dominant element in Scottish society with its chaste ethical standards, its sensible patronage of philosophical writers whose views were penetrating but un-subversive, and its sensitivity towards tenants' interest, was the ideal aristocracy which the French had lacked, which could have channelled popular feeling towards the crown. He was not foolish in seeing veneration of the monarchy as an important prop for social stability in Scotland. But his enthusiasm for it produced the ridiculous, if endearing, spectacle of a writer famous and loved all over Europe whipping up a pageant of tartanry in 1822 to honour his liege lord, fat old George IV – a man as hedonistic, licentious and un-martial as any decadent French aristocrat could have been. It is often pointed out how paradoxical were his simultaneous rejoicing in new inventions – Watt's steam engine, gas lighting – and his failure to comprehend the social and moral changes which industrialisation was bringing. It could be that his youthful reactions to the French Revolution and to Burke's rebuttal of Paine explain why the man whose novels were revolutionary, both in their application of fictional form and their new depth of historical imagination, never wrote with outstanding success about contemporary, industrial Scotland. This in turn would make the Revolution important in the genealogy of the Kailyard. Scotland's most powerful writer in the first third of the nineteenth century was fixated by the idea that a quasi-feudal order dominated by rural landowners was imperative if the excesses of revolutionary France were to be avoided in Scotland. This city-born man insisted, by omission, on a rural conception of Scottish identity.

It must have been the case that the 'licentiousness' of the French, as he thought he saw it displayed rampant in revolutionary Paris, powerfully reinforced the Calvinistic prudery which makes his treatment of sexual relations in his novels much less than convincing or compelling. Montesquieu and Voltaire, he saw clearly, were extremely talented writers. But the free and worldly treatment of sexuality in the work of such writers had contributed to appalling consequences.

All this said, Scott clearly drew strengths from brooding about revolution at an impressionable age. His masterly treatment of the Porteous Riots in *Heart of Midlothian* shows a remarkable understanding of the self-made discipline characteristic of the eighteenth-century mob – contrast Dickens' hysterical treatment of (an admittedly much more severe) riot in *Barnaby Rudge*. And even if *Old Mortality* ends with a woebegonely chaste hero marrying a virtuous cypher in an idealised version of the Scottish countryside of the 1690s, Scott in that novel creates a classic account of a revolutionary movement, governed by understanding of the dynamic by which counter-revolutionary challenges push such movements into the hands of extremists. The noble and up-to-a-point chivalric royalist, Claverhouse is marked out as an extremist as dangerous as the heroic Covenanting zealot, Ephraim MacBriar.

(1990)

6

Scott and Goethe: Romanticism and Classicism

It was, of course, entirely by accident that Scott and Goethe died within a few months of each other (Goethe on 22 March 1832, Scott on 21 December) – though it was also an accident that they never met despite Goethe's warm invitation of Scott to Weimar. The coincidence is entirely opportune if it prompts us to delve for likenesses and contrasts between the two men who have become prime symbols of the revolutionary shift in European consciousness which has been labelled Romanticism.

One contrast can be shortly set out like this: both men worked away from the metropolitan centres of cultural production, London and Paris. But in historical retrospect, their sites on the periphery look very different. The Scottish Enlightenment with which Scott grew up became less and less peripheral as Edinburgh became a publishing centre to rival and even eclipse London and as the triumphs of its literati harmonised with those of British imperialism. Before it was consumed by it, Edinburgh culture contributed gladly to 'British' culture, and helped to reshape it. Its thinkers and artists found and knew their place in 'History' as it proceeded. Whereas Goethe's Weimar culture 'fits into' History by anticipation. During Goethe's lifetime it remained, even in his own view, peripheral: only the later achievement of German unity absorbed it into a national culture able to throw its weight about, into the 'mainstream' of European history.

Goethe was born in 1749. Scott was twenty-two years his junior. Both witnessed the culmination of a struggle meriting the adjective 'titanic' for world hegemony between two national states which had developed precociously along with potent and distinctive national cultures. England and France clashed on the mountains of North America and the plains of India and their rivalry extended from the West African slave trade to the islands of the Pacific. Louis XIV's France had been the dominating influence not only on European battlefields but upon European culture, and had even, in the age of Dryden (who was, more than incidentally, Scott's great hero) exercised a spell over the fecund literary culture of England. But the 'Glorious Revolution' of 1688 had represented the shrugging away by commercial England of France's old-fashioned pretensions, and by the second quarter of the eighteenth century leaders of French art and intellect – Voltaire, Montesquieu, Prévost – had begun to contrast tolerant, pragmatic England favourably with dynastic France. We can only understand the Europe-wide deification of Shakespeare, the discovery of his 'universality', if we associate it in our minds with the victories of Marlborough on land and those of the Royal Navy under both Pitts at sea.

Addison and Steele and Defoe and Swift had been in the vanguard of cultural conquest, along with the scientific heroes Bacon, Locke and Newton. Then Richardson, Sterne and 'Ossian' followed through the breach. The peripheral cultures of Europe – Catherine's Russia, for instance – were fertilised by complex chemical interactions of the classicism of Racine and Voltaire's discourse of Reason on the one hand, Shakespeare and the proto-Romantic discourse of 'feeling' on the other. With Goya, and with younger men such as Rossini and Pushkin, Goethe and Scott represent the prodigious energies which were generated.

Nationalisms evolved in response to the thrusts of imperial England and revolutionary France. It was Goethe as 'German', not as Frankfurter or Thuringian, who was reconstructed after his death so as to provide an apt effigy for a Deutschmark, but it was Scott as Briton or 'Englishman' who influenced poets and historians, patriots and novelists, all over Europe. Neither remained after death what he had thought he was or had wished to be. It is impossible to conceive of two more intriguing, and hardly of two better-documented, biographical entities than theirs, yet their 'greatness' is not *individual*. These persons touched and were touched by more of the collective experiences, more cultural trends, of their times than others. Each was remarkably open to a range of discourses – romantic and neo-classical, evangelical, medievalist, experimental, positivist and nihilist – flourishing in that age of revolutions. Each stood, as it were, admiring the blaze of Enlightenment while listening to the banshees and war drums which sounded in the encircling darkness.

Definitiveness must be, when one thinks about it, a product of limitation: which does not make it any the less attractive or important. The names 'Austen' and 'Keats' evoke wonderful openness but also specialism, refinement out of and so perhaps away from the central fluencies of their period. Scott and Goethe were institutions before they died and were transmitted into monuments. Both have been misunderstood because of our craving for definition. Daily we read that Scott was a 'romantic', and this term is applied to him at best condescendingly ('knights in armour – great fun'), often pejoratively ('faked things up'). He is seen as submerged in discourses which in fact he encompassed and circumvented. Goethe suffers from having been old and wise and from posthumous official favour. That stony blandness which his name evokes masks the dialectical interplay, calm hovering over chaos, delight courting misery, of his response to the turmoil of times in which Voltaire wrote of a civil war in every soul.

Scott planted trees by the Tweed at Abbotsford: Goethe laid out a beautiful riverside park in Weimar. That interest in landscape gardening, which they shared with most 'cultivated' persons of a period when our modern metaphor 'culture' was under formation, was not a commonsense desire for tame beauty and genteel tidiness. It was an excited response to the new capacity of aristocratic and bourgeois Europeans to control nature through science and technology, mixed with pangs of remorse for wild beauty violated, ancient pieties profaned. Follies were not so foolish as they seem to us, nor was there anything skittish about ha-ha's. Both involved effort for balance between the organic and the experimental, the 'natural' past and the man-made future. The civil war between religious awe and intellectual freedom, between the principles of Burke and those of Paine, raged in many 'souls' besides those of Scott and Goethe, but it was their distinction to express it with breadth that can fairly be called 'Shakespearian'. As the liturgical, biblical and classical shells in which European thought had been imprisoned cracked open, Scott and Goethe were at hand to re-position humankind and its intellect.

Hazlitt wrote that Scott's works were 'almost like a new edition of human nature'. The 'almost', which might seem grudging, is judicious. Shakespeare, and certain Germans, helped form Scott's vision (just as Gibbon and Burke assisted him in the invention of 'history' as we now understand it). They helped him to develop his apprehension (in more than one sense) of the clash between aristocratic and bourgeois values and world-views into an animated model of Scottish society changing by revolutions, in time.

During Goethe's youth in bourgeois Frankfurt, both bourgeois realism and bourgeois sentimentalism, along with bourgeois *success*, were identified with English culture. When the courts of Europe were still dominated by the literary culture of Louis XIV, the impatience with outdated hierarchical forms felt by some young intellectuals was bound to take sides with Shakespeare in his titanic posthumous struggle with Racine. Around the time of Scott's birth, J. G. Herder was teaching Goethe to venerate Shakespeare, associated by both with folk poetry, with Homer and, of course, with 'Ossian'. Goethe's retreat from the 'storm and stress' of his twenties into the Latinate classicism of his middle years was accompanied by a recoil on his part from the revolutionary forces which overthrew the Bastille. But his early work was still read, most momentously by the young Scott. By a nice coincidence it was a lecture in 1788 on the new German drama given by Henry Mackenzie, whose *Man of Feeling* had vied with *Werther* among 'sentimental' novels, which enthused Scott, with other young Edimbourgeois, to form a language class. From this came Scott's earliest creative writings, translations of Burger, and of Goethe.

Scott was steeped in the literature of England and France as well as in the folk poetry of Scotland and the verse of Burns, but it was contact with German writings in the movement associated with Herder which launched him as 'minstrel' of the Scottish border. In 1799, furthermore, he translated Goethe's *Goetz von Berlichingen*, and this was his first extensive work in any form. He was returning at second hand to the influence of Shakespeare which had formed Goethe's drama. Events helped confirm him in his nationalistic allegiance to the literature of England or, as he preferred to think of it, 'Britain', or 'Albion'. A revitalised France and a revitalised French culture challenged the sceptred isle of shopkeepers. Scott's passion was to drill on horseback as a Volunteer, prepared to defend Edinburgh against Napoleon.

Goethe, ambivalent, watched Napoleon spellbound as he conquered Europe, including Weimar, inciting nationalisms to rise against him which, alongside rampant British nationalism, finally vanquished him at Waterloo. Scott, magnanimous in victory, attempted to write in the 1820s an impartial life of Napoleon, but Goethe was disappointed when Scott sent the vast work to him – it was so obviously a product of *English* nationalism.

'England' had won the struggle for cultural and imaginative hegemony. Even in France itself, by 1827, the young Victor Hugo, in his preface to a play about Cromwell, was advocating Shakespearian variety rather than Racinian unities. Five years earlier, a journalist had dined in Vienna with Beethoven. The composer 'spoke of England and the English, and of how both were associated in his thoughts with a splendour incomparable'. He had 'no kind words' for the French. Beethoven was devoted to Shakespeare. Most days he went to a cafe or beerhouse to peruse newspapers, but, as another visitor, Schindler, recorded, 'when the English Parliament was sitting the *Allgemeine Zeitung* was regularly read at home for the sake of the debates.[1] Scott's own conquest of Europe (and that of Byron) coincided with the triumph of England as obviously as, in our own day, the empire of rock music matches the rise of the United States to world hegemony.

Scott's imaginative relationship with England was problematic. Just as the labels 'Romantic' and 'Regency' (c.f. 'neo-classical') seem to fit him equally well, or badly, so it won't do to project him either as a smug North British quisling or as a straightforward Scottish patriot. Love of Scotland dominated his life, and the best of the non-Scottish Waverley novels are those (*Durward*, *Nigel*) in which Scottish heroes take Scottish themes abroad with them. But *Marmion* can only be decoded as a 'British' nationalist polemic.

It was published in 1808 and sold 36 000 copies in British editions alone between that year and 1825. Its context was war with Napoleonic France. Its aim is to conflate Scottish and English military traditions. It contains much of Scott's most attractive verse, and indeed is perhaps the best introduction to that now-neglected area of Scott's output.

Its very form demonstrates the impotence of the term 'Romantic'. While the narrative is varied in metre, displaying the freedom which Scott had learnt from Wordsworth and Coleridge as well as from mediaeval models, each of its six cantos is prefaced by a introductory epistle to a friend. Though these are composed in flowing octosyllabic couplets which recall Milton's *L'Allegro*, with an occasional longer line thrown in for 'Spenserian' effect, the device itself is un-, even anti-, Romantic. Contemporary allusions, familiar conversation with friends, break up the narrative and distance the reader from its mediaeval doings. Furthermore, the text is swathed in learned footnotes in scores. The first line of Canto First, 'Day set on Norham's castled steep', prompts Scott to a page-long note in the Appendix describing in plain prose the ruins of Norham and their history, and 'donjon keep' in line 4 elicits from him not only an erudite definition of 'donjon', but also an etymological disquisition. Scott, as Hazlitt put it, is only the amanuensis of truth and history. He would despair if his far-fetched fable fostered an erroneous view of the past.

The proud English lord Marmion, famous warrior, journeys north, just before the battle of Flodden, on a mission to avert war. Meanwhile, unbeknownst to him, his erstwhile mistress, Constance, has been tried by a secret monastic tribunal and buried alive in a cell on Holy Island after the discovery of her plot to murder her rival Clare. Greedy for Clare's lands, Marmion once 'framed' as a traitor her lover, Ralph de Wilton, who fled as a pilgrim to the East. Clare herself escaped from Marmion's clutches to become a nun in Whitby – and so has arrived in Holy Island as part of the train of the Abbess who serves on the tribunal which condemns her rival.

Marmion is guided through the Border country to Edinburgh by a Mysterious Palmer. His mission fails, James IV is set on war, and Marmion admires the assembled Scottish army. Naturally, the Abbess of Whitby and her followers have been captured at sea by a Scottish ship. James now proposes that Marmion shall take the ladies, including Clare, back to England, stopping first at extremely picturesque Tantallon Castle, the seat of old Archibald Douglas, Earl of Angus. Inevitably, it turns out that the Mysterious Palmer is none other than Ralph de Wilton. Moved by the tale of his wrongs, old Douglas re-dubs Ralph knight, and the latter then speeds south to Flodden, as does Marmion. In the battle, de Wilton heroically proves his fidelity to the Tudor dynasty, and survives to marry Clare, who has meanwhile tended the wicked Marmion in his final agonies. The latter proves himself, whate'er his faults, to be a patriot, as he hears the war-cry of the victorious English:

> With dying hand, above his head,
> He shook the fragment of his blade,
> And shouted 'Victory! –
> Charge, Chester, charge! On, Stanley, on!'
> Were the last words of Marmion.

The tale makes *Rigoletto* seem like an everyday story of city folk, and Scott would never have pretended that it wasn't preposterous. But, like that of *Star Wars*, it offers pretext for all kinds of special effects – Gothic chill in the secret tribunal, picturesque description of Edinburgh from Blackford Hill, historical panorama as the Scottish army is assembled, and a projection of the battle of Flodden from a distance which owes something to Goethe's *Goetz* and anticipates Tolstoy's *War and Peace*. *Marmion* could be recommended without reservation as sheer fun, to all who enjoy a good opera or a good Western (both genres, of course, owe much to Walter Scott) were it not for its blatant nationalistic thrust. The spirit of chivalry with which Douglas, heir to the name and tradition of Bruce's companion in arms, knights Ralph so that he can slaughter Scots at Flodden, is designed to provide ideological cement for the British nation in its hour of trial. The introductory epistle to Canto I, with its mournful reference to 'my Country's wintry state', and the famous eulogy of Pitt which follows, rubs in the point that all hatchets must be buried in face of the French challenge by reconciling in death Pitt with his arch rival Fox:

> And ne'er held marble in its trust
> Of two such wonderous men the dust.

This inspired the Whig critic Jeffrey to fury. Scott said that Fox's 'errors should be forgotten, and that he *died* a Briton – a pretty plain insinuation that, in the Author's opinion, he did not live one: and just such an encomium as he himself pronounces over the grave of his villain hero, Marmion'.[2]

Scott's frankness, as usual, spares his admirers embarrassment. He is unashamedly writing propaganda, just as he uses the supernatural (which features in episodes of *Marmion* omitted from the plot-summary above) without superstition or the wish to delude. That interest in spooks which Scott had found attractive in German poetry was for him only a kind of hobby. He never lost touch with the 'real world', represented for him by the practical energies of Pitt and Fox, of Nelson and Wellington and, not least, of a great hero of his, James Watt. His own commercial and artistic feats as a writer swam easily in England's – or Britain's – tide of triumph. Scott was able so easily to encompass and adapt so many different discourses because success dissolved contradictions. His marvellous generosity was that of a victor.

To return to terminology. Byron's 'Song to the Isles of Greece' and Keats' 'Ode to a Grecian Urn', are surely 'typical' Romantic poems if such exist in any language? Yet each relates very obviously to the 'neo-classical' discourse which had emerged from the mid-eighteenth century. The prose of Scott's novels, deriving in part from Johnson and Gibbon, is nothing like De Quincey's or Carlyle's, is not Romantic at all, really, however 'romantic' may be some of the events which it narrates, and however central the Waverley series was in the development of European Romanticism. By the second decade of the nineteenth century, each of the larger discourses which we seek to separate as 'classicism' and 'romanticism' proves on inspection to be composed interchangeably from a common stock of lesser discourses. And British culture, supremely self-confident in its hour of victory, was particularly fitted to create broad and protean syntheses, so that the arch 'Romantics' Scott and Byron are also in method and spirit transmitters of Henry Fielding's 'realism'.

Goethe's position as minister in a petty ducal court in German lands which were politically disunited and culturally raw was far more difficult. Scott's modesty, which was genuine, was paradoxically a product of pride. He could gladly subsume himself and his intense Scottishness in Britain's success. He was a pleased little fish (he believed he was little) in a vast pool. He was proud that Pitt and Fox had both spared time to read and commend his writings. Goethe was like a whale in an aquarium.

His curious, fascinating novel *Elective Affinities (Die Wahlver-*

wandtschaften) was published a year after *Marmion*. After the battle of Jena in 1806, the French army had occupied Weimar, yet Goethe's story seems wholly remote from the topicalities of its period. It is a formal fable, opera-like, highly abstracted, schematic, in two exactly equal parts. Eduard (we are given no surname) is a wealthy land-owner who has recently, after the death of his wife, married Charlotte (no surname), the love of his youth. They share a passion for land-scape gardening. As they re-shape Eduard's estate, they invite two outsiders to join their idyll – Eduard's dearest friend 'the Captain' (Christian name Otto), and Charlotte's niece Ottilie.

The novel's strange title derives from a theory in chemistry ac-cepted by Goethe though not invented by him. Some chemical substances are naturally attracted to each other. The Captain explains:

What we call limestone is more or less pure calcium oxide intimately united with a thin acid known to us in a gaseous state. If you put a piece of this limestone into dilute sulphuric acid, the latter will seize on the lime and join with it to form calcium sulphate, or gypsum: that thin gaseous acid, on the other hand, escapes. Here there has occurred a separation and a new combination, and one then feels justified even in employing the term 'elective affinity' because it really does look as if one relationship was preferred to another and chosen instead of it.[3]

He and his friends whimsically apply it to their own situation but do not suspect the real pattern of 'Affinities'.

Eduard falls for Ottilie, Charlotte for the Captain; their feelings emerge in subtly worked out relationship to their projects in land-scape gardening. The Captain and Charlotte conquer their passion, but Eduard succumbs entirely and, to escape, goes off to fight in the war. He returns after Charlotte has borne his child, whose eyes are Ottilie's, whose face is the Captain's. Hopes of disentanglement come to nothing. Eventually Ottilie drowns the baby by mistake, renounces Eduard, dies; and the broken-hearted Eduard also dies. The lovers are buried together in a chapel where an architect patron-ised by Eduard has, with Ottilie's help, painted angels, all of which resemble Ottilie. The novel's resolution makes a nod towards supersti-tion, when a child is miraculously restored to life as her limbs touch the dead Ottilie's dress, and more than token concessions to conven-tional morality; the sternly self-controlled Captain and Charlotte outlive the romantic lovers. The novel's psychological subtlety makes it much more than a period piece – it is like a brilliant cross between Henry Mackenzie and Henry James – but it represents Goethe at his most 'Enlightened'. It is a book to set beside the fictions of Diderot and Voltaire.

Yet for all its formality and implicit caution, the book projects ideological instability. Passion and satire coexist uneasily, as do 'Enlightened' and 'Romantic' discourses. The book's thrust is really *self*-critical. Goethe sharply inspects his own situation, among under-employed aristocrats in a stagnant corner of Europe. In *Werther* years before he had momentously symbolised the superfluousness of the educated youth in a society unable to occupy him; absurdly excessive and self-destructive feeling results from the absence of an adequate object for Werther's intellectual and emotional energy. Eduard's irritating personality floats all-too-free on its own whims in the half-baked world of *Elective Affinities*: he goes to war merely because he is in love, he transforms his estate to match his private feelings.

At his very best, Scott projects similar unease. *Waverley, Old Mortality, Redgauntlet* are not complacent books at all. But elsewhere he could be *safely* 'Romantic', for *fun*, because his culture worked. Scottish culture worked. Scott stood in easy relationship to the comprehensive achievements of Hutcheson and Hume, Robertson and Smith, Ferguson and Black and Watt, whose ideas had, so to speak, been validated by economic success. Scottish Enlightenment had glowed for decades in a compact, increasingly thriving society where men sighed with relief that they had escaped from the nightmare of history, but felt secure enough to follow as Scott beckoned them back to the vanished strife of Covenanters and Jacobites. German Enlightenment had been quite different. Mere coincidence made Weimar a centre. Ideas flashed, thundered and sparked ineffectually in an arena of political fragmentation and economic underachievement; only in retrospect could it be clear that this firework display prefigured the consummation of a major philosophical school and the development of German unity.

Goethe wrote out of a culture not 'young', perhaps, but self-consciously 'immature', which had neither a Shakespeare nor a Racine. The grounds of its very existence had to be established. As in the not dissimilar conditions, rather later, of Turgenev's Russia, 'Romantic' passion was necessary as an escape from petty, boring reality, yet had also to be seen as feeble and time-wasting; Werther and Eduard, fine-souled, intelligent, achieve nothing but self-destruction. Science was a matter of speculation, not of application, so that Goethe himself wasted time trying to refute Newton. While Scott in a sense was a scientific romancer, establishing history as a science, Goethe was a Romantic chemist, toying with matter.

Goethe once remarked that Romanticism was sickness, Classicism was health. Yet he had to be more Romantic than Scott. *Faust Part I* is of course one of the fundamental books in European culture. There is nothing 'classical' about it at all. It is based on folk-tale; it includes an archetypal tragedy of humble life. Its discourse is Gothic and Shakespearian, its energy stems from impatience with all cut-and-dried solutions and with conventional morality. It projects Germany unhistorically – in order to construct an imaginatively effective Germany which can enter contemporary history, Goethe has recourse to magic, devils, witches. In deploying a kind of secularised superstition Goethe anticipated the nationalistic late-Romanticism of Wagner. I need hardly point out that Scott's construction of Scotland was very different – despite astigmatisms and some cheating, it is one of the most impressive breakthroughs in the development of 'scientific' thought, a triumph of 'realism' which should overawe those who now seek to write off 'realism' as merely bourgeois ideology.

(1983)

7

Tartanry

George IV's visit to Edinburgh in August 1822 seemed historic at the time because no ruling King of Scots had set foot in the country for a century and three quarters. It commands special interest again now for two reasons.

First, recent discussion of the horrors of 'tartanry', of our celebration of non-existent nationhood through bogus symbolism, has rightly pointed to the profusion of purportedly Gaelic dress in the ceremonials devised for the King as a culmination of the process of 'Ossianising' the Highlands which had been going on for sixty years. Walter Scott's role as pageant-master has been used as a stick with which to beat that complex, sensitive man. Readers of John Prebble's *The King's Jaunt*[1] will learn of bad news for eagles, whose feathers were much in demand to adorn bonnets, but excellent news for John Callender and Co. of Stirling and the Wilson brothers of Bannockburn. The former wove the tartan for the King's costume (but presumably did not supply the flesh-coloured tights which modestly covered the gap between His Majesty's belted plaid and his stockings.) The Wilsons were older hands at this game – they had long been supplying tartan to Highland regiments, and had invented a comprehensive range of clan tartans, now greatly in demand from Scots who had learnt from Sir Walter's anonymous *Hints* on etiquette for the Royal visit that the Garb of Old Gaul was flavour of the month.

Second, Tom Nairn's *Enchanted Glass*[2] has served to open overdue debate about the function of monarchy in the 'Ukanian' or 'Great British' state. Drawing on research by Linda Colley, Nairn's book, and the TV programme based on it, have pointed to the decades after the French Revolution as a key phase in the monarchy's history. In reaction against 'Jacobin' ideas, 'Jacobite' devotion to Royal persons seemed an excellent notion after all. The British ruling classes were happy to see cult worship developed around the unlikely figures of demented George III and libertine George IV, now somehow symbols of British identity. Adulation of monarchs filled the space which bourgeois nationalisms in Scotland and England might have occupied. Byron spotted royalism nestling amid the Evangelical cant which he so detested, the religion of pious suburban ladies and Jekyll-and-Hyde capitalist employers. His riposte to Southey's ridiculous apotheosis of George III in *A Vision of Judgement* is misunderstood as a jocular flyting against a poem of no importance: Southey's nonsense was attuned to the taste of the times. Byron went on to assail, at the end of his satire *The Age of Bronze* (1823), the figure cut by Sir William Curtis, fishmonger, banker, Lord Mayor of London, friend of George IV, when, old and corpulent, he wore tartan at the King's levee at Holyrood:

> . . . Sir William Curtis in a kilt!
> While throng'd the chiefs of every Highland clan
> To hail their brother, Vich Ian Alderman!
> Guildhall grows Gael, and echoes with Erse roar,
> While all the Common Council cry 'Claymore'!

But Byron loved Sir Walter, man and works, and may well have felt that the purity of his brother poet's conception had been marred by a vulgar upstart. Nairn, on the other hand, sees Scott as hardheaded organiser of 'the first really modern Royal spectacle', forerunner of many more 'inventions of tradition'.

Of course, tradition had to be invented. There were no precedents at all for the entry into his Northern capital of the monarch of a Union constituting the most thriving commercial nation in the world. Scott felt compelled to transmogrify the Company of Archers, founded in Edinburgh in 1676 as a sporting club for nobles and gentry, into the ancient bodyguard of the Kings of Scots, parading in Lincoln-green with bright yellow bows.

John Prebble is just the man to make sartorial details like this telling. In a series of books, he has contributed powerfully, not so much to a revision of Scottish historiography, as to shifts in perception of their own history by Scots, budding historians included. He has de-Ossianised the Highlands with his accounts of Glencoe, Culloden, mutinous regiments, the Clearances, which have presented brutality and betrayal with novelistic 'realism'. In the course of debunking the traditions of many of our 'noble' families, he has erected his own counter-myth of the tragic Gaelic commoner – unfitted for the new spheres of commerce and 'improvement' which opened up for Scots after the Restoration, loyal to clan, attached to land, victimised over and over again. He attempts to incorporate this dualism into the structure of *The King's Jaunt*.

Prebble's great strength has always been his capacity to 'recreate', from exhaustive study of sound primary sources, the physical detail and moral atmosphere of dramatic events – battles, confrontations, in this case pageants. Used now to his methods, we willingly suspend disbelief and relax historiographical prudery. When he tells us early in his new book that on the first Thursday of March 1820, Sherrif Donald Macleod of Geanies left Dingwall to enforce writs of eviction upon the people of Culrain, 'in a well-sprung, well-upholstered carriage, his old but resolute body warmly wrapped against the cold breath of the lingering snow',[3] the vigour of the realisation persuades us not to worry about where documentation ends (is the upholstery vouched for?) and plausible supposition begins (well, an old man would be warmly clad . . .). Maybe a local source reported on the weather that day, maybe not.

For the King's activities in Lothian during his two-week stay, source material is so abundant that Prebble's imagination has had few gaps to fill. No better account of the details of those days is ever likely to come our way. Prebble handles his wealth of material with good judgement and restrained wit:

Despite the planning of Scott, and the eager ambition of Glengarry, the first man to greet the King upon his landing was not a figure representative of Scotland's noble past, but a Mr Kent who did not wait for the King to set foot upon land. He was given a modest immortality in one newspaper report the next day, though it was lamentably incomplete.

'When he was some distance from the shore, his Majesty was saluted by Mr Kent, who was walking upon the water, to whom his Majesty bowed.'[4]

Paradoxically – perhaps against his own will and judgement –

Prebble communicates a sense of how much fun the King's Jaunt provided for so many Scots. About one in seven of the population, 300 000, turned up to see him. This was a forerunner not only of such mummeries as the investiture of our present-day Charles as Prince of Wales, but also of the atmosphere of a good Edinburgh Festival – one suspects that the city never again enjoyed such bustling life in the century and a quarter between 1822 and 1947.

Prebble, furthermore, accords to many of the leading figures a surprising degree of sympathy. Sir Walter, as always, looks like a good man – working tirelessly at his home in Castle Street to set things up, while afflicted with a nasty skin rash, cheered by crowds in the High Street as if he were royal himself, but modestly playing down his own centrality, and finding time to be kind and hospitable to the elderly poet Crabbe, who had picked this of all times to visit him from England. The King, overweight, ailing, tried hard to please. He had a real affection for Scottish music, played for him on all occasions, and a strong liking for Glenlivet. He was deeply moved not only by Mary's apartments in Holyrood where Rizzio had been murdered, but also by the delight with which his Northern subjects welcomed him – a pleasant relief, as Prebble must be right to suggest, from surly, *blasé* Londoners. He genuinely liked and admired Scott, and attended a theatrical version of his *Rob Roy*.

That hero's clan, the MacGregors, still outlawed within the memory of many of its members, were a striking component of the Highland army which Scott's fiery cross gathered in Edinburgh. Prebble is almost unmanned by respect for their chief, Sir Evan MacGregor, a handsome veteran of East Indian wars, 'battle scarred, brave and considerate.' He is generous also to the 4th Duke of Atholl, Sir Evan's father-in-law, though the latter, worried about the danger to public order of too many armed Gaels thronging the city, did not summon his own well-drilled tenants to Edinburgh. Atholl thought the proceedings 'daft', but gave his time, as a leader of the Order, to the Masonic project for a National Monument on Calton Hill modelled on the Parthenon which the Earl of Elgin (Ensign-General of the Archers in the King's escort) had recently deprived of some notable sculptures. The King didn't manage to attend the ceremony at which the foundation was laid during his visit.

But Prebble is clearly determined that we don't lapse into merely enjoying his abundance of character and anecdote. He begins each charming chapter with an epigraph containing testimony about the Sutherland Clearances. He argues, eventually, that the true value of the Royal Visit to many great Highland land-owners was that 'a theatrical display of Gaelic splendour on the part of conscientious chiefs' had demonstrated that critics of the Clearances 'were liars, and that the Highland people knew that they were being improved for their own good alone. Although some must leave their glens or their country forever, they could be confident that their dress, their customs and their language would be safely preserved by their evictors.'[5] He supports this by quoting a letter from the Countess of Sutherland, who sent a contingent of her own to parade in the Black Watch tartan.

With equal justice, Prebble relates the enthusiasm of prosperous Scots, and the motives of politicians involved in the Visit, to the scare of the 'Radical War' of 1820. A *grande peur* had seized the Edimbourgeoisie at the prospect of a mass rising by disaffected Western weavers. *The King's Jaunt* opens with the execution at Stirling of Baird and Hardie for their part in the tiny insurrection which had eventuated. The Jaunt was used both to cement the loyalty of Scots to King and Union and to convince Southerners that the ghosts of Scottish Jacobitism and radicalism were well and truly laid. Lord Melville, 'manager' of Scotland for the Government like his father before him, wrote to George as the Jaunt was ending:

When your Majesty announced your intention to visit Scotland, Lord Melville had no doubt that the people of that country would not be deficient in dutiful respect to your Majesty; but he did not anticipate to its full extent the determined and deep-rooted Monarchical feeling which evidently pervaded the great body of the people.[6]

The King was now 'Chief of Chiefs', the focus of all the clannish loyalties once utilised by Prince Charles Edward, and true successor – as he himself saw it and others believed – to the mighty Bruce himself. The vast sums of money deployed on the Jaunt had been well spent in the interests of the ruling class.

After all the high spirits in rain and shine, the fun in the streets and at balls and dinners, which Prebble has evoked so delightfully, his final judgement on the Jaunt is caustic:

Scotland could not be the same again once it was over. A bogus tartan caricature of itself had been drawn and accepted, even by those who mocked it ... With the ardent encouragement of an Anglo-Scottish establishment, and under the patronage of successive monarchs who took to kilt and cromach with Germanic thoroughness, Walter Scott's Celtification continued to seduce his countrymen, and thereby prepared them for political and industrial exploitation. It gave them a picturesque national identity where none had been wholly satisfying since the Union, and reminded them, as Scott had hoped of 'all those peculiarities' which distinguished them as Scots. It also, and pre-eminently, united Lowlander and Borderer as one nation with a diminishing Gaelic minority whose existence had once aroused uneasy guilt or derisive contempt, but whose costume and history might now be honourably assumed by all. Finally the pageant devised by Scott ... encouraged Scots to believed that of all the peoples of the United Kingdom they might perhaps consider themselves to be the most favoured by God and the Monarchy (which they, indeed, had supplied).[7]

As far as it goes, this is admirably astute. What Prebble might be hard pressed to explain, though, is how, 'politically', Scots were more 'exploited' after 1822 than before. His implication that 'industrialisation' involved, for Scots, only their exploitation, presumably by non-Scots or Anglo-Scots, might also arouse worthwhile argument.

So far from being, all of them, helpless victims, emigrant Gaels controlled the entire fur trade of British North America and much else in that arena beside. At the cost of poverty and foul conditions for many, Glasgow would outstrip Manchester and Birmingham as the Empire's greatest industrial city, and among those who profited would be numerous manual workers. Scotland in 1822 was in the process of acquiring a large, prosperous middle class which would set its impress on many parts of the world. What did the Jaunt mean to them? Prebble doesn't ask.

He is always very strong on the foreground, the event close up. Here, this power means that, willy-nilly, the pleasure and bustle of the Visit are so strongly conveyed that loyal monarchists and Unionists will find *The King's Jaunt* enjoyable rather than discomforting. More thoughtful souls will indeed respond to his irony: for instance, the absurd figure of MacDonnell of Glengarry, a notable Highland Clearer, dashes about Prebble's pages attempting to establish himself before King and people as the most Gaelic and important of Gaels, founder of the Society of True Highlanders. But Prebble misses

completely political issues, class issues, at least as significant in
Scottish history as Loch's 'improvements' in Sutherland.

The Scots who packed their capital, crowding its hills and streets
to behold their King, were not a people entirely consisting of landlords of ancient lineage, loyal Gaelic dupes, and weavers tied to
obsolescent artisan traditions. Edinburgh was the centre for a legal,
financial, and professional middle class, as Glasgow was for an
industrial and commercial bourgeoisie. The streets of Glasgow emp-
tied as people used the new Forth–Clyde canal to get to where the
Royal action was. Visitors from the North were impressed by the
convenience of the new steam-boat ferry across the Firth of Forth.
Sir Walter (Prebble does not miss this irony) was an enthusiast for
the new gas lighting, which flowered brilliantly in the capital. ('The
Edinburgh Gas Company seized this chance with enthusiasm . . .')
This was a land of pioneering industry and exciting opportunity.
The New Town, which, to Cockburn's regret, was now spilling over
into the Earl of Moray's pleasure grounds where he had listened 'to
the ceaseless rural corn-craiks, nestling happily in the dewy grass'
was not mostly populated by Highland Clearers, but by members of
an uppity middle class, intellectually stiffened by Enlightened ideas,
morally braced by a vigorous Church life, and still touched with
patriotic feeling. Sir Walter Scott, lawyer's son, lawyer himself,
successful literary entrepreneur and *nouveau riche* landowner in the
Borders, was the representative hero of the Edimbourgeoisie. He was
adored even by Whigs such as Cockburn, whose *Memorials* have
nothing to say about the King's Jaunt, but a great deal about the
public meeting in December 1820 which had called on the King to
dismiss his Tory ministry and had launched a petition signed (so
Cockburn himself calculated) by about 85 per cent of the Capital's
adult male inhabitants. Cockburn noted with gratification 'the rise of
booksellers and haberdashers', or 'ordinary trading citizens', to prominence in the movement of self assertion preceeding the Reform Act
of 1832 and prefiguring the total eclipse of Toryism in the Scottish
burghs for half a century.[8]

Politics within the property-holding classes were bitter, and disfigured at this time by violence – as when the Whig Stuart of Dunearn
killed the Tory Sir Alexander Boswell (son of the biographer) in a
duel in March 1822. But the anti-Tory *Scotsman*, sniffy about the

101

Royal Visit, could not help acknowledging the fine spectacle. As Nairn's *Enchanted Glass* has reminded us, the potentially revolutionary growl of the rising British bourgeoisie subsided by about 1860 to a toothless mumble. The *ancien régime* was superseded in 1832, but the mystique of royalty helped to maintain the hegemony of the landed-financial ruling class of south-eastern England.

Trends in Scottish history before and after the Jaunt must be fully acknowledged if we are to focus its full significance. Firstly, it was no accident that Scott's pageantry had an overwhelmingly military aspect. The incorporation of Highlanders into the British state machine as soldiers had begun even before Culloden. Tartan, by 1822, symbolised not only the tragic loyalty of Prince Charlie's followers, but also the valour of kilted warriors, such as Sir Evan MacGregor, on imperial battlefields all over the world. Anyone innocent enough to believe that the British have never been bombastic nationalists like those noisy Frogs and Krauts should be gently led into the Crypt of St Paul's Cathedral, England's Panthéon, with its startling and oppressive collection of monuments to heroes of the Napoleonic Wars. Other North Britons felt they had every reason to be as proud as Sir Walter himself was of the Scottish contribution to an epic series of wars against the French and their would-be world conqueror. Scotland's Old Regime – the Dundas-Melville system whereby Scottish magnates had controlled the country with no real interference from London – had provided not only Jobs for the Boys but Wealth for Warriors and Hauls for Heroes. Seven years after Waterloo, the panorama of kilts and Volunteer uniforms which Scott assembled was bound to be very stirring.

However, the King's Jaunt was to be the last occasion on which 'all Scotland' assembled in the capital to recharge national feeling. The figure of Robert Peel, who was less interested in the pageantry than in his plans, as Home Secretary, to bring into line with English ways certain Scottish legal practices which were 'rather repugnant to English feelings',[9] cast no shadow over Scottish self-congratulation in August 1822. But by the 1840s, when Queen Victoria picked up the habit of visiting Scotland, much would have happened to reduce the country's separateness. Middle-class Scottish Liberals, vindicated in 1832, identified more easily with universal principles of political economy than with Scottish tradition, and English co-thinkers of theirs would become MPs in Scottish constituencies (whereas in Dundas' time, the traffic had all been the other way). The new railways would make life easier for MPs, land-owners and sportsmen based in the South as they did for Victoria herself, slashing travel-time between Edinburgh and London, whence George IV had pro-ceeded slowly by sea. The Disruption of 1843 would fissure, as little secessions before had not, the monolith of Scottish Presbyterianism. Scotland by mid century was not yet a 'province' of England, but its distinctiveness was far less secure than it had been when Sir Walter had greeted his King at Leith, the Wizard of the North and Bard of All the Clans welcoming home the descendant of the Stuarts, the Chief of Chiefs.

I am arguing, *pace* Prebble, that the tartanry and frolics of 1822 are less significant as a facade masking the dispossession of Highland Gaels than as an episode in the transition from the Dundas-Melville era of aristocratic management to the New Scotland of Liberalism and manufactures. They typified the ideological means by which a Union of practical convenience became a Union of irrational love and fears, sublimated in militarism, tartanry, royalism and, eventually imperialism.

What we need if we are to understand this process, and with it the history of Scotland since 1822, is more and better work on the social, cultural and political history of the Scottish bourgeoisie. Certain limitations of T. C. Smout's *Century of the Scottish People* arise from the lack of integrative studies of Scotland's employing and professional classes. We have economic history in some abundance, and plenty of good 'labour history' about the victims and challengers of the Scottish bourgeoisie. But we cannot understand what has happened to us until we know more about what went on in the minds and later lives of middle-class children taken to see George IV process through their capital in the rain in August 1822.

(1989)

Two

Unionised Scotland

8

Social Centuries

In his *A Century of the Scottish People, 1830–1950*[1] T. C. Smout has had the difficult task of providing a sequel to a book which now looks like a landmark in Scottish historiography. Published in 1969, his splendidly written *History of the Scottish People, 1560–1830*[2] combined economic, social and cultural history to provide a new overview of Scotland in transition which dissolved mythologies and liberated imagination. Its effects have been seen in many valuable monographs published since. As the Scottish landscape was once transformed by lairdly improvers, so Smout and his followers have created fertile fields where there were once intellectual bogs.

The Duke of Atholl's estates straddled Highland and Lowland. A Gaelic poem of 1781 salutes the Duke's lovely province:

> You lie in the middle of Scotland,
> Your air is pure, your water is fast flowing . . .
> Your straths are pleasant and productive,
> Clad with grass and corn . . .
> Your people live in tranquillity and sufficiency . . .

As Dr Leah Leneman points out in her *Living in Atholl: A Social History of the Estates, 1685–1785*, this helps to confirm the judgement of an English traveller six decades earlier (Captain Burt), that Atholl and its people were exceptional in the generally 'gloomy' Highland vista.[3]

Though the gentry – including some of the ducal family – were Jacobite in 1715 and 1745, ordinary countrymen showed little enthusiasm for that cause and had to be bullied to fight for Prince Charlie. A recruiter complained that the men of Dunkeld were 'quite degenerate from their Ancestors, and not one spark of Loyalty among them.'[4] But Atholl highlanders who had eagerly welcomed the Hanoverian Campbells, supposedly their traditional foes, were rewarded by brutal oppression from Cumberland's soldiers, acting on their general's belief that all Gaels were Jacobites. Dr Leneman's lengthy quotations from documents point to a complex situation, contradicting mythological simplifications, yet showing where the roots of such may be found.

Likewise, she confirms, so far as this area goes, the traditional view that lower-class Scots showed unusual thirst for learning – as when the people of remote Glen Tilt petitioned the 3rd Duke in 1769 for a school convenient for their 'bairns', who would otherwise 'be lost for want of education' – but undermines the myth that Scottish education was egalitarian. Free and cheap instruction was deliberately limited in scope: 'for the majority, all that was considered necessary was to be able to read English in order to understand the Scriptures', and there was little chance to go further, since charity schoolmasters were 'expressly forbidden' to teach Latin.[5] On the other hand, the assumption that coal-miners in Scotland, as serfs, must necessarily have been downtrodden, is called into question by evidence from the Dukes' Lowland mine at Blairingone in Clackmannan, where colliers in 1740 earned wages eight or nine times as high as the average for agricultural workers.[6]

Overall, Dr Leneman's study insinuates pretty effectively the view that the Atholl estates were successfully managed in a spirit of 'enlightened paternalism'. Perhaps the jocundly pastoral, fresh-faced musicians and dancers in David Allan's famous painting of a 'Highland Wedding at Blair Atholl' are less idealised than one has supposed.

Whatever good there was in eighteenth-century ways of life in Scotland – and notwithstanding the brief Jacobite irruptions it was on the whole a more peaceful land than England, and increasingly dedicated to improvement – industrialisation wrought transformation. T. C. Smout covered the early stages of the process in his *History of the Scottish People*. Despite his realism about conditions in the new industries and the sad fate of the handloom weavers, despite his evident regret for the eclipse of Enlightened rational optimism as Evangelicalism secured a blighting grip on the blackening cities, and despite his conclusion that the tendency for decades before 1830 had been for the culture to become 'more British and less specifically Scottish', that book ended with a sense of upbeat. Smout had explored and attempted to explain an astonishing afflatus of intellectual discovery, creative talent and entrepreneurial drive – a 'cultural golden age' in one small country which had, and went on having, world-wide consequences.

But *A Century of the Scottish People* takes up the story again in a different, sad spirit. One reason for Smout's change of temper may be that, whereas in 1969 he could half-hint at a coming upsurge in favour of home rule, he now writes in the aftermath of the abortive referendum of 1979. He extols the belief, partly inherited from Enlightenment, which he finds in Scottish radicalism down to the 1920s – that 'by the exercise of political will, the people hold their own future in their own hands.' In 1979, offered some measure of greater democratic control, two-thirds of Scots preferred to leave their future in the hands of Southerners. This, Smout seems to believe, was already prefigured by 1950, the terminus of his oddly inflated 'century'. Scots then seemed mostly content to opt, under Westminster governance, in a capitalist and inegalitarian order, for 'The fruits of the collectivist State, of the rule of the expert, and of a policy of welfare determined from above and afar . . .' He admits that the material quality of life went on improving, down to the mid-1970s, but laments the loss of 'vibrant political culture'.[7] So his instincts as a radical democrat are at odds with his role as compassionate historian of everyday life.

Further, he finds that 'the perspectives of the social historian and the economic historian show our century in very contrasting lights.'[8] The latter sees a 'triumphal progression' from the success of textiles in the first phase of industrialisation through that of iron and coal in the second, followed by a surge in 'steel, ships, jute, tweed and high farming' which crashed dismally with the post-1920 depression. But the social historian notices that life in the heydays of success was commonly brutish and that the interwar years show marked improvement for ordinary people in terms of health and housing, real income and recreation. The grandchildren of 'vibrant' Scots who worked for heroic industrial success under Beardmore or strove for a new world order with Keir Hardie have settled cannily, Smout's overview implies, for bread and circuses, *alias* sliced loaf and *EastEnders*. This he most controversially tends to attribute to what he sees as the malign effects of the famous Scottish education system – so complacently admired still by many of those whom he deems to have been its victims.

The general ethos of Scottish education, he argues, was throughout his 'century' anti-egalitarian. It aimed

firstly at providing, as cheaply as possible, the bulk of the population with the bare minimum of education combined with adequate social discipline, and secondly, at giving a small number of children of all classes, but especially of the higher classes, a more respectable academic education, to qualify them for their role as a controlling élite.[9]

Following the Education Act of 1872, old burgh schools which had given some kind of general access to learning were either transformed, as in thirteen cases, into 'Higher Class Schools', fee-paying at first, or made into essentially elementary board schools. Edinburgh's professional middle class successfully captured for its own purposes the funds of the Merchant Company schools and of the Heriot Trust, which had originally been intended for the unprivileged. (As a present-day resident, I can confirm that educational snobbery is uniquely rife in Edinburgh.)

For the mass of the population, education thus came to involve a syllabus restricted to the three Rs, thrashed home with the tawse, instilling what A. S. Neill called 'a gigantic inferiority complex'.[10] Smout sees this as the key 'to some of the more depressing aspects of modern Scotland', where there are 'too many people who fear what is new, believe the difficult to be impossible, draw back from responsibility, and afford established authority and tradition an exaggerated respect . . .'[11]

Well, followers of George Davie and his vision of the 'democratic intellect' in Scottish education might dispute Smout's emphases while necessarily admitting many of his facts. Readers of certain recent Scottish fiction and poetry, on the other hand, will find the image of the crass and brutal dominie vividly present, as with Tom Leonard's 'Mr Johnstone':

> Jenkins, all too clearly it is time
> for some ritual physical humiliation;

and if you cry, boy, you will prove
what I suspect – you are not a man.[12]

But comparison with other educational systems is needed to prove Smout's case. And is contemporary Scotland, relatively speaking, so servile and depressing? Its teachers were long engaged in industrial action which commanded wide public support, and which they seem to have conducted with greater *élan* and skill than their English counterparts, against a Conservative Government for which, currently, only some 15 per cent or 20 per cent of Scots are prepared to vote, and of which the middle-class supporters seem increasingly demoralised. Much fresh creativity is to be seen in literature and other arts. Smout is perhaps out of touch with the manifold local sources of liveliness. The stultification which his book purports to explain is not now so dominant as he suggests, and may not have been so even in 1950.

Had Smout explored in this new book the same range of materials with which he coped so well in his *History of the Scottish People*, he might have avoided the tone of humane gloom against which I reacted on first reading his *Century* and which made me, as I now find, underestimate it greatly. In the *History* he discussed literary culture with great verve, and responded zestfully to Scottish achievements in architecture. In this sequel, he has narrowed his aim to the exploration of a 'complex world of deprivation and social division', and has decided to minimise treatment of 'artistic or intellectual endeavour'. It is true that many who strove in these fields expatriated themselves, but this had also happened in the eighteenth century, and Orchardson, Robert Louis Stevenson and the later Haldanes did not spring from nowhere. Still less, so to speak, did Lewis Grassic Gibbon. Such large mainly home-based figures as Rennie Mackintosh, MacDiarmid, Joan Eardley, still inspirational today, are not admitted into Smout's pages to tease us or to cheer us up. More seriously, Smout neglects, not indeed all popular culture – his pages on football, so far as they go, are insightful if joyless – but some of its most important forms.

It is sad that Smout does not respond to the continuing vitality of folk music in Scotland, a subject of surprised envy in some other parts of Europe. It is amazing that he can write a book with such a title without referring once to the D. C. Thomson press or to Harry Lauder. Inspired by Tom Nairn, the Grigors and Colin McArthur, much interesting acerbic comment has latterly been passed on the semiotic nexus of kailyardism, *Brigadoon*-ery, *Sunday Post*-ity and tartanry wherein tourists and also many Scots have perceived regional or national identity. The sound of the pipes is not heard in Smout's pages, nor is the swish of the kilt descried – and this is because he also leaves the very significant position of the army in Scottish life out of his survey. I do not suggest that deconstruction of 'Loch Lomond' or Barthesian analysis of *Beano* and the Broons would have uplifted Smout's spirits greatly, still less that Scottish militarism is other than a distasteful subject. But perhaps the vigour, however perverted, of popular culture, might help to explain how Scots have survived the dire conditions to which Smout draws our attention. The book would have been not only livelier, but also analytically more cogent, had he kept it steadily in view.

But I am being ungrateful. Within the scope which he has chosen, Smout's book is consistently excellent. He writes with due shock about the 'dark exterior' of life in industrialised Scotland. 'What was the point of all those triumphs of the great Victorian age of industry if so many people were unspeakably oppressed by its operations?'[13] The 'triumphs' of the shipbuilders and the juteocracy depended on low wages. Along with these went peculiarly bad housing conditions, which middle class persons who profited from them contrived to attribute to the fecklessness of the poor themselves.

In 1861, 34 per cent of all Scottish houses had only one room and two-thirds of the entire population lived in one- or two-room houses. 'The "but-and-ben" and the "single end" were, in fact, the normal environment in which to bring up a family.' Fifty years later, half the population were still so housed, compared to 7 per cent in England and Wales. Even in 1951, 15.5 per cent of Scots still lived more than two to the room, when the figure for England was 2.1 per cent.[14] Smout attributes this disparity to the absence of a poor law in nineteenth-century Scotland, which led people to favour the cheapest possible housing rather than face disaster when unemployed, and to the feuing system, under which sellers of land demanded the highest possible annual duties as well as big down-payments, so encouraging builders to maximise returns as fast as possible by rushing up small tenement homes.

From the Addison Act of 1919, which conceded subsidies to local authority housing, matters should have improved vastly. But in fact this and subsequent legislation contributed further to the dismal aspect of urban Scotland. 'Our hearts sank at the grimness of the towns', said Simone de Beauvoir when she and Sartre toured Scotland after the Second World War.[15] Working-class people were decanted from centres which were 'at least compact' to 'segregated and ill-served housing estates'. The tendency towards social *apartheid* was, typically, taken furthest in Edinburgh, but even in Glasgow, under Labour control from 1933, council officials 'perpetuated the ancient distinctions between the respectable and the unrespectable poor'.[16] The latter were given 'Re-housing' homes in a ghetto which became a by-word for sickness and violence, the former received 'Ordinary' accommodation.

Smout is acute about 'respectability'. The Lowland Scottish artisan or skilled worker (and around 1900 over 70 per cent of employment in the Glasgow region was more or less skilled) was, but was not, radically inclined. Samuel Smiles was a Scotsman, and self-help and thrift were in his native air, inspiring the growth of co-operative societies and a most significant temperance movement, which argu-ably played the same role in the origins and early days of the Labour Party as Nonconformity did in England. The appalling 'whisky culture' of urban Scotland was finally given its quietus not by militant teetotalism but by the Chancellor of the Exchequer's discov-ery in 1909 that the Government could make money by taxing spirits heavily. However, the movement enjoyed a last moment of glory in the 1922 general election when a prohibitionist, Edwin Scrymgeour, defeated Winston Churchill in Dundee. One tragic aspect of the interwar period was the battering of traditions of respectable 'inde-pendence' by slump in the great industries and by mass unemploy-ment. If the Scottish workforce was demoralised – and Smout has a clear case here – it was, more likely, by this crude economic factor rather than by tawse-wielding schoolteachers.

But the language of class throve. Independent working men had found it strongly present in the usage of the Liberal Party which attracted their support and dominated Scotland electorally for dec-ades, but when Gladstone spoke of the war of 'class against masses', this was a rallying-cry against aristocrats and rural landlords. With many signs of reluctance, from the 1880s through the First World War, more and more Scottish workers realised that their interests were not, as they had supposed, identical with those of their employers. The insecurity of skilled men in the first two decades of the present century underlay those famous displays of militancy on the wartime Clyde, then the precociously large Labour vote in the West in 1922 which firmly attached the adjective 'Red' to the river. Both were reactive rather than revolutionary. Smout deplores seemingly ingrained class feelings, believing that Sweden and Japan have shown how harmony can bring economic success. But they seem to have been the inevitable outcome of that disparity between 'economic' and 'social' history to which he is so sensitive. So long as the economy was buoyant, evil material conditions could be tholed. When it faltered, working-class mistrust was inevitable.

Meanwhile, kailyardism and tartanry were pulling Scots' sense of identity yearningly towards regions of clean air, to the 'wee bit hill and glen' invoked in our recent nationalist anthem, 'Flower of Scotland'. Regarding what really went on in the country places, Smout is admirably judicious and balanced. Reaction against Highland clearances, and then the later 'crofter's war' of the 1800s, dramatised a development of class feeling beside lovely lochs which preceded and influenced urban bitterness. Whatever pastoral unity had existed, as maybe once in Atholl, between lord and commoner, was destroyed as the values of industrialism advanced into glens now over-populated. Smout can sympathise with the special attachment of the Gaels to their ancestral lands. But he is alert to ironies. People imagine that the Highlands were drastically depopulated by the clearances which certainly occurred and which were in some cases without doubt crassly insensitive, if not brutal. But Argyll had a population of 66 000 in 1755 and 63 000 in 1951. Half way between these dates, the seven Highland counties, well after certain classic episodes of clearance had occurred, reached the historic peak of their populations.[17] Pressure on the land was intense, and the famine caused by potato blight in 1846 vividly demonstrated that it could not reliably support so many. Recognition of this, rather than cruel landlordism *per se*, seems to have been the decisive cause of heavy emigration. The hard-won Crofters's Holding Act of 1886 made it virtually impossible to evict a Highlander from his land – yet population over the next half century fell markedly faster than in the rural Lowlands, where, up to this point, it had declined at the same rate. Smout has risked odium by exposing coolly the truth, anathema to passionate mythologists, that the Gaelic Highlands were not an arena vindictively, even racialistically, singled out for peculiar oppression, but one highly distinctive region, among many in Europe, over which the normal processes of industrialisation acted nastily.

Highlanders flocking to the United States and the colonies of settlement commonly throve, as did Lowlanders. It is a vast pity that Smout says so little, even speculatively, about the effects of emigration on Scotland over his 'century'. Exodus on a significant scale was a perpetual feature of Scottish life, Lowland as well as Highland. It peaked in the first two decades of the twentieth century at about 50 per cent of the natural increase of the population. Scottish consciousness has been enormously affected by this factor. To oversimplify: Scots who have emigrated and done well have looked back with mingled guilt and nostalgia. They provided bases for the enormous commercial success of Kailyard novels and of Harry Lauder. They have responded avidly to *Brigadoon*-ish sentimentalisations. The international fame of such representations, brought home by ancestor-hunting tourists, has impressed Scots still in Scotland and has convinced them that such kitsch is their true heritage. Tom Nairn's 'great Tartan monster' is a creature we have to live with since we now possess no alternative national symbolism.

But the wonderful array of photographs which Smout has assembled provides many haunting depictions of tartan-free ordinariness. They are an important feature of an important book, one which is sure to become, like its predecessor, a source of reference for many further studies and both stimulus and corrective to the imaginations of all who read it.

(1987)

9

Thomas Campbell's Liberalism

The funeral of Thomas Campbell in Westminster Abbey on 3 July 1844 was a memorable occasion. While friends and admirers thronged inside, spectators crowded the area outside the west entrance of the church, hoping to see the procession which took the coffin to Poets' Corner. The pall was carried by nine peers of the realm, including the Duke of Argyll, Campbell's clan chieftain; Lord Brougham, former Lord Chancellor but before that, like Campbell, a contributor to the *Edinburgh Review*, and Lord Aberdeen, once nicknamed 'Athenian Aberdeen' by Byron, who had shared his ardent phil-hellenism. The one commoner among the pall-bearers was Sir Robert Peel, Britain's Conservative Prime Minister. Among the many distin-guished mourners were Benjamin Disraeli, T. B. Macaulay and W. M. Thackeray. A deputation of Polish notables in exile was also present:

When the coffin was lowered into the grave, the crowd closed gradually around the spot, eager to catch a glimpse of all that was yet to be seen of the author of 'The Pleasures of Hope' and 'Gertrude of Wyoming'. When the Rev. Mr Milman arrived at that portion of the ceremony in which dust is consigned to dust, an additional interest was thrown around this part of the proceedings, by the significant tribute of respect which was paid to the memory of the Poet by the Poles . . . One of their number, Colonel Szyrma, took a handful of earth, which had been taken for the purpose from the tomb of KOSCIUSKO, and scattered it over the coffin of him who had portrayed in such glowing terms the woes and wrongs of their country.[1]

The presence of the current Prime Minister and two of his succes-sors at this imposing event is harder to explain than that of the Poles. When, aged only twenty-one, Campbell had first stunned with admiration the British reading public, his *The Pleasures of Hope* had contained some extremely memorable lines about the Polish insurrection of 1794, crushed by Russian and Prussian armies. Tadeusz Kosciuszko, who had served brilliantly under Washington as a volunteer in the American Revolution, had led the Poles in this last doomed attempt to preserve their country's freedom. Campbell's poem imagined him as Warsaw's champion leading 'his trusty warriors' into their final battle:

> In vain, alas! in vain, ye gallant few!
> From rank to rank your volley'd thunder flew:–
> Oh, bloodiest picture in the book of Time.
> Sarmatia fell, unwept without a crime;
> Found not a generous friend, a pitying foe,
> Strength in her arms, nor mercy in her woe!
> Dropped from her nerveless grasp the shattered spear
> Closed her bright eye, and curbed her high career,
> HOPE, for a season, bade the world farewell,
> And Freedom shrieked – as Kosciuszko fell!

After some tremendous rhetoric regarding the carnage which ensued, Campbell had broadened his theme:

> Departed spirits of the mighty dead!
> Ye that at Marathon and Leuctra bled!
> Friends of the world! restore your swords to man,
> Fight in his sacred cause, and lead the van!
> Yet for Sarmatia's tears of blood atone,
> And make her arm puissant as your own!
> Oh! once again to Freedom's cause return
> The patriot Tell – the Bruce of Bannockburn![2]

The reference to Scotland (like the Scotticism which gives 'arm' two syllables) raises a question for later discussion. But let us stay for a while with Campbell's interest in Poland, of which the third and last partition was completed by 1796. Napoleon's creation of a duchy of Warsaw in 1807 was doomed by his defeat of 1812. Tsar Alexander I became nominal King of the rump of Poland in Russian possession. In November 1830 a rising occurred in Warsaw against his brother and successor Tsar Nicholas I, 'The Flogger', inspired by revolution in France and revolt in Belgium. The Polish forces were defeated by September 1831 and a regime of relative tolerance and autonomy established by Alexander was replaced by brutal repression. Thousands of Polish exiles clamoured all over Europe against it. Prussian and Austrian Poland suffered in similar ways.

All this affected Thomas Campbell greatly. Abandoning his editorship of *New Monthly Magazine* in 1830, he, with his faithful lieutenant, Cyrus Redding (who actually did the hard editorial work) moved on to similar roles with *The Metropolitan: A Monthly Journal of Literature, Science, and the Fine Arts.* They soon left that, too, but while they were there, they thundered about freedom. These were exciting times as events moved towards the great Reform Act of 1832:

Our politics are before our readers. We are the unflinching advocates of a Reform in State and Church; not on a wild, theoretical, abstract plan, but a rational reform which shall give back to the people of England those rights, furtively abstracted from them, and grossly abused ... We ... hail the cause of liberty everywhere – in the lofty and noble-minded Poland – in France – in the boastful and noisy Belgium – among the remotest nations of the earth ... We shall make it a matter of importance to gather intelligence from all parts where the glorious flame breaks forth ...[3]

Verses by Campbell on Poland, and other matter on Poland, duly followed. *The Metropolitan* of October 1831 carried an unsigned article 'Poland – Its Fate and Consequences' lamenting the defeat of the rebellion:

The robbers have been successful ... The knout and the dungeon of the northern despot are to be gorged anew with victims in the noblest cause that can adorn human nature.

Now England

must either ally herself with the semi-barbarians of the north, in their conspiracies against the freedom of the world, or she must take the side of the free nations and France ... Russia is resolved to be the arbitress of Europe.[4]

Whether or not Campbell penned these lines himself, the sentiment was certainly his. Earlier that year he had written to a friend:

All continental Europe, I distinctly anticipate, will be enslaved by Russia! France and Austria will worry each other till they are exhausted; and then down will Russia come on all the south of Europe, with millions and millions, and give law and the knout both to Germany and France.

Quoting these lines his friend, doctor and biographer Beattie called the poet's work 'thrillingly prophetic'.[5] They do, indeed, anticipate quite remarkably certain notions about Stalinist Russia prevalent among Western liberals after 1945.

Campbell was by this time obsessed with Poland. On 6 July 1831 he wrote: 'My zeal for Poland has put me half mad.' At the end of that month, his continued engagement in the cause was ensured when Count Jelski, President of the Bank of Poland, in London for a loan,

showed me a column of matter inserted in every Polish newspaper that touched me deeply, or rather with deep melancholy. The Poles call me the stanchest [sic] friend they have in England. In large characters it is printed – 'The gratitude of our nation is due to Campbell.' They conclude by comparing me with Byron . . .

News of the fall of Warsaw according to one witness drove him nearly demented. 'In fits of abstraction and absence of mind, he used frequently to start from reveries of long continuance, with such exclamations as "Poor Poland!" . . . "Warsaw is taken!" . . . "the miscreant Autocrat!" . . . "The murderer of this brave people . . ."' In March 1832 a 'literary association' was founded to disseminate information about Poland. Several MPs were members. Campbell was permanent chairman.[6]

Three months later, he exulted that the carrying of the Reform Bill would be the 'making of' his Polish Association – quite how, is not clear. Pressed to stand as a Whig candidate for Glasgow, his native city, in the first election for the reformed Parliament, Campbell at length refused, though he stood a very good chance of success, on the grounds that his Polish Association was consuming so much of his time. At one stage, according to Redding, he changed his routine to dine at 2 o'clock so as 'to have the longer afternoon for his Polish labours.'[7]

Campbell had always been a man for a good cause. He had been hot against black slavery and in favour of Catholic emancipation. He edited a volume to raise funds for Spanish and Italian liberal refugees, attached himself to the cause of freedom in Germany, and was conscious of the wrongs of Ireland. But his Polish Association was his most significant involvement in public affairs, expect perhaps for his role in university life in the 1820s. He associated universities with liberty. Elected Lord Rector by the students of Glasgow in 1827 (they would re-elect him twice, once against no less an opponent than Sir Walter Scott), Campbell told them in his inaugural discourse:

It was mainly through her Universities that northern Europe, at least, first learnt to distinguish between the blessed light of religion, and the baleful gleams and false fervours of bigotry.[8]

Some years before this, he had proposed the creation of a university in London which would not, unlike Oxford and Cambridge, be confined to adherents of the Established Church. He claimed to have invented the scheme, and certainly played an important role in the early stage of promoting University College London, which was chartered, along with the Anglican King's College, as the University of London in 1836. According to Redding, his old friend Brougham, to whom he confided his idea at the end of 1824, later hijacked it as his own.[9] But whoever could justly claim priority, the University must be seen as a joint project between English Benthamites and Unitarians and the people whom Peacock derided as 'Scotch feelosophers'. Anand Chitnis points out in his study of the influence of the Scottish Enlightenment on Victorian England that six of the twenty-four members of the University's first council, including Brougham, James Mill, George Birkbeck and Lord John Russell, had been students at Edinburgh University under Dugald Stewart, Professor of Moral Philosophy and most eloquent of Adam Smith's disciples. He had also taught Campbell and had become a personal friend and mentor.[10]

What I have said so far should have suggested that there was nothing very distinctive above Thomas Campbell's liberalism. He was a Whig of the *Edinburgh Review* school. He was attached to principles of laissez-faire in economics and tolerance in religion. Though his passion for liberty was expressed with a vehemence which impressed his contemporaries, it was aligned with the foreign policy of George Canning, a Tory statesman whom the lifelong Whig

Campbell greatly admired: he was much downcast by Canning's early death soon after his accession to prime ministerial office.[11] When Canning had replaced the reactionary Castlereagh as Foreign Secretary in 1822, this had permitted Britain to stand forth as a friend of freedom in Latin America and Greece, though E. J. Hobsbawm can easily demonstrate that concern for British interests shaped policy in both these arenas.[12] A Whig of Campbell's disposition could feel fellowship not only for Canning but for Sir Robert Peel, a Tory of 'reforming' bent – and Peel, as we have seen, reciprocated Campbell's high regard.[13]

It is not surprising that the Tory Walter Scott, also a former student of Stewart's, had a lifelong liking for Campbell as man and poet. Nor is it odd that Byron should rate him, in his journal in 1813, above the Lake Poets, though below Scott. Campbell, after all, was a Whig like himself, attached to Holland House. Byron's esteem was not based only on partisan grounds: there is evidence that he genuinely admired the older poet.[14] It is said that Shelley imitated Campbell's *Pleasures of Hope* in his own early revolutionary poetry, and Godwin accused him in a letter of December 1812 of overestimating Campbell, along with Scott. But Shelley was clearly not deeply touched by a poet whose liberalism was initially orthodox and became at last inertly consensual.[15]

There is no reason to dispute the judgement of time. For most of the nineteenth century Campbell was generally regarded as a great poet. If his lack of energy and originality – and also his relatively small output – meant that Byron, Shelley and Keats inevitably overtook him in the judgement of most critics – his major status was still confirmed by edition after edition. In the twentieth century, J. Logie Robertson, collecting his poems for Oxford University Press (1907) was already complaining with 'indignation' that Campbell was neglected. He now survives as the author of a handful of martial poems inspired by the Napoleonic Wars, which were hailed when they first appeared and still attract anthologists.

What is striking now about Campbell, compared with his major Romantic contemporaries, is how very smoothly he accomplished his ideological transition, from Friend of the People, in the early days of the French Revolution, to national bard honoured with burial in the Abbey. This is not to suggest that his life was calm and successful.

He was born in 1777, the last child of an elderly Glasgow merchant. His father's bankruptcy meant that Campbell, from his earliest adulthood, was striving not only to support himself, and from 1803 a wife and children, but also to help his mother and unmarried sisters. He depended always on journalism, editing and hackwork. The persistent writer's block which made these things painful for him, and restricted his output of verse, can be related to a depressive disposition, perhaps exacerbated by the syphilis which he had picked up from a charming Jewess in Altona, Germany, around 1800.[16] Of his two sons, one died in childhood, the other was confined to a mental asylum. The enduring reverence accorded to him as author of 'Pleasures of Hope', 'Gertrude of Wyoming' and popular war poetry could not fully compensate for the cool reception, even by the friendliest reviewers, of his later long poems, especially as he was morbidly sensitive to criticism. His sorties into public life, marked as they were by financial gestures and sacrifices of time beyond his precarious means, can be seen partly as a way of escaping from the dreadful consciousness that he had failed his many admirers, producing nothing of much consequence after 1809.

To summarise Campbell's political history: the American War of Independence ruined his father, who traded in Virginian tobacco. Nevertheless, Campbell was always firmly convinced of the justice of the cause of the Thirteen Colonies. He wrote in 1822: 'The loss of our colonies was a blessing, compared with the triumph of those principles that would have brought Washington home in chains.'[17] As a student at Glasgow University, which he entered in 1791 at the age of 14, he came under the influence of the great liberal professors John Millar and Thomas Reid, who in that year shared the chair of the meeting in Glasgow of the Friends of Liberty. Millar was very much a Whig, who was firmly in favour of the limited type of monarchy established in Britain by the Revolution of 1688–9. Like other Foxites he was smeared with Jacobinism, but in fact he was alienated by the development of the French Revolution.[18]

Campbell's early opinions were further affected by Dugald Stewart, whose lectures in Edinburgh he attended later. Directly accused, in 1794, of arguing subversively in one of his books of philosophy published during the anti-Jacobin witch hunt which disfigured Edinburgh life, Stewart replied by denying that he approved of the French philosophers or favoured revolution. He wrote that he 'was aware of the mischiefs to be apprehended from the spirit of innovation', and said that he always concluded his moral philosophy course by enlarging in 'the warmest and most enthusiastic of terms' upon 'the peculiar excellencies' of the English constitution.[19]

Campbell wrote *The Pleasures of Hope* as a struggling young literary hack in Edinburgh. Its vast success permitted him to travel to Germany. Here, in 1800, he saw the French army capture Ratisbon. Horrified though he was by the carnage of battle, his affection for the 'Marseillaise' dates from this era: dying in Boulogne four and a half decades later, he got his niece to play it for him on the piano. An acquaintance later claimed that he returned to England confirmed by his travels in a 'decided preference for the British Constitution'. Nevertheless, when his fame had prompted Lord Minto to take him up and use him as a secretary, he told his patron that his 'principles were republican' and that his opinion of the practicality of a republican form of Government 'had not been materially affected by all that had happened in the French revolution.' His relations with Minto, who carried him off to stay in his stately home in Scotland, seem to have been marked by a social unease on Campbell's side characteristic of his excursions into aristocratic society, with the exception that he always felt comfortable with Lord Holland – or so he told Redding.[20]

He met Holland in London in 1801. Next year he contracted to compile *The Annals of Great Britain from George II to the Peace of Amiens*. This was hackwork, and he insisted on anonymity. Nevertheless, his work on providing a Whiggishly sound account of recent history was probably in the minds of the Whig leaders when they briefly assumed office in 1805 and Campbell received a royal pension of £200 per annum for life.[21] Fox, now Prime Minister, was an admirer of Campbell's verse: all the more reason to secure the poet's loyalty.

Whatever republican sympathies he may for a while have retained, his 'naval ode' 'Ye Mariners of England', published in the *Morning Chronicle* in 1801 and reprinted in the several editions of his work which soon followed, was an immediate success and remained popular throughout his lifetime and beyond. His father had been fond of singing sea songs and Campbell added this uninhibitedly patriotic item to the tradition, summoning seamen to launch their 'glorious standard' again 'To match another foe' – Napoleonic France. His poem 'The Battle of the Baltic' put together in 1804–5, with the help of friendly criticism from Walter Scott, celebrated the victory of the British fleet over the Danish at Copenhagen. It has some metrical originality – it impressed Hopkins with its use of what he called 'sprung rhythm' – but its patriotism, again, is orthodox and unqualified. The Danes are represented as grateful to Nelson as he calls on them to yield:

> Then Denmark blest our chief,
> That he gave her wounds repose;
> And the sounds of joy and grief
> From her people wildly rose . . .[22]

This poem too was highly successful. Campbell thereafter was always as ready to celebrate British arms as to call for liberty in this or that part of Europe. Perhaps his most interesting poem in this vein is his 'Lines Written at the Request of the Highland Society in London, When Met to Commemorate the 21st of March, the Day of Victory in Egypt'. This dates from 1809. It reconciles with apparent ease the claims of British and of Scottish patriotism:

> Triumphant be the thistle still unfurled
> Dear symbol wild! On freedom's hills it grows,
> Where Fingal stemmed the tyrants of the world,
> And Roman eagles found unconquered foes.

The specific achievements of Highland soldiers are applauded, fighting 'First of Britannia's host'. But the Unions of Scotland and, very recently, of Ireland with England are invoked:

> Is there a son of generous England here
> Or fervid Erin? – he with us shall join
> To pray that in eternal union dear,
> The rose, the shamrock, and the thistle twine.[23]

Scott in *Marmion*, published the year before, had worked, from his profound historical knowledge, to produce a poem which fully confronted the ancient enmity of England and Scotland but harmonised this into a vision of two fierce military traditions united, now, against

Napoleon. Campbell had once thought of confronting such subject-matter, and had backed away. After the success of 'Pleasures of Hope' his next project was to have been a poem about Scotland, set in Edinburgh, celebrating the glories of the country's independence, 'as recorded in history and tradition', displaying 'in a series of martial episodes, the characters and achievements of her great men' and aiming to 'rekindle in the national mind her ancient spirit of freedom and independence.'[24] But 'The Queen of the North' came to nothing. The fact that he composed 'Ye Mariners of England' while in Germany without apparent difficulty in the very period when he was blocked in his big Scottish project is highly suggestive. Campbell not only lacked Scott's learning, he lacked the courage and honesty which enabled Scott to stand forth both as an emphatic Scottish patriot and as a staunch upholder of the Hanoverian monarchy and the Union Parliament's war against France. To return to his mighty obsession with Poland: it is impossible not to suspect that Campbell's manic dedication to the cause of a faraway nation gave relief to some guilty awareness that he had deserted that of his own people, choosing, as he did, to reside and write in London – that he comprehensively displaced his national feeling. Cyrus Redding had found it unaccountable that Campbell would not admit his early poem 'The Dirge of Wallace' into a new collection of his work which Redding was preparing for him. This, too, might be attributed to his unease over his Scottish identity.[25]

Campbell was a man of considerable charm and uanffected generosity. Contemporaries were not deterred from vast admiration of his early poems by the feeble verse and hack prose which he produced over the last three and a half decades of his life. His burial as of right in Poets' Corner, conveyed there by such exalted men of rank and power, must have some significance for our understanding both of early Victorian political society and of the digestion of Romantic poetry into bourgeois ideology.

Campbell's liberalism, which never prompted him to rash defence of the lower orders in Britain itself, was Romantic-seeming, but unlike the ideas of Byron and Shelley, and essentially uncontentious. So, of course, were his patriotic sentiments. Because his verse was so evasive about ideological tensions and contradictions implicit in Campbell's life-experience and sometimes explicit in his private correspondence, it never ran much risk of deeply offending either Whig or Tory. I have written elsewhere about the exemplary ideological inertia which he achieved in his very famous and much admired narrative poem *Gertrude of Wyoming*, published in 1809.[26] The silences and sentimentalisations which make this poem seem ludicrous now were essential to its popularity then even with judges – Jeffrey, Scott, Hazlitt – who really should have known better. Campbell's place in literary history is assured: 'Pleasures of Hope' can be seen as the first long poem which we can call 'Romantic' to attract a large public, and general critical esteem, in Britain. There is every reason for specialists in the period to read him. But there is no case for rescuing him from the neglect into which he has fallen for the benefit of any non-specialist readership. His oeuvre has dissolved, so to speak, into the ideological history of the period which made him celebrated.

(1992)

10

Samuel Smiles: The Unexpurgated Version

If Samuel Smiles had possessed a less smirky surname – if he had had a horribly dour cognomen like his Scottish compatriot Andrew Ure, author of a Philosophy of Manufactures – he might not now be so horribly misunderstood. 'Urian' would not have quite the ring of 'Smilesian'. The name immediately evokes an utterly smug exponent of the key Victorian idea of 'self-help'. Any man, of whatever rank in society, can advance himself by sober dedicated effort on his own account. As crudely transferred to the Thatcherite 1980s, this idea is taken to imply that rich men have every right to the swimming pools in their barricaded mansions, and young blacks in Brixton and yobs on Tyneside have only themselves to blame if they are unemployed. Poverty is a result of indiscipline, sin, insufficient strength of character. 'On your bike . . .'

But in fact Smiles' thought derived from the same milieu as produced, not only the Victorian trade union movement, but also the co-operative wholesale societies which helped poor workers keep their families fed and clothed. He would have been bewildered by the Thatcherite assertion that there is 'no such thing as society'. He did not define 'self help' in terms solely of material advance: his criteria were cultural. He thought it was better to be very learned than to be very wealthy. His treatise, *Self-Help*, of 1859, needs to be read in its entirety, not raided for selected quotations. It is in fact the work of a confused left-wing moralist, blundering into imperialism as a refuge from the implications of the collapse of Chartism and the corruption of working-class radicalism by prosperity.

V. G. Kiernan has suggested that imperialism, in its heyday around the time of Smiles' death in 1904,

126

may seem the outcome less of capitalism's own inner structure, as it was then, than of a peculiar, unique amalgam in Europe and Japan of feudal-monarchical elements still strong and industrial capitalism young and ambitious but still unsure of itself . . .[1]

This reminds us of Joseph Schumpeter's influential view that imperialism is the outgrowth of pre-bourgeois, pre-capitalist forms of life – of atavism rather than calculation. A close look at Smiles suggests certain routes by which the rationalist, utilitarian, free-trading, anti-government, anti-imperialist ideology characteristic of the triumphant manufacturers of Britain when that country was the 'Workshop of the World' elided into emotional and practical support by British businessmen and workers for jingoistic British expansionism.

Smiles' view of the state, as expressed in *Self-Help*, is characteristic of the mid-Victorian period . . . 'The function of government is negative and restrictive, rather than positive and active, being resolvable principally into protection – protection of life, liberty and property.' He is against something he calls 'Caesarism', which he would identify, like other patriotic Britons, with the bluster of European rulers such as Napoleon and his nephew.

Some call for Caesars, others for Nationalities, and others for Acts of Parliament . . . Caesarism is human idolatry in its worst form – a worship of mere power, as degrading in its effects as the worship of mere wealth would be. A far healthier doctrine to inculcate among the nations would be that of Self Help; and so soon as it is thoroughly understood and carried into action, Caesarism will be no more.[2]

Self-Help is implicitly 'anti-imperialist'. The spirit of the remarks just quoted is not easy to reconcile with the ideology of Joseph Chamberlain and Cecil Rhodes. The Smiles familiar to us from the works of social historians is a minor prophet of Social Darwinism, a missionary for the middle-class world-view among the labouring people who helped make his book a best-seller, a complacent man representative of his times in nothing so much as his complacency. But if one actually reads his most famous book, an intense, confused Smiles appears – and his multifarious other writings confirm the impression that he was deeply self-contradictory. He often seems less a realist than a romantic, less a pragmatist than an idealist, less a man of his times than an anachronism.

127

Smiles (as surprisingly few people know) was a Scot. He came from Haddington in Lothian. It was a small country town of no more than 4000 people, relatively remote from the 'industrial revolution'. It gave him a model in his head of how things should be, of 'a society of interlocking duties and privileges based an intimate human knowledge.'³ Born in Haddington in 1812, the son of a small shop-keeper, he lived in this arena of *Gemeinschaft*, except for medical studies in Edinburgh, until he was twenty-six years old.

Jane Welsh who married Thomas Carlyle was a childhood friend, and coming from their home town Smiles was deeply ill-at-ease with a wider British society dominated by what Carlyle called the 'Cash Nexus'. Co-operation, brotherly feeling, small-town decency, were denied by what he saw in Leeds and London. He had a horror of mobs and crowds, of conformity. He loathed the characteristic 'respect-ability' of the grand Victorian middle classes based, like that of Dickens' Veneerings, on mere appearances. 'It means', he wrote in *Thrift* (1875), one of the sequels to *Self-Help*,

wearing fine clothes, dwelling in fine houses, and living in fine style. It looks to the outside, the sound, the show, externals. It listens to the chink of gold in the pocket. Moral worth or goodness forms no part of modern respectability.⁴

What Smiles wanted was a *cultured* nation – not a nation of aesthetes, but a community steeped in the disinterested intellectual concerns which had been part of his own upbringing. Haddington in the 1820s had been profusely supplied with schools, libraries, evening classes, self-made entertainment, all reflecting the Scottish educa-tional tradition associated with John Knox, who had himself been born in the town. Knowledge, in this tradition, is seen as crucial to man's salvation.

But Smiles found that he could not prosper as a doctor there: too much competition. 'I wanted to make a living . . .'⁵ He travelled on the Continent awhile, then went to London, where he experienced acute culture-shock:

I had been brought up in a country town where I knew everybody, even the cocks and hens running about the streets. Now I was in a great city of some three millions of people . . . The inhabitant of the West End knows as little of those of the East End, as the latter do of Wales or the Highlands ... Though there is no scandal, there is no help. The people are strangers to each other; each is intent upon his own business, knowing nothing, and caring less about what his neighbours are doing, or feeling, or suffering ...[6]

In London, Smiles lived for a while in the same lodging-house as Giuseppe Mazzini, the exiled leader of Young Italy, a prime inspirer of the 1848 revolutions and the Italian Risorgimento. He was greatly impressed, not only by Mazzini's philanthropy towards his fellow Italians in London, but by Mazzini's patriotic ideas.

He continued devoted to the idea of the united nationality of his country, and still spoke hopefully of the revival of cosmopolitanism, of the brotherhood of all men, and the amelioration of all through the work of all.[7]

Smiles moved on to the north of England, as a journalist. He edited, in Leeds, a radical newspaper which was a rival to Feargus O'Connor's famous *Northern Star*. He was, in modern terms, less 'left wing' than the fiery O'Connor, but he was within the broad Chartist movement. He agitated for household suffrage and the repeal of the Corn Laws. He identified with working-class aspirations.

Leeds, a city of 80 000 people, was overwhelmingly working-class. Housing conditions in some areas were as bad as in Engels's Manchester. *Respectable* workers lived crowded in tiny back-to-back dwellings. Sickness and unemployment attacked and destroyed their meagre savings. Yet Smiles was impressed by the 'life, industry and energy' he saw. 'Although trade was bad, and they had much misery to contend with, they were anxious to help themselves by all conceivable and rightful methods.'[8]

He disagreed with the Owenite socialists he met, though he praised their intelligence. He thought that strikes were a way of throwing away capital which could have been used to buy land or buildings – or to set up co-operative production. Yet he admired, in the strike wave which hit the north of England in 1840, the unity of the workers. It showed him what great moral power they had at their command in their beneficent principle of co-operation.[9]

'Self-help', as he met it in Leeds at this time, was simply the consciousness of the emerging working class. It was the ideology of the leaders of trade unionism and the co-operative movement, and it was fuelled by evening classes. Self-education became Smiles' most obsessive theme. In Leeds workmen naturalists, workmen poets, were commonplace. In *Self-Help* Smiles' greatest approbation, among all the people whose improving biographies he cites, clearly goes to such men as Robert Dick of Thurso, the baker-geologist, Thomas Edwards of Banff, the cobbler-naturalist, James Sharples of Lancashire, the blacksmith-artist. The West Riding in the early 1840s was well stocked with young men of similar bent, eager to collaborate in mutual improvement societies.

In March 1845, Smiles was asked to give a lecture to such a society. In it, he made his own position on the 'Education of the Working Classes' plain. It was to be seen

not as a means of raising up a few clever and talented men into a higher rank of life, but of elevating and improving the whole class ... What matters it how much steam power we employ, if it keep man more than ever yoked to the car of toil? Man, I insist, has a *right* to leisure ... leisure to think, leisure to read, leisure to enjoy.[10]

This lecture was the germ of *Self-Help*. It was well received, and Smiles began to think that a book written in the same spirit might be useful. So he started to enlarge the lecture, adding examples of virtuous self help.

Smilesian self help relates in its origins to the motivation which took British workers in hordes at this time to the frontier settlements of North America and Australasia. Smiles himself wrote guides for intending colonists. 'The guide to America was especially successful.'[11]

118 592 people emigrated from Britain in 1841, 128 344 in 1842, even before the vast spate of Irish emigrants during and after the famine and even before the lure of the gold rushes. The figure for 1852 was 368 764.[12] Men sold their few belongings, added the price to hard-won savings, and ventured on the hazards of the ocean in quest of prosperity – and leisure. These far outnumbered the 70 000 or so people who subscribed to Feargus O'Connor's Land Plan, where the idea was that a Chartist company should buy up and divide smallholdings or estates in Britain itself. Only 250 members were eventually settled.[13] But the pull was the same in both cases. The worker in the new industrial cities was commonly still, at heart, like Smiles himself, a countryman, not reconciled to long hours of mill work or the squalid street of back-to-back houses.

Smilesian self-help, in its origins, was an ideology arising at the point of conflict between agrarian values and the pressures of 'industrial revolution', in an atmosphere charged with democratic social protest and in a growingly literate society. Its initial direction was as much outward, away from Britain as it was inwards, into British society. It was, for Smiles himself, an internationally valid creed appropriate to the 1840s when men and women all over Europe were seized with patriotic and democratic ideas. And, indeed, Garibaldi admired Smiles as much as Smiles admired Mazzini. The rhetoric of Smiles' extraordinary *History of Ireland* (1844) evokes at times the choruses of operas in which Verdi insinuated the patriotic imperative. Smiles denounces Henry VIII of England as a 'monster', describes Elizabeth I as 'heartless and selfish enough for anything' and characterises her reign in Ireland as 'one of the darkest and bloodiest passages to be found in history'. Things got even worse, it seems, in the eighteenth century – Smiles cannot describe, he says, 'the daily and hourly sufferings of a whole people, endured, without intermission, from infancy to old age – from the cradle to the grave', until Grattan's Irish Parliament after 1782 'began to sympathise with the nation, to imbibe its patriotism, and to lead it onward in its struggles for liberty.' No wonder Smiles could sell America so effectively to emigrants: at this point in his life he was in effect a democratic republican. If only the Irish peasantry had been better armed and led in their 1798 rebellion, it 'would have taken rank in history with the struggles for National Independence, of Switzerland, Scotland, and the United States of America.' Smiles went over the top in his praise of Daniel O'Connell, leader to greatness of the Irish 'People' (Smiles' capital) while 'the civilised world looked on in admiration.' In Ireland,

The people themselves – did they but know it – hold in their own hands all the powers of the State ... it only requires their united will and energy to accomplish their own complete emancipation – social, political, and religious.[14]

Smiles links the claim of democracy with that of the working class. He believed that abolition of the Corn Laws was in the interests of the British working class, and his greatest political hero was without doubt Richard Cobden, the Manchester free-trader who led the anti-Corn Law agitation which succeeded in the mid 1840s. Detestation of aristocratic privilege, in both Smiles and Cobden, led to language inciting class war. In Smiles, it was linked to the romantic vision of free and united peoples, in Britain, in Ireland, all over Europe, throwing off the shackles of want and toil and reaping in leisure the fruits of hard-won culture. A thinker more remote from the author of 'the great textbook of Victorian casuistry', as Humphrey House once described *Self-Help*,[15] it is almost impossible to conceive . . .

But where do we find traces of the romantic Smiles in *Self-Help*? Alas, in precisely those pages where he evokes the spirit of the 'English' in India during the 1857 Mutiny and ignores behaviour by them similar to that which he had condemned in Ireland in 1798: indiscriminate massacre, in revenge, of native rebels.

What happened to Smiles between 1845 and 1859? In 1842 he got married. His union proved contented and fecund. He was neither the first nor last man to be diverted from radical politics by domestic claims. He had failed to make much money as doctor or writer. So he got a steady white-collar job. He became secretary of the Leeds and Thirsk Railway Company. He set up house in a genteel suburb. Then, in 1854, he rose socially again, moving to Blackheath, a very desirable area near London, as secretary of the South Eastern Railway Company.

He lost touch with the working class as he identified himself, through the railways, with the 'industrial revolution' of which he had been suspicious. He worked for years on a biography of Stephenson, the railway pioneer, published in 1857. This was his first best seller – its popularity meant that John Murray was prepared to bring out the treatise on *Self-Help* which another publisher had turned down a few years before.

But Smiles now rewrote *Self-Help*, hundreds of miles from Leeds, with sensationalist tales of the Indian Mutiny fresh in his mind. He had changed, and the world had changed. Chartism's last outburst was in 1848. The great boom of the 1850s had surged through Britain, taking the edge off working-class resentments, bringing full employment and some improvement in living conditions. Emigration had removed many radical, impatient working-class men. The industrial middle class, which, in Anti-Corn Law days had seemed to have revolutionary fire in its belly was now, to Cobden's disgust, pervaded with deference to aristocracy. Smiles himself, on certain pages of *Self-Help*, tactfully praised hard-working aristocrats . . .

Smiles was now, in a sense, stranded in Blackheath, amid philistines who worshipped money. The Cobdenite ideal of a nation of citizens rather than classes seems unattainable. Smiles yearned. And his yearning took imperialistic expression.

Self-Help is not primarily a book about success. It is a book about heroism. Smiles intends to offer a heroic model of conduct. The aim of striving is not wealth, but salvation. Commerce is not an end in itself, but a trial – trade 'tries character perhaps more severely than any other pursuit in life. It puts to the severest tests honesty, self-denial, justice and truthfulness.'[16]

Where, as Smiles looked around him, were fit heroes? The humble life could still itself be heroic, but it needed to be inspired by lofty examples. Livingstone was at hand, 'with a heroism greater than that of Xavier.'[17] But the self-made engineers who pioneered the industrial revolution – the likes of Stephenson and Arkwright – had passed on leaving opulent but unexciting successors. The heroes of the anti-slavery movement had won their struggle, and they also were dead. Life was too settled, too comfortable.

So Smiles, who spoke with a strong Scottish accent till he died, fell into naïve English nationalism. He blundered into an imaginary vision of the English people, *il popolo*, as they should be – and had proved, in India, they *were*.

We read near the beginning of *Self-Help*:

Such as England is, she has been made by the thinking and working of many generations; the action of even the least significant person having contributed towards the production of the general result. Laborious and patient men of all ranks – cultivators of the soil and explorers of the mine – inventors and discoverers – tradesmen, mechanics, and labourers – poets, thinkers, and politicians – all have worked together, one generation carrying forward the labours of another ... This succession of noble workers – the artisans of civilisation – has created order out of chaos, in industry, science and art.[18]

As I have pointed out elsewhere, such passages align Smiles with the greatest novelists of his age – with George Eliot questing in *Middlemarch* for a model of heroism, with Dickens creating in *Great Expectations* the portrait of a heroic working-class 'gentleman', Joe Gargery.[19] Smiles, however, now lacked the edge of radicalism which we find in both novelists. He can sound, in fact, rather like Dickens' Podsnap. The English exhibit what has so long been the marvel of foreigners – a healthy activity of individual freedom, and yet a collective obedience to established authority – the unfettered energetic action of persons, together with the uniform subjection of all to the national code of Duty.[20]

The concept of the 'gentlemen' is as important in Smiles' best seller as that of self help. The two are in fact inseparable. It is not wealth but *moral worth* such as the gentleman displays which is the end of self-help. And, like Dickens and George Eliot (whose *Adam Bede* came out in the same year), Smiles insists that a poor man with gentlemanly attributes is thoroughly superior to a rich rotter, 'gentleman' in class terms though the latter is.

The Indian Mutiny

... served to bring out the unflinching self-reliance and dormant heroism of the English race. In that terrible trial all proved almost equally great – woman, civilians, and soldiers – from the general down through all grades to the private and bugleman.

In the capture of Delhi

All were great ... men taken from behind English ploughs and from English workshops and those trained in the best schools and colleges, displayed equal heroism when the emergency arose ...

Several times Smiles returns to India and to the Mutiny:

Notwithstanding the wail which we occasionally hear for the chivalry that is gone, our own age has witnessed deeds of bravery and gentleness – of heroic self-denial and manly tenderness – which are unsurpassed in history ... It was in the hour of the great trial in India that the qualities of our countrymen shone forth the brightest [to] inspire the conviction that the best and purest glow of chivalry is not dead, but vigorously lives among us yet. ... Even the common soldiers proved themselves gentlemen under their trials.

Only war, it seems, can bind all classes together like this and show the English 'character', Smiles' great theme, as a *unified* phenomenon. By accepting the propagandist, idealised view of its events purveyed in Britain, he can use the Mutiny as confirmation that the result of 'self help', seen as the key trait in national character, is not sordid but beautiful. The working class in whom the spirit of self-help is innate take their place in a social structure hallowed by moral values shared by all:

At Agra, where so many poor fellows had been scorched and wounded in their encounter with the enemy, they were brought into the fort, and tenderly nursed by the ladies; and the rough, gallant fellows proved gentle as any children. During the weeks that the ladies watched over their charge, never a word was said by any soldier that could shock the ear of the gentlest.[21]

Smiles does not hurl abuse at the Mutineers. He was not a racist, except in so far as he took on occasions a characteristically naïve and confused interest in the very fashionable subject of race. He was happy to use a French Huguenot as an example of self-help, and to quote Russian proverbs approvingly in his book with the Crimean War barely over. The spirit of romance lures him into accepting the nonsense he reads about the Mutiny. He finds in it what he needs, in 1859, to permit him to believe that British society, which makes him uneasy, is really sound at heart. He offers a vision of Greater Haddington, in which the English stand together in the spirit of Scottish clan-feudalism as interpreted by that hero of *Self-Help* and profound influence on the younger Smiles, Walter Scott.

Around this time, the popular premier Lord Palmerston had shown a precocious awareness of the power of jingoistic demogoguery to distract opinion at home from domestic issues. The aristocracy were successfully reasserting their hegemony after the Cobdenite challenge to it over the Corn Laws. The public school system was emerging as a basis and nursery for the crucial concept of the 'English gentleman'. Smiles had picked up the Palmerstonian and Arnoldian rhetoric. 'Talk to me of the aristocracy of England!' Palmerston had cried to Parliament when defending the conduct of the higher command in the Crimean War.

Why, look to that glorious charge of the cavalry at Balaclava – look to that charge where the noblest and wealthiest of the land rode foremost, followed by heroic men from the lowest classes of the community, each rivalling the other in bravery.[22]

Smiles echoes this very audibly in *Self-Help*:

The bleak slopes of Sebastopol and the burning soil of India have been witness to the . . . noble self denial and devotion on the part of our gentler classes . . .[23]

As *Self-Help* went through many editions. Smiles took opportunities to change its text. Drake, a hero in 1859, was expunged from later editions, perhaps because Smiles remembered his part in massacring Irish persons. But as the book's sales rolled on – 20 000 copies in its first year, 150 000 by 1889, innumerable foreign translations including those into Arabic, Japanese and the native tongues of India – Smiles never changed his mind about the significance of the Mutiny. Just as only Livingstone's heroism can validate a Christianity tottering at home, so only the imagined triumph of *il popolo inglese* in India can validate *Self-Help* in an era when, to Smiles' own disgust and outrage, this idea is made by others a beggar-my-neighbour prescription for winning wealth.

Cobden, vehemently against imperial expansion in general, had made a significant exception for India. After all, that was where Manchester's markets lay. As the century wore on, more and more of his free-trading co-thinkers accommodated themselves more and more to Empire. When Smiles died in 1904, even those who regarded him as a prophet for the very successful co-operative wholesale movement would have found nothing egregious in his patriotic witterings. Thatcherites in the 1980s had a right to appropriate his name, but not for the reasons they supposed. He was not quite the advocate of possessive individualism they wanted: the edition of *Self-Help* which appeared in Penguin's 'Business' list in 1986, with an introduction by Keith Joseph, was significantly abridged.[24] But Smiles had unwittingly anticipated one of Margaret Thatcher's characteristic means of ideological mystification. When the results of wealth-getting at home seem sordid, and the long-term success of free enterprise is problematic, it's a good idea to start a war and kill off a few heroes.

(1992)

11

'A Mania for Self-Reliance': Grassic Gibbon's *Scots Quair*

'When I read or hear of our new leaders and their plans for making of Scotland a great peasant nation, a land of little farms and little farming communities, I am moved to a bored disgust with those pseudo-literary romantics playing at politics, those refugees from the warm parlours and lights and policemen and theatre stalls of the Scots cities. They are promising the New Scotland a purgatory that would decimate it. They are promising it narrowness and bitterness and heart-breaking toil in one of the most unkindly agricultural lands in the world . . . This life is for no modern man or woman – even the finest of these.'

Lewis Grassic Gibbon, in *Scottish Scene*[1]

*

Lewis Grassic Gibbon's trilogy about life in the Mearns has the status in Scotland of a modern classic. Elsewhere its reputation is not wide, though critics on the Marxist left commonly respect it as one of the most remarkable of 'proletarian' novels.

The three books of the *Quair*, published individually from 1932 to 1934, take the story of Chris Guthrie from childhood to death. *Sunset Song* (1932) projects the life of a peasant community from 1911 through the First World War. The Guthrie family have moved from Aberdeenshire to a peasant croft at 'Kinraddie' in the Mearns. Here John Guthrie's wife, finding herself pregnant again and fearing the pain of another childbirth, poisons her young twins and herself. His son Will revolts against him and emigrates. Guthrie himself soon dies after a stroke, leaving his highly intelligent daughter, Chris, with a choice between going elsewhere to complete her education or turning peasant farmer in her own right. She decides on crofting, then marries a labourer, Ewan Tavendale. They produce a son, also named Ewan.

Their idyll is barely touched at first by the outbreak of war, which indeeds bring unwonted prosperity to the area. But eventually Ewan enlists. His death in France, shot as a deserter, and those of Chae Strachan the socialist crofter and Long Rob the freethinking miller represent the end of a peasant tradition.

Chris marries Kinraddie's new minister, Robert Colquohoun, who was gassed at the front and has come home a socialist. In *Cloud Howe* (1933), which spans the 1920s, Colquohoun transfers to the manse of 'Segget', a small Mearns town where shopkeepers and craftsmen stand disdainfully apart from the workers in the local jute mills. Gibbon's evocation of this place is as remarkable as his handling of peasant life in *Sunset Song*. The General Strike of 1926 is central to the second novel. Robert commits himself to the workers' side, and the loss of his child, which Chris is carrying, just as the cause founders, betrayed by its leaders, matches the destruction of his revolutionary hopes. He slumps into sentimental Christian mysticism, and when he rallies at last, to preach radically again, his gassed lungs give way and he dies in his pulpit.

His stepson, Young Ewan, brought up an English-speaking, middle-class child of the manse decides, at the opening of *Grey Granite* (1934) not to live off his mother but to become an apprentice in a steel works in 'Duncairn', a city on the Mearns coast. Moving there with him, Chris becomes part-owner and manager of a lodging-house. Young Ewan, despite his initial contempt for working-class 'keelies', is drawn, at the height of the slump, into left-wing agitation, and suffers at the hands of the Duncairn police. Chris is married for a third time, to Ake Ogilvie, a joiner from Segget who has migrated to the city. But Ake soon decides to go further, to seek work in Canada. Young Ewan leaves at the head of a hunger march to work for the Communist Party in London, and Chris goes back to farm alone the croft in Aberdeenshire where she was born.

Few characters in fiction have endured such a series of calamities as Chris. Yet her personality seems to survive unmutilated. She is courageous but not domineering, warmly human yet strong in detached reflection. 'Chris Caledonia', as Robert calls her, could be taken to symbolize Scotland in a most attractive way. She is so alive in a credible modern world that her eventual retreat to solitude on the land is disappointing, and she is so appealing that readers do not want to believe that Gibbon kills her off, still barely forty, on the last page of the trilogy where, meditating on a hill top, she slips from consciousness into death. By contrast, even left-wing readers tend to recoil from the callous, arrogant militancy of her son. The common opinion is that *Grey Granite*, despite some brilliant writing, fails. Those who want it to be a Scottish nationalist text can hardly be happy with a conclusion which might suggest that Scotland, personified by Chris, is dead, while those in search of the Great British Proletarian Novel may be uneasy about the inhumane crudity of Young Ewan's commitment.[2]

I aim in this essay to explore the *Quair*, in relation to Gibbon's life and times, so as to promote a way of reading the text which will permit us to say that *Grey Granite*, despite flaws in execution, does complete the trilogy adequately. My main argument is that in it Gibbon completes a critique of peasant 'independence' which he began in *Sunset Song*. His fictional methods exclude direct authorial comment. If we identify him too closely with either Chris or Young Ewan we misread the trilogy and are liable to underestimate its achievement.

The action of the *Quair* is conveyed to us by a flow of voices. Even when it isn't clear that Gibbon's prose is dialogue or internal monologue, it remains intimately within the point of view of a character or characters. Here Young Ewan is falling in love with Ellen Grant:

And she tripped beside him, sweet, slim and demure in act and look, dark cool kitten, and inside was frightened at the wildness there. So up Windmill Steps through the sheet of the snow, a corner with a mirror, here the snow failed, Ewan halted panting while she made to run on.

But he caught her arm and drew her down, she wriggled a little, the light on her face, startled, eyes like stars and yet drowsy, he drew her close to him and they suddenly gasped, with wonder and fear and as though their hearts broke and were shattered in the kiss, sweet, terrible, as their lips met at last.[3]

Could 'omniscient' prose be more inward? The procedure through comma after comma, characteristic of Gibbon, suggests the unpunctuated nature of human thought and speech, as well as, in this case, the breathlessness of two youngsters hurrying home from a dance, excited by love. 'Dark, cool kitten' is Ewan's appraisal, foreshadowing, in its more-than-hint of a sneer, his eventual discarding of Ellen. The latter part of the same sentence gives us Ellen's feelings.

Every sentence in the *Quair* is creating character, evoking experience; there is no room for detached comment. Though Gibbon gives special prominence to the voice and consciousness of Chris, he cannot be implicated in her views of life – still less in those of Young Ewan. And as Gibbon adapts his technique, through the trilogy, to the social worlds which he projects, his separation from Chris becomes more obvious.

In *Sunset Song*, the narrative voice of Chris is not far from the gossip voices of Kinraddie, where, although they have a habit of sneering, folk exhibit strong communal feeling in moments of celebration and crisis, till the war brings economic success and social disaster. Gibbon, it has been pointed out, uses the pronoun *you* in moments when Chris, narrating, addresses herself:

So mother had worked and ran the parks those days, she was blithe and sweet, you knew, you saw her against the sun as though you peered far down a tunnel of the years.

Here the effect of the *you* is to bring the reader into special intimacy with Chris. But the previous page (we are close to the *Quair*'s beginning) has established another usage for *you* (even within Chris' narrative voice:

You could go never a road but farmer billies were leaning over the gates, glowering away at the weather, and road-menders, poor stocks, chapping away at their hillocks with the sweat fair dripping off them . . .

Chris is using 'generic *you*', implying that everyone in Kinraddie has shared, or could have shared, her observation. The 'overlap' between Chris's voice and the 'gossip' narrative voice which also employs generic *you*, helps Gibbon to draw us into the whole community of which Chris herself is so much a part.[4]

But city life did not allow the novelist, still committed to narration through characterized voices, the same ease of continuity. In *Grey Granite*, the passages of narrative-monologue employing *you*, whether 'self-referring' or 'generic' *you*, are distributed between sharply different voices. Four are given to Chris, three to the Anglicized Ewan, seven to a 'keelie' worker named Bob (briefly a socialist, and as important a centre of consciousness in the novel as Ewan or Chris), four by unidentified workers, and one by a draper's clerk,

John Cushnie, overheard, comically and yet movingly, as he begins
to revolt against lower middle-class proprieties.[5]

In *Sunset Song*, all voices converge towards one, and Chris dominates. In *Grey Granite*, social distances keep the voices apart, and
Chris's relative stature is diminished by the prominence given to
centres of consciousness very different from hers; we cannot be
enthralled by her view of the world. The diminution of her role
makes sense if we see Chris as inheriting a tradition of peasant self-
reliance, and her end as figuring the exhaustion of that tradition in
the Scotland which Gibbon surveyed in the early 1930s.

*

In 1933, James Leslie Mitchell, who had recently begun publishing
fiction in Scotticized English, or Anglicized Scots, under the pseudonym of 'Lewis Grassic Gibbon', proposed a collaboration to C. M.
Grieve, whose poetry in 'synthetic Scots' had already enjoyed a
certain fame. They had been introduced to each other by John
Strachey,[6] and an interest in revolutionary Marxism was one of
several things which these leaders of 'Scottish Renaissance' had in
common.

Each was an autodidact, reared in an anachronistic community
on the periphery of industrial 'civilization'. Gibbon, the son of a
peasant farmer from north-eastern Scotland, viewed that civilization
with as little reverence as Grieve, whose father had been a rural
postman in a small mill-town near the English border, and who was
currently praising the 'immense genius' of Major Douglas on the
significant grounds that Social Credit would 'establish the economic
independence of the individual.'[7] The scalding contempt for gentility
which flavours Gibbon's writings matched the class-conscious radicalism passed on to Grieve by his father, but both men felt separate
from the urban 'masses', about whom both wrote scornfully on
occasion.

Their collaboration produced a mischievous volume called *Scottish
Scene*. Gibbon's essays and short stories were written amid the
creature comforts of Welwyn Garden City. Grieve's (or to use his
pen-name, Hugh MacDiarmid's) poems and essays arrived from the
Shetlands, where he endured a more strenuous kind of exile. The
book makes it hard to accommodate either writer in the mainstream
of Marxism. While Gibbon jeers at his colleague's panacea, Social

Credit, as 'that ingenious scheme for childbirth without pain and – even more intriguing – without a child', he unveils his own 'Diffusion-ist' view of history (which leaves many traces in the *Quair*). A a self-taught archaeologist, he believed that in a distant Golden Age the naked hunters in Scotland's forests had been free and happy. Agri-culture, civilization, rule by lairds, had been imposed by alien sea-farers. Though Gibbon admired William Wallace, who had briefly roused and led the 'Pictish' poor, he despised Robert Bruce – a nobleman. The industrial revolution had eventually brought complete disaster.[8]

One might see Gibbon and MacDiarmid quite plausibly as brilliant provincial eccentrics whose main obsessions were essentially reli-gious. MacDiarmid was writing 'hymns' to the messianic figure of Lenin. In his masterpiece, 'On a Raised Beach' (1934), he addresses an audience of stones – 'I would scorn to cry to any easier audience' – and other people are for him 'human stones'. Towards the end of Gibbon's trilogy, in that novel significantly entitled *Grey Granite*, Young Ewan, long associated with granite in his mother's mind, is at work as a labourer for a granite mason, 'getting interested in granite'. Not to be outdone in stoneyness, Chris herself dies surrounded by stones.

This obsession with stones of two writers who were currently influencing each other might be explained in terms of what both drew from Scottish Calvinism, which had made God as alien as his universe, of which Scotland is one of the stonier portions. While neither is in the least a mystic, their evocations of the vastness of time and space, which mocks the puny lives of individuals, might seem to give each man's materialism an impractical appearance. And Gibbon did write very consciously in a Scottish tradition shaped, for better and worse, by the most intellectual and least ingratiating variant of Christianity. When he died in 1935, he was working on a novel about the Covenanters, whose grim and gentry-hated lives are a point of reference in *Sunset Song*, and in whose traditions of martyrdom Young Ewan is tortured by the politico-legal establish-ment. But I think that in the context of the early 1930s, his stony views, and those of MacDiarmid, had as much to do with existing conditions in Scotland as with inherited cultural factors.

The 'Scottish Scene' was very ugly. After the First World War the country's characteristic heavy industries – coal, iron, shipbuilding – had lost export markets, but although new consumer-goods industries maintained prosperity for many in southern England, Scotland neither created nor attracted such industries. Mass employment, led to mass emigration. In the ten years leading up to 1931, nearly 400 000 Scots (say about one person in twelve), left Scotland, and despite high natural increase, population actually declined. Politically, Scotland had swung precociously to the left. In 1922 Labour had returned the largest bloc of Scottish MPs and the eccentric constituency of Mother-well had actually elected a Communist. But the abortion of the General Strike was followed by further disillusionment in 1931 when a Scottish premier, Ramsay MacDonald, defected from the Labour Party to head a 'National' government, and his former party, which had held over half Scotland's seats, was reduced from thirty-seven to a mere seven.

In 1932, when *Sunset Song* was published, over a quarter of all Scottish workers were unemployed; in the worst hit areas well over half; in Greenock, three-quarters even two years later when the slump had abated somewhat.[9] Though Gibbon lived in an 'affluent' part of England, he frequently revisited his homeland, and the 'granite' ruthlessness of Young Ewan must be understood in terms of what he saw there. Gibbon was not escaping into religious fantasies about Lenin-like young heroes, so much as asking himself how an educated young Scot might react to social disaster. He did not *invent* the corruption, where they had local power, of some Labour politi-cians, nor the battles between workers and the police, nor the hunger marches. As MacDiarmid harangued pebbles in the Shetlands, the political and cultural situation in Scotland was desperate, and Gibbon's would-be 'granite' hero makes a plausibly drastic response to a horrific crisis.

One aspect of the crisis was the destruction of a proud Scottish tradition: the 'independence' of several classes of literate, disputacious manual workers. This is marked in *Grey Granite* by the emigration of Chris's third husband, Ake, a small-town joiner and vernacular poet unable to find a job in the city to which the collapse of his rural trade consigns him. Burns, so often mentioned in the *Quair*, had been these classes' representative hero. The Lowland peasant culture for which Burns spoke had been wrung by capitalist agriculture since

143

the eighteenth century. The related culture of handloom weavers had peaked and declined in the nineteenth. But the lead miners of Wanlockhead maintained the remarkable library which their forebears had started in the eighteenth century, right up to the closure of the mines in 1934.[10]

The worst shock Scotland suffered after 1918 was the collapse of the Clyde shipbuilding and engineering industry. Skilled engineers had attitudes closely comparable to those of the archaic 'independent' classes.[11] David Kirkwood, a leader of the Clyde Workers' Committee during the First World War, looked back admiringly to the 'mania for self-reliance' of his father, a labourer in a weaving mill, yet a devoted Calvinist who idolized the Covenanters and Burns. But Kirkwood himself by the 1930s epitomized one kind of Labour MP whom Gibbon mistrusted – sentimental, conceited, reformist, collaborationist at heart – and the fact that Kirkwood's autobiography appeared with a foreword by Winston Churchill, praising its author and the 'strong type he represents', might prompt us to question the real virtue, in twentieth-century society, of that kind of 'self-reliance'.[12]

Hammered by post-war slump, the Scottish working-man's tradition which had produced Burns and Carlyle, Carnegie and Livingstone, was at last deprived of a social basis. This might help to explain the prominence of Scots in British Marxist organisations. The tradition which said 'A man's a man for a' that' might well mutate into self-identification with the workers of the world, and a grounding in Calvinist theology was not the worst basis for a delight in dialectics. If we took Grassic Gibbon in *Grey Granite* to be simply endorsing Young Ewan's view, we could see him as exemplifying the process whereby the cult of self-reliance gave way to one of self-obliteration in the impersonal forces of history.

But there is strong evidence that Gibbon stands apart from Young Ewan. 'A hell of a thing to be History, Ewan!' his mentor in Communism, Jim Trease, tells him – at which Young Ewan thinks, enraptured, 'not a student, a historian, a tinkling reformer, but LIVING HISTORY ONESELF, being it, making it, eyes for the eyeless, hands for the maimed!' Masochistically, he supposes that the Party, historically speaking, *are* the workers, yet when the proletariat finally rise, 'most likely' he and Trease will be 'flung aside or trampled under', and, racing on through the commas with which

Gibbon punctuates interior monologue, 'it didn't matter, nothing to them, THEY THEMSELVES WERE THE WORKERS and they'd no more protest than a man's fingers complain of a foolish muscle.' (*Grey Granite*, 160–61, 195)

Trease gives History only an initial capital. The slogan-like capitalisations which follow belong to Young Ewan and serve to characterise him. He is very young. Beneath his composure, he is sentimental in his extreme anti-sentimentality. It must finally seem a weakness in *Grey Granite* that Gibbon cannot persuade his readers that Young Ewan, despite the truly heroic aspects of his role, is not a spokesman for his creator. But he could only have done this at the high cost of lapsing from that closeness with his characters which makes the *Quair*, though it has its faults, such a powerful work overall.

Young Ewan despites 'bunk symbolism'. But his mother is made to think symbolically. The titles of the three novels are, as it were, provided by Chris's symbolizing proclivities. The first is not called 'Twilight of the Peasants'. Nor is it called 'Gloaming Sang', as nationalistic critics might wish. It is *Sunset Song*, and its shape and force depend on symbolic linkings 'made by' the part-Anglicized Chris. She *sings* the old lament over Flodden, 'Flowers of the Forest', during the celebration of her marriage to the first Ewan. At the end of the book, clearly at her suggestion, it is played by a piper at the ceremony where her next husband, the minister, unveils a monument to Ewan and the three other Kinraddie men killed in the war. The symbolism of this monument must likewise be of Chris's devising. Above her own croft, on one of a circle of standing stones, the names have been cut after the style of a tribute to persecuted Covenanters at Dunnottar Castle where 'the Covenanting folk had screamed and died while the gentry dined and danced in their lithe, warm halls.' (*Sunset Song*, 126) Chris and Ewan had seen it on a jaunt in the early days of their love. Chris inherits her peasant father's class feeling against the gentry, but she does not make an intellectual connection (e.g., that the ruling class had been responsible for the carnage of the war). Like her theatrical deployment of bagpipes, an easy way to induce tears which blur over the historic conflict between Highland and Lowland, this suggests that her vision of Scotland and of history is inadequate. The end of *Sunset Song* could not be so moving if Gibbon did not expect his readers to implicate themselves in temporary acceptance of the sentiment. But this does not mean that in *Cloud Howe* and *Grey Granite* we are to regard Chris as an oracle rather than a character, to accept her mythology and to attribute it to her creator.

One critic makes this mistake when he claims that Gibbon's point is 'All is change, nothing endures but the land, while the forms of social organisation are blown away like chaff.'[13] This is, in fact, what Chris thinks. But despite a certain obvious truth in her notion, we should not attribute Chris's fatalism to Gibbon himself.

The contrast between Chris's view and her son's has prompted the suggestion that Gibbon sees history in terms of struggle between 'the masculine' and 'the feminine'.[14] Not continually, but in significant crises, Chris does indeed struggle with the men in her life. Her confrontation with her son gives us the last conversation in the trilogy. Chris denies the validity of all creeds:

Yours is just another dark cloud to me – or a great rock you're trying to push up a hill.

He said it was the rock was pushing him: and sat dreaming again, who had called Robert dreamer: only for a moment, on the edge of tomorrow,/all those tomorrows that awaited his feet/by years and tracks Chris would never see,/dropping the jargons and shields of his creed,/thinking again as once when a boy,/openly and honestly, kindly and wise:

There will always be you and I, I think, Mother. It's the old fight that maybe will never have a finish, whatever the names we give to it – the fight in the end between FREEDOM AND GOD (Grey Granite, 20)

The italics are Gibbon's, who thus avoids the conventional separation of speech from the surrounding narrative. The division into verses, of four beats each, is mine. David Craig has objected to Gibbon's 'mechanical metre' in certain passages, to his resort to 'a sort of soaring operatic highnote . . . whenever he wants that sort of kick.'[15] But its function in this particular passage is clear. The flight into rather flatulent 'poetry' is consonant with Ewan's drift into 'dream'. The rhythm characterises his state of mind, as he blurs over the prospect of his mother's death and looks forward, sentimentally, to moving *back*, past his creed, to childhood candour.

He hankers, for a blink, to regress. His mother has actually regressed and will regress further. This is not because she is a woman, and Gibbon does not typify 'eternal feminity' through her.

Gibbon was ahead of his time in his understanding of the legitimate demands of women from life. Contraception is a major issue in all three books. Want of it drives Chris's mother to suicide. Having it enables Ellen Grant to restore Ewan's relationship with his own body after the Duncairn police have tortured him. Ellen, like Maggie Jean Gordon in *Sunset Song*, Cis Brown and Else Queen in *Cloud Howe*, shows us that Gibbon's appreciation of the capacity of women for self-emancipation was not exhausted in his creation of Chris. On the contrary, Chris – though, paradoxically, by an unconventional act of will – throws up the chance of a wider life which her success at school might have given her. The emancipation of other characters shows up her relative conservatism, and their actions contradict her own association of 'creeds' with men. While most of the men in the *Quair* aren't ardent believers in anything, Maggie Jean, going off with her Labour doctor to organise farm workers, obeys the call of a 'creed' long before Young Ewan does. Is the latter talking nonsense perhaps in his last dialogue with his mother? While we may be prepared to associate him with FREEDOM, does anything we have read in the *Quair* entitle him to identify the atheistical Chris with God? Is he not splurging like some literary critic (most likely Scottish!) projecting some big fanciful theory?*

Cairns Craig is not such a nonsense-talker, when he argues that the absence, since 1707, of a distinctive Scottish political history has given the Scottish novelist special problems of applying narrative patterning to social experience. 'What Scottish novelists have had to do again and again in recent times, is to link their novel to some moment of historical dynamism which intrudes upon the historyless Scottish community: Scotland can only be known through narrative in those moments when narrative possibilities are forced upon a society that has lost all sense of its own narrative.' So the Great War and the General Strike are, in this view, necessary 'intrusions' in the *Quair*. Cairns Craig admires Gibbon's commitment of Young Ewan to 'history', to 'the only possibility there is for transforming an inhumane environment', but argues that Chris's role, balancing his,

---

* His remark is actually less absurd if we assume that he equates GOD with HISTORY and sees Chris as aiming for FREEDOM from HISTORY. But I am just not clear what Gibbon could have intended us to make of it.

is to deny history. She is 'identified at the end of the novel with the eternal principles of a landscape that is untouched by human changes, its granite permanence implacably opposed to human transform-ations.'[16]

This might make sense of what Young Ewan says: if Chris equals landscape and landscape equals eternal principles, then Chris equals God – the stony, impermeable God of Calvinism brooding over the puppet shows presented by humankind with its useless freedom. But if this is so, why is is that when she perishes Gibbon explicitly sits Chris not on *stone*, but on 'a great mass of crumbling cement', left by astronomers who came up the hill to make observations a hundred years before? (*Grey Granite*, 174) Chris herself denies the existence of anything 'permanent' in her last reverie. The dreams of men are transient. Intellectually she accepts the tyranny of change, which the cement represents not only in its relative newness, but also because it is already as much an archaeological relic as the 'standing stones' of ancient men. But by going back to the land, Chris has turned from the possibility of constructive change which the city offers.

History has destroyed her family and her childhood community, killing her first two husbands and her second baby, now taking her third husband and her son away from her. She cannot accommodate further her 'wearied body' and her battered self – or selves – to changes within history. She regresses to infantile peasanthood, from which she was educated to be a 'second Chris', an intellectual girl, and removed in class terms by her marriage to a minister.

Her relationship with Ake is as significant in the *Quair*'s scheme as those with the elder Ewan and with Robert. 'I'm no body's servant, the Broo folk's, or the bobbies'' is a saying of his which wins Chris's liking – he'll stand neither with the unemployed nor with the Establishment. Ake, with his 'slow independent walk', gives her, not rapture with marriage, but 'ease'. In his company she slides back to the values of her childhood, those of dour, uncommunicative Mearns folk who think it daft to say goodnight to their wives. He is, she thinks, 'crude and clean as she herself had been before a playing at gentry enslaved her'. He has in her eyes the 'sneering, half-kindly, half-bull-like face, the face of the folk of the Howe throughout, canny and cruel and kind in one facet, face of the bothies and the little touns.' And one of her lodgers muses, 'Queer the resemblance between her and Ogilvie – chips of the same bit of stone in a way.' (*Grey Granite* 70, 137, 157, 178) Unromantic though their relationship has been, Ake's going is not her wish. Defeated by history, but still a skilled man, he can move on to Canada. Skilled in nothing but housework and farm-work she can think only of return to the croft of her origins.

*

Gibbon's politics were heterodox. MacDiarmid alleged that Gibbon was a Communist, but was kept out of the CPGB by his adherence to Trotsky. One awaits further evidence of this 'Trotskyism'. His writing left him no time for activism. In an article published in *Left Review* just before his death, he wrote: 'I hate capitalism; all my books are explicit or implicit propaganda. But because I'm a revolutionary, I see no reason for gainsaying my own critical judgement.'[17] His nationalism was equally reserved. He wrote that he was 'some kind of Nationalist', but only 'temporarily, opportunistically'. He believed that nationalism was a temporary cultural aberration and must give way to cosmopolitan community, but saw 'a chance that Scotland, especially in its Glasgow, in its bitter straitening of the economic struggle, may win to a freedom preparatory to, and in alignment with, that cosmopolitan freedom long before England.'[18] So his nationalism was not cultural, but strictly political, and was subject to the conviction that politics must be about class.

He thought that Glasgow workers could destroy capitalism. He knew that the old Scottish radicalism of self-reliance could not. Ake – and Chris – vote Liberal in the 1929 general election. Raymond Williams has argued that in the *Quair* 'the radical independence of the small farmers, the craftsmen and the labourers is seen as transitional to the militancy of the industrial workers.'[19] It is true that Young Ewan is summoned, as a boy in *Cloud Howe*, to the deathbed of Moultrie, Segget's old radical saddler, and receives unspecified instruction from him. But he himself is middle class by upbringing and is converted to socialism by an English girl schoolteacher. None of the keelies whom he sets out to lead has a rural background or expounds artisan 'independence'. Since Gibbon's plotting has no place for a David Kirkwood, the *Quair* suggests disjuncture more strongly than transition. Gibbon may in this be untrue to history,

149

perhaps because his judgement was affected by bitter consciousness of how peasant independence had furthered its own destruction.

Ian Carter has shown how 'family' farming, on tracts of less than 100 acres, persisted tenaciously in north-eastern Scotland along with, and even symbiotically with, capitalist agriculture. The peasant farmer depended on hired labour to some extent, except when his children were old enough to work but had not yet left to set up on their own. Peasant agriculture had proved more resilient than capitalist farming during the agricultural depression of the late nineteenth century, but as increased demand for small farms forced up rents, the small man needed a higher cash profit – and was driven towards more thorough exploitation of the labour of sons and daughters.[20]

Hence the nightmarish character of John Guthrie in *Sunset Song* is not a melodramatic creation. He typifies the peasantry of his time. The rapidity of his movements, so much emphasized, suggests the ferocious pace of work which maintaining independence now entailed. His bad relations with his son Will, who escapes to Argentina, show the economic pressure on family relationships. So, in part, does his tragic sexual drive. More children will mean more workers. And the ideal of patriarchal self-sufficiency has obvious psychological consonance with incest; Guthrie's lust for Chris while he is mortally ill matches the rest of his peasant mentality.

Increasing numbers of peasant children fled, like Will Guthrie, from a life of bondage. The selective migration of boys and girls with initiative meant that peasant society lost power to resist just as outside factors conspired to sweep it away. The First World War brought a boom in sales of produce, and triggered a move from mixed-farming self-sufficiency into specialised work for urban markets, exemplified by the Munros in *Sunset Song*, who 'clean stopped from farming every park except one to grow their potatoes in, all the rest with covered with runs and rees for the hens, they'd made a fair fortune with their poultry and all.' (*Sunset Song*, 248–9)

Choosing when her father dies to remain on the croft alone Chris, as a girl, makes a momentous, even scandalous, assertion of independence. But, tragically, her decision coincides with the moment when self-reliance meets nemesis. In *Grey Granite*, her peasant values drag her into regression, stasis, and death.

Yet Chris has stood for something positive. Gibbon himself clearly feels at home with her, more than with the notion which he gives to middle-class-reared Young Ewan – that the masses, unthinking yet all-powerful, are sacred. In his *Left Review* article, he insisted on his own 'critical judgement'. Chris's independent thoughtfulness is her most attractive quality.

The opposition of Chris and Young Ewan at the end of the *Quair* suggests a dialectic of thoughtfulness – in itself, without action, useless and even potentially crippling – and militancy, which may, like Young Ewan's, be rash, cruel and opportunistic. Gibbon's trilogy can be related vividly to recent discussion on the left in Britain of the limitations of 'Leninist' militancy and the need to apply within socialist politics lessons learnt from the success of the women's movement, with its more flexible and responsive methods of organization.[21] The right synthesis of critical spirit and action might produce a mature socialism.

But Chris's negative aspects are travestied in Ake, her male look-alike, egotistic and complacent in fiction as David Kirkwood was in the Commons. Like countless 'independent' Scots before him, Ake transports himself to the New World, where the success of some such men has its monuments in the foundations of Carnegie and the banks of Toronto.

(1982)

12

Miss Jean Brodie and the Kaledonian Klan

The Protestant sectarian politics of Edinburgh during the thirties have interested historians in recent years. The question must be asked: where did the most celebrated *Edimbourgeoise* of the period stand in all this?

We know a good deal about Miss Jean Brodie's religious views and habits. 'At the same time as adhering to the strict Church of Scotland practices of her youth, and keeping the Sabbath' she was 'now, in her prime, attending evening classes in comparative religion at the University. So her pupils heard all about it, and learned for the first time that some honest people did not believe in God, nor even in Allah.'[1] This 'Edinburgh spinster of the deepest dye' impressed her pupil Sandy as an archetypal Calvinist. 'She thinks she is Providence . . . she thinks she is the God of Calvin, she sees the beginning and the end.'[2] From her biographer, Mrs Spark, we learn that 'she was not in any doubt, she let everyone know she was in no doubt, that God was on her side whatever her course.'[3] But she is in her Sunday behaviour – up to a point – sedulously tolerant. 'She always went to church on Sunday mornings, she had a rota of different denominations and sects which included the Free Churches of Scotland, the Established Church of Scotland, the Methodist and the Episcopalian churches and any other church outside the Roman Catholic pale which she might discover. Her disapproval of the Church of Rome was based on her assertions that it was a church of superstition, and that only people who did not want to think for themselves were Roman Catholics.'[4]

Her flat was in Church Hill. Living there it was quite impossible that she should not be conscious of the anti-Catholic riot which took place in nearby Canaan Lane in 1936. The Catholic hierarchy set up a Scottish Eucharistic Congress in Edinburgh. About 30 000 Catholics were to assemble in Canaan Lane Park, celebrate Mass and then march along Princes Street. John Cormack, leader of Protestant Action, organised a riposte against this 'propagation of a Blasphemous and Idolatrous worship of a Wafer-God'. Between 35 000 and 40 000 Protestants surrounded Canaan Lane Park when the day came. Police on horseback charged them and considerable violence resulted. The protest succeeded. The Catholic march was cancelled.

How did Miss Jean vote, if at all, in the November elections that year? These marked the zenith of Protestant Action's influence. Its representation on the Council rose from three to nine. It outstripped Labour in the vote – 32 per cent to 29.8 per cent – while the 'Moderates' took 38.2 per cent. It is hard to imagine the excessive Jean Brodie voting 'Moderate', let alone Labour. But could she have stomached the populist xenophobia of Cormack, who had his special cadre within Protestant Action – Kormack's Kaledonian Klan? This appropriated symbols from the Southern US racist Klan and sang, to the tune of 'The Old Rugged Cross':

> We will forever be true
> To the Red, White and Blue,
> And British will always remain.[5]

We know that Brodie had admired 'Mussolini's marching troops', but regarded Hitler as 'a prophet-figure like Thomas Carlyle, and more reliable than Mussolini; the German brown-shirts, she said, were exactly the same as the Italian black, only more reliable'.[6] However, her love for Teddy Lloyd suggests that she had no animus against individual Catholics.

It is curious that her pupils learn (or recall) nothing of her response to the most colourful element in the dreich, provincial politics of Scotland's stagnant capital. It is even odder that Mrs Spark offers us no comment on the matter. Spark, nee Camberg, is of Jewish parentage. Though her conversion to Catholicism came long after she had left Edinburgh, growing up in the city she must surely have sensed parallels between Cormack's rhetoric and the anti-Semitism of Nazi Germany. Perhaps the autobiography which she has been writing will reveal how she viewed Cormack's bully-boys.[7]

Meanwhile, it seems not to have been wholly fortuitous that Miss Brodie was betrayed for inspiring another pupil to fight and die for Franco in the Spanish Civil War, by a pupil who chose Catholicism. There was no logical connection between Sandy Stranger's anti-Falangism and her conversion to Catholicism. Much Catholic opinion supported Franco against the Republicans, who were largely anti-clerical and were accused of anti-Church atrocities. However, in choosing Rome, Sandy was implicitly rejecting genteel, and not-so-genteel Protestant Edinburgh, which harboured the fascistic Cormack.

As for Spark, her short account of her Edinburgh days in Karl Miller's *Memoirs of a Modern Scotland*[8] indicates a paradoxical relationship with the city's hegemonic Protestantism. She describes herself as 'puritanically nurtured' and imbued with 'puritan virtues' such as industriousness, horror of debt, 'polite reticence about sex' which are regarded as eccentric in the south of England.

She writes:

All grades of society constructed sentences bridged by 'nevertheless' ... I believe myself to be fairly indoctrinated with the habit of thought which calls for this word. In fact I approved of the ceremonious accumulation of weather forecasts and barometer readings that pronounce for a fine day, before letting rip on the statement, 'Nevertheless, it's raining.' I find that much of my literary composition is based on the nevertheless idea. I act upon it. It was on the nevertheless principle that I turned Catholic.

She associates 'nevertheless' with the 'primitive black crag' of Castle Hill 'rising up in the middle of populated streets of commerce, stately squares and winding closes ... like the statement of an unmitigated fact preceded by "nevertheless".' The Castle, it seems, represents for her human sinfulness standing in apposition to all the business and beauty of life. The weather forecasts are good – nevertheless, it's raining. Charlotte Square is gracious – nevertheless, standing in it you can see the unaccommodated crag on which the Castle sits. But why become a Catholic rather than embracing Calvinist doctrines which stress the ubiquitousness of sin, the likeli-hood of damnation? How does Edinburgh inspire someone to turn to a creed alien to the city's traditions?

Miss Brodie's self-contradictions may help to explain this. She represented an Edinburgh cast of mind derived from Calvinism – élitist, antinomian, the psychology of the 'justified sinner' – yet without efficient theology. A local person – Sandy Stranger or Spark – sincerely attracted by Christianity, would find in Edinburgh's Protestantism no satisfactory answer. Not only did Cormack's people represent unsavoury impulses – it was also the case that genteel Protestantism between the wars combined killjoy puritanism with doctrinal *insouciance*. There was no longer much call for tales of the Covenanters. Publishing of books from and about the seventeenth-century heyday of militant Calvinism had more or less ceased around the time of the Great War. Protestantism was socially dominant, ethically on top, but the Church of Scotland had replaced theology with homilies, eschatological vision with petty prudery. Miss Jean Brodie's ecumenical explorations typified the new doctrinal vagueness. The tragi-comedy of her life derived from her ethical revolt against a decadent tradition which – 'nevertheless' – had conditioned her personality. She had, to quote Sandy again, 'elected herself to grace'.[9] Spark comments: 'Just as an excessive sense of guilt can drive people to excessive action, so was Miss Brodie driven to it by an excessive lack of guilt.' Brodie 'was by temperament suited only to the Roman Catholic Church; possibly it could have embraced, even while it disciplined, her soaring and diving spirit, it might even have normalised her.'[10] 'Nevertheless', like her famous ancestor, she acted out the double life of a justified sinner until one of her accomplices betrayed her.

(1989)

13

Labour and Scotland

Just seventy years after Friday 31 January 1919, when troops and tanks stood by to quell a mass rally in George Square of West of Scotland workers campaigning for a forty-hour week, the event was remembered in the People's Palace on Glasgow Green. A bronze bust of Willie Gallacher by Ian Walters was not so much unveiled as proclaimed. It sits at the top of the building, in the room where Ken Currie's controversial Rivera-style murals of working-class history can be seen around the ceiling, but the speeches were in the Winter Garden downstairs, where heavy rain dripping through the glass roof and a chill which gnawed one's bowels did not dismay perhaps 200 people who had gathered to honour in their movement's own way the man who from 1935 to 1950 was Honourable Member for West Fife (Comm.), and an activist long before that in the Clyde Workers' Committee, arrested in George Square on that day recalled now as 'Bloody Friday'.

Speaker after speaker suggested that the bust was a tribute to countless nameless fighters as much as to Gallacher himself. The tradition of 'Red Clyde' was being celebrated, and this was an occasion for stirring songs and warm hearts, not for pedantic historians. Gallacher was one of those who put it about that John Maclean was out of his mind, literally hallucinating, when he ran his Scottish Workers Republican Party in opposition to the infant Communist Party of Great Britain. Nevertheless, the name of the great Marxist dominie was repeatedly invoked, and Pat Lally, Glasgow's Labour Provost, was much applauded when he seemed to promise that the Council would erect a statue of Maclean in George Square. The roll-call of Red Clyde heroes was fondly recited, Labour men, ILPers,

156

CPers, heretics – Wheatley, McShane, Maxton . . . And why was I there myself if not because I'd read as a boy a book about Maxton and fallen at once under the twin spells of the Red Clyde and of Labour history?

The People's Palace sells a postcard of Maxton. In an election advertisement of 1922, a man with a lovely smile in a huge cloth cap is holding up a solemn tot: VOTE FOR MAXTON AND SAVE THE CHILDREN. The image assimilates itself with that of Christ on the Sunday school wall: SUFFER THE LITTLE CHILDREN TO COME UNTO ME. Complex crossovers between religion and politics help to explain why a version of 'socialism' which is sentimental as well as pragmatic still dominates the political map of Strathclyde. *Breach of Promise*, the title of Clive Ponting's study of Wilson's Governments of the 1960s,[1] evokes, with its suggestion of sordid betrayal, a polarity which dominates structures of feeling within the labour movement. The shades of men like Maclean and Maxton whose failure in politics expressed refusal to compromise are invoked against 'traitors' like MacDonald and Jenkins and wheeler-dealers such as Wilson. In particular, the highly intelligent Scottish politicians now so prominent on Labour's front bench have to live with the oral history of folk-song, and comparison in young minds with Harry McShane, that Marxist saint who fought beside Maclean and died only recently, and Mick McGahey, happily still with us, beaming serenely at the back of that throng in the People's Palace.

In this context, Gordon Brown MP's biography of *Maxton* is a brave venture. Maxton did indeed try to 'save the children', with a furious oratory at Westminster (sneered at as 'pink' by Maclean back home). He told how his own wife had lost her life struggling to save her baby's. He denounced as 'murderers' those who had voted to withdraw milk from the list of entitlements of mothers and children. In 1932, he led the Independent Labour Party out of the Labour Party. Jennie Lee was a fellow Scot who went with him. 'Yes, you will be pure all right', Nye Bevan chided her. 'But remember, at the price of impotency.' Others accused Maxton of being too lazy to want Government office. Brown's summing-up, which is more generous, sheds light on his own political values. Maxton was a 'visionary'. When he died in 1946, 'The determined rebels of the 1920s had given way to the dark suited grey men of the Labour establishment.'

Maxton was an ethical socialist who stood for individual freedom – 'We must not allow ourselves to become ants in an ant-hill' – and had 'an inherent sense of human equality'.[2]

For Brown and others who preserve a sense of socialist mission, it was difficult to incorporate the heritage of protest into the public profile of Kinnock's Labour Party. In Glasgow, exceptionally, people who know little history seem still to feel that Maxton and Maclean are somehow mixed in with the ethos of local councillors whose canny city-centre yuppifications stand in bizarre contrast to the miseries of the housing estates. To be a (non-Ramsay) MacDonald is to have fought with Brave Charlie; every Glaswegian inherits the Red Clyde. Elsewhere in Britain traditions have been 'breached' by the Wilson–Callaghan years when the 'dark suited grey men' compromised most ideals which the Party had ever represented and Labour's chief *raison d'être* appeared to be to ensure that moderate trade unionists and liberal dons got their shares of chauffeur-driven transport and expenses-paid trips.

Clive Ponting's survey of the first phase of 'breach' is comprehensive, careful and acute. Its chief limitation is that it is political history written by a former civil servant (albeit one very critical of Whitehall) who looks at events from 'inside'. A lot can be explained from this position, but not the most remarkable fact of all: that the Labour Party survived the behaviour – cynical, baffled, or plain incompetent – of the collection of Oxford graduates and self-made men who sat in its Cabinets. Why couldn't Wilson get rid of George Brown earlier? The man's conduct in public was often preposterous, and he would offer or threaten resignation two or three times in one private meeting. What connections did Brown have, in or out of This Great Movement of Ours which made him seem indispensable? What part did Wilson's association with the well-known swingingness of the 1960s play in preserving his credibility – which he had almost wholly destroyed by 1969 – just sufficiently for him to come back as Prime Minister in 1974? Ponting mentions the defeat of England's football team in the 1970 World Cup, just before an election which Wilson lost, not its victory in 1966, when the result at the polls was likewise different. The Beatles are referred to only in connection with the cosmetic democratisation of the honours system (they got MBEs), not as working-class lads of anti-Establishment bent.

The Labour Party, one might conclude, survived because it gave its poorer supporters just enough, and presented a humanitarian and liberationist face to middle-class campaigners. 'The Government', Ponting points out, 'had a good record on one of the most important areas for any Labour administration – economic equality.' Its attempts at incomes policy did the lower-paid little good, its fiscal measures against the rich were ineffectual. But it increased pensions, supplementary benefits and family allowances. Public expenditure rose from 34 per cent of GDP in 1964–5 to 38 per cent in 1969–70. More went on health, social services and education. This record, Ponting concludes, 'is all the more commendable since it was achieved in the face of an awful economic legacy, economic difficulties throughout the period, and considerable opposition from Jim Callaghan.'[3]

Feminist aspirations were acknowledged in the Equal Pay Act of 1970. Though it was private members whose bills legalised abortion and adult homosexual intercourse, and got rid of the death penalty, the Government was helpful in these cases. Theatre censorship was abolished despite Wilson's personal opposition. Divorce became easier. 'Trendy lefties' had every reason to suppose, then and throughout the 1970s, that Labour was more likely to pass, or let through, liberal legislation in such spheres than were the Tories. And it was Labour's two Race Relations Acts which began to outlaw blatant manifestations of prejudice.

These points aside, Ponting's book makes very depressing reading. Wilson, former Liberal, former don, former civil servant, had persuaded the Bevanite Left in the 1950s that he was their man. But Ponting presents him as an opportunist who enjoyed power and its trappings for their own sake and, still more fatally,

loved the Whitehall system. He admired its superficial efficiency in producing papers and moving work smoothly through a hierarchy of committees, and tended to believe that this was equivalent to dealing with and resolving real problems. Wilson would certainly have made a better permanent secretary than prime minister.

His confidant Crossman recognised for the first time in September 1968 that Wilson didn't 'feel himself representing the Labour movement, really caring about the trade unions or feeling great loyalty to the party.' He cared 'about politics, about power'.[4]

Such strategy as Wilson had in 1964 soon broke down in face of economic problems and Whitehall sabotage. The new Department of Economic Affairs produced a National Plan in 1965, but there was no mechanism for implementing it, and within months it went into the dustbin, victim of the priority given to defending the pound and deflationary measures which made its targets unrealistic. The new Ministry of Technology, intended to fan the 'white heat' of revolution, merely collected problems piecemeal as industries continued to decline. Labour opposed monopolies – but favoured mergers. Share of world exports of manufactures fell from 12.7 per cent in 1960 to 8.6 per cent in 1970, reflecting Britain's slow rate of economic growth and poor productivity. Socialists might have argued that national wealth was not the be-all and end-all of civic striving, but except in wartime such appeals rarely work. What was needed, it seems in retrospect, was a socialist strategy for shifting responsibility, along with power, from Whitehall and the City to the people, a return in a new context to the young Gallacher's vision of workers' control and to the ideals of municipal self-help. Ken Livingstone would later show that Labour working with the people could get somewhere. Wilson's Labour Party, in the person of slick Dick Marsh, could do no better than renationalising steel under a board which included a token working trade unionist but was headed by a conservative Old Etonian with no experience in industry.

Some Cabinet members – Crosland, Castle, Benn – retained elements of socialist vision and occasionally mentioned principles. Even George Brown was not entirely incapable of gut reactions in the movement's tradition. In January 1968, the Cabinet, discussing a package of cuts, was 'split largely on class lines' over a proposal to postpone the raising of the school-leaving age to 16 – a commitment envisaged in the 1944 Education Act steered by the Tory Rab Butler. Just two graduates, Crosland and Benn, sided with formerly working-class ministers, among whom Brown challenged the Education Minister directly:

Brown: I want a straight answer to a straight question. If you had to choose between these 400 000 fifteen year olds and university students, which would you help?

160

Gordon-Walker: If I had to make such a choice I suppose I'd help university students.
Brown: May God forgive you.

The vote went 11–10 in favour of postponement for two years.[5]

Since this would ensure fresh cohorts of the underprivileged for Jennie Lee's new Open University to recruit, one could argue that Brown set up a false opposition. But nothing can justify certain lies which ministers told to their party because they knew that what they were up to was unacceptable.

The most nauseating case was deception over sanctions against Rhodesia. Wilson appears at his worst in relation to this issue. The Government was very anxious to expand trade with South Africa, and was terrified of being pressurised into sanctions against Pretoria; this in itself was enough to ensure that action against Smith's UDI régime was merely cosmetic. Since all Smith had to do was to keep saying 'no' to any solution acceptable to Commonwealth and world opinion, Wilson's efforts in personal diplomacy were palpably ridiculous. Parliament was lied to over the role of Shell and BP in sanction-busting, against which the Government took no action, while prating about the delinquencies of other nations.

The labour movement stood for colonial freedom and increased aid to the Third World. About these issues Wilson's cabinets were less than lukewarm. Britain's support for Nigeria against Biafra was defensible. Further Balkanisation of Africa was not self-evidently desirable. Despite having an arguable case, Wilson's Government lied about the extent of British export of arms to Nigeria (70 per cent of the total acquired by that country in 1969). It did not even talk about its action in clearing some 2000 reluctant people off the Diego Garcia Islands in the Indian Ocean in order to hand these to the United States as a base. This operation, which cost over £15 million, was carefully hidden from Parliament's view. The Cabinet panicked in 1968 over the possibility of an influx of Kenyan Asians and passed an infamous Immigration Act invalidating the right of these British passport-holders to enter the United Kingdom – which, as it was told, 'would have been unconstitutional in any democracy with a written constitution.' It is hardly surprising that the percentage of British GNP spent on overseas aid fell from 0.53 in 1964 to 0.37 in 1970.[6]

The British Empire was finished, but Wilson and his colleagues didn't want to admit it. A more atmospheric historian than Ponting might have made something, in blame or extenuation, out of the role of the press in the 1960s in sustaining belief in Britain's greatness and the 'Powellite' racialism which fed on that faith. Wilson, as Ponting shows, was obsessed with 'defusing' issues, such as immigration and Rhodesia, which might aid the Tories at the next election. He emerges, not for the first time in print, as a paradoxical mixture of over-confidence (in his clout as international statesman and his capacity to steer the economy) and paranoia (over the media and over real and imagined intrigues to oust him in favour of Brown or Callaghan). To move from judgement on his personality to world-historical considerations, his addiction to jetplane statesmanship diverted him from the horrible realities of the economic position inherited from 'thirteen wasted years' of Tory government.

Devaluation of the pound was overdue. From 1964 to 1967, Wilson's Government fought to avoid it, until there was really no alternative. Why?

Wilson presumed to take over from Macmillan the role of 'mentor to the brash and inexperienced Americans in the complexities of world affairs'. The reserve currency role of sterling gave Britain illusory economic status at a time when it was slipping further and further behind West Germany and France. Its role in NATO was seen as second strongest, and East of Suez it had traditional commitments which the United States were unwilling to take over. By maintaining what was thought to be a special relationship with the United States, Britain could, it was imagined, remain a great power. (Entry into the EEC, the alternative finally pursued, was, it should be stressed, not the only one. There were Scandinavian models of effective social democracy outside the Treaty of Rome.)

Ponting has looked at previously secret American documents which show that in 1965 a series of 'undertakings' were arrived at with the United States which gave Wilson, with his tiny majority, a basis for short-term electoral success. They were so secret that most of the Cabinet heard nothing of them. The US Government did not want devaluation because it would put the dollar under pressure. In return for US support for the pound, Callaghan, as Chancellor, would deflate. Though Wilson resisted pressure to send British troops to

Vietnam, diplomatic support for the US presence there was ensured, and it was understood that Britain would not cut its commitments in Germany and the Far East.

George Brown was off the mark when he told a colleague that the Prime Minister was 'bound personally and irrevocably to President Johnson and had ceased to be a free agent.'[7] Wilson did not want to devalue and claimed to have always been 'an East of Suez man'. He had freedom to pursue his own preferences. By 1967, however, when sterling entered a decisive crisis, Wilson had been converted to devaluation. The purchase of US F 111 aircraft was one of the cuts which followed devaluation, and withdrawal from East of Suez was brought forward. The US Secretary for Defense, Clark Clifford, expressed the scorn of his Government at this display: 'The British do not have the resources, the backup or the hardware to deal with any big world problem . . . They are no longer a powerful ally of ours . . .' Devaluation, then, marked the effective End of Empire.[8]

But meanwhile Britain's overcommitment to defence, including the shibboleth of the 'independent deterrent', had cost the country dearly. Large savings could have been made by scrapping Polaris, which was ridiculed in Labour's 1964 manifesto. It was kept. Britain badly needed to spend more on industrial research and development. Nearly 60 per cent of all input into this came from the Government – and nearly two-thirds of that went on military projects. For all Wilson's blather in the 1964 election campaign about new technology, little thought was put into this problem. When Lord Zuckermann, as the Government's Chief Scientific Adviser, produced a report in 1969 suggesting diversion of effort into the civil field, Wilson rejected it: 'I am afraid there is no political capital in this because nothing we decide will have any effect until years after the next Parliament gets going.'[9]

By this time, Labour was consistently well behind in opinion polls. Its appeal to the electorate in 1970 would perforce be based not on any achievements in restructuring British institutions or economy, but on the 'sound' management which produced, in 1969, a huge balance of payments surplus of £440 million. That year saw two truly spectacular political disasters. A strange, half-cock plan for reforming the House of Lords proved impossible to force through the Commons, and Wilson, thrusting his most loyal colleague,

Barbara Castle, in front of him for safety, took on the trade union side of This Great Movement of Ours and lost.

Trade unions were increasingly unpopular. The proportion of the public which saw them as beneficial had fallen from 70 to 57 per cent since 1964. Strikes were seen by nearly half those polled as the unions' main problem. Legislation concerning strikes worked out with Trades Union Congress consent might have embodied a sensible response to public opinion, though it would still have faced left-wing distaste. Wilson's anti-TUC fervour created a position where his rival Callaghan could gain support by public opposition (breaching the convention of collective responsibility for Cabinet decisions) and the proposals in Barbara Castle's White Paper *In Place of Strife* could not be pressed forward. Obsessed with wresting the strike issue out of Heath's hands, Wilson merely made rational discussion of it within the Labour movement a short- and long-term impossibility.

Since 1951 the overall Labour vote in the United Kingdom has been in decline. Between 1964 and 1970, individual membership of the party dropped by half. Yet the party recovered sufficiently to win two elections in 1974. Two overlapping factors may explain the persistence of Labour. Firstly, however dismal the party's recent record, there was no appetising alternative for the poor, the militant and the visionary. Maxton's ILP, Gallacher's CP, had failed to provide scope on the left, and the Liberal Party of Grimond and Thorpe was hardly likely to fire the urban masses or the young activists in CND and Anti-Apartheid. Secondly, the movement in which the party was rooted had a life of its own. I can recall, even from the early 1980s, a Co-op store which was still the centre of social vitality in a former shale-mining village. The values of co-operation and trade unionism originated in mid-nineteenth century self-help, a concept which Tories have illegitimately hijacked. Maxton, Jennie Lee and other 'visionaries', however often their argosies of hope foundered on the rocks of bureaucracy, did articulate cries for fairness and friendship against greed and selfishness which had deeply rooted popular support.

If Labour in England has lost credibility as the voice of such values, it does not follow that they are dead. Mrs Thatcher received lower shares of the poll in successive elections after 1979. Scotland, of course, contributed mightily to this effect in 1987. Scottish Tories polled over 50 per cent in 1955. Their fortunes have steadily slumped since. Meanwhile, the Labour vote has been remarkably steady in urban Scotland.

When the Party broke through in 1922, it took 35.9 per cent of the poll. In 1935, a poorish year, the figure was 36.8 per cent. Against the 1974 onslaught of the SNP, which became Scotland's second party with 30 per cent, Labour retained 36.3 per cent. The bad year of 1983 – 35.1 per cent – was followed by Labour's recovery to 43.9 per cent in the regional elections of 1986 and general election triumph in 1987 when Labour took a record 50 out of 72 Scottish seats on a similar poll, not too far off the 1945 result of 47.6 per cent, though well below the apogee of 49.9 per cent in 1966.

In the fine Scottish tradition of self-righteousness against the odds, Tories talk as if there is a temporary timewarp; Thatcherite policies remorselessly applied in defiance of three-quarters of Scottish opinion will privatise council housing, make schools and hospitals opt out, replace old heavy industries with nice light ones and reduce the mental dependence on public funding of which they accuse their fellow Scots. These Tories can no more explain than I can why social categories (e.g. home owners) likely to vote Tory in England vote against Tories in Scotland. They tend to blame the insufficiently Murdoch-ised Scottish media. They may have a point. The *Scotsman* and the *Glasgow Herald*, rival claimants to the title of 'Scotland's national newspaper', targeted at AB readers, both gave Mick McGahey a good send-off when he retired from the NUM leadership. Photographs of a Grand Old Man smiling in sunlight registered him as part of the Pageant of Scottish History, not as a Red Bogey.

Perhaps the labour movement's respectability in Scotland has partly depended on the modesty with which it has pressed the claims of socialism in local and Westminster Government. The many facts recited in *Forward!* rarely seem to justify its uplifting title.[10] This is a valuable, long-overdue book, but perhaps it has been as well for Labour that no such general history of its record has previously appeared. One is struck constantly by the fact that until the recent emergence of bright, youngish MPs amongst whom Gordon Brown is by no means the only star, effective Scottish contributions from the Labour front bench have been tiny relative to the disproportionate number of seats which Scotland has delivered to the party over the years. Ramsay Macdonald is still the most eminent politician to have risen from among the Scottish poor.

It is true that John Wheatley, of Housing Act fame, was the only creative minister of the 1923–4 Government. But Willie Ross, Wilson's Scottish Secretary, hardly gets a mention in Ponting's book. His most important Labour forerunner in the Scottish Office, Tom Johnston, during the Second World War, lived down his Red Clyde past to become a man above politics. In particular, his earlier enthusiasm for home rule – widely shared in Scottish Labour circles before the war, and endorsed by a party *Plan for Post War Scotland* in 1941 – was apparently sated by his own success at 'Government by consultation', strengthening the country's postwar prospects by the use of powers delegated from Westminster. He gave Scotland what he thought was good for it. There were now lots of Plans. After the war, planners with more clout imposed UK-wide plans, including centralised nationalisation, on Scotland, and the Labour tradition of support for home rule was increasingly left in the hands of the CP.

Michael Keating in *Forward!* takes on the difficult job of explaining Labour advance in Scotland and Tory decline in 1951–64. He attributes this to the 'resilience of class divisions'. Scottish Labour MPs, 'compared to their English counterparts . . . were older, more working class, more likely to have been local councillors and less likely to lose their seats.' They were mainly unambitious and parochial in outlook. Only one in the whole 13 years was elected to the party's Parliamentary Committee.[11] The continuing mediocrity of Scottish Labour representation at Westminster must have helped the SNP in its surge of 1967–74.

However, there were other factors bearing on that development and on the simultaneous and apparently unconnected afflatus of Plaid Cymru in Wales and growth of the Civil Rights movement in Northern Ireland. This was precisely the moment when Britain's loss of prestige was felt in devaluation and reduced international status. The benefits of belonging to the United Kingdom were less obvious than before. All over the world nationalist movements or ethnic minorities had asserted or were asserting themselves. Sympathy for Biafra drew on the feeling in the air that self-determination was just. If Tanzania could govern itself, why not Scotland? Civil Rights and Black Power agitation in the United States exemplified a confused but exciting world-wide move towards raised 'consciousness'. The Scottish Executive of the Labour Party, which had killed off home rule as a policy commitment on 'compelling economic grounds' in 1957, found its spectre rising from the grave.

In some respects the most original and important contribution to *Forward!* is Frances Wood's on 1964–79. The author was a fully engaged Labour activist and conveys some of the pain and confusion which the movement suffered over 'devolution' in the 1970s.

Labour's sketch 'National Plan' had been scuppered by 1966. Labour's policies for regional assistance, assessed as 'moderately creditable' by Ponting, did not prevent palpable decline in Scotland's traditional industries, symbolised above all by the Upper Clyde Shipbuilders' agony of 1971. In 1968, the SNP polled 30 per cent in Glasgow and briefly robbed Labour of overall control of the heart of the Red Clyde. By 1974, mounting Nationalist pressure had forced Scottish Labour to move back to home rule, despite the opposition of Willie Ross.

The Labour Party was now divided between those well-entrenched, mostly older elements who hated the idea of devolution, those, mostly Communist-influenced or younger, who positively liked it, and those, probably in a majority, who found the issue confusing if not downright boring. Labour did not really deserve to get away with the half-baked proposal for devolution which failed to arouse sufficient enthusiasm in the 1979 referendum.

Since then, opposition to home rule within the party has gradually fallen silent and there has been a steady advance of 'neo-nationalism' in its ranks. Two possible interpretations of this are not incompatible. As in the 1930s, there has been acute frustration that a party strong in Scotland has faltered in the South. 'Visionary' and pragmatist alike have been tempted to imagine a Scotland where Thatcher's writ would not run. But a longer-term development, dubbed by the Nationalists a 'sea-change', has affected people inside and outside the Labour Party. Since the 1960s – or so everyone says – Scotland has been enjoying a cultural renaissance, led by poets and painters who give little heed to English example, by touring drama companies which utilise Scottish music hall and folk traditions, and historians (including the editors of *Forward!*) who have refused to accept accounts of the past which relegate Scotland to footnotes or appendices. Along with this, and largely through the debates over devolution in the 1970s, a distinctive 'political culture' comparable to those of other medium-sized countries, and embracing relevant sections of the media, has emerged. Hence the Labour defeat by the SNP at Govan, in November 1988, comparable statistically with by-election débâcles in England during the Wilson era, caused less gloom than excitement, in which a veteran trade-unionist spoke up for independence and Tory home rulers flew frail but surprising kites. Debates were conducted with backs turned on London and eyes towards Europe. Constitutional reform, dead as a dodo according to Hattersley, was a live issue for Dewar and Cook. Could it be that Labour in Scotland is moving, together with broader Scottish opinion, towards a version of democracy which would obliterate any possibility of Wilson-style 'breaches of promise'?

(1989)

Three

Modern Literati

14

Edwin Muir

'Late in the evening the strange horses came . . .' Though I first read Muir's poem 'The Horses' more than thirty years ago, and have often returned to it, it still gives me the same impulse to shiver. At his best Muir was supremely able to govern pain and despair with serenity. His vision is distinctive. If he echoes Yeats frequently in his cadences, so have other major poets. While the Eliot of *The Waste Land* and the Ariel poems is often an obtrusive influence, it is arguable, I think, that in *Four Quartets* Eliot shows signs of influence from Muir. Histories of Scottish literature invariably set Muir beside MacDiarmid, not merly as an important adversary, but as the other big poet of the 'Scottish Renaissance'.

So why does a 'complete' edition of Muir's poems appear so long after his death in 1959?[1] And why is it published by the admirable Association for Scottish Literary Studies, whose imprint has normally rescued neglected texts and authors, rather than by Faber or Carcanet? Any temptation to blame 'English prejudice' should be resisted. Muir's reputation in England, and America, was high before he died. Professor Butter tells us where all his poems were first published – and that was normally in major London weeklies and prestigious literary journals.

I think the case may be that 'complete' Muir isn't really very appetising. His poems are commonly sturdy and intriguing when read individually. They suffer from inspection *en masse*. He was a late developer – thirty-eight before his first book was published in 1925. As he started, so he continued. Though his work of the 1940s and 1950s shows him at his best, in its themes and methods it marks no enormous development. When I received this book I dipped in and got the expected thrill from old favourites. Settling down to read it from the beginning, I grew increasingly depressed and bored.

His remarkable wife Willa related how, in 1941, a love poem to her sent her 'into a passion of tears, because I knew too well that I was only a botched version of what I was meant to be.' This was 'The Confirmation':

> Yes, yours, my love, is the right human face,
> I in my mind had waited for this long,
> Seeing the false and searching for the true,
> Then found you as a traveller finds a place
> Of welcome suddenly amid the wrong
> Valleys and rocks and twisting roads . . .

Marrying Willa had indeed been Edwin's salvation. But this poem, with its conventionally 'high' diction, gives no sense of her personality at all. Instead, we are set off at once on one of those innumerable journeys – more emblematic than allegorical – which feature in Muir's verse from beginning to end.

A book called *Journeys and Places* (1937) might arouse expectations of actual travel to actual territories. Instead we get a 'Stationary Journey' expressing Muir's incessantly repeated belief that all time is present in eternity, a 'Mythical Journey' to a dreamland where 'the gods' recline and converse 'from summit to summit', a journey by Tristram, an imaginary journey by the real German poet Hölderlin. Since the 'places' are likewise mythological (Troy, etc.) or visionary, to see that Muir's next volume (1943) is called *The Narrow Place* tests patience, in my case, to snapping point.

Yeats once wrote somewhere, I think, that 'the Muse prefers the embraces of gay, warty lads.' The very purity of Muir's obsessions becomes repulsive. One begins to long for bad taste, bad temper, even bad jokes.

And yet . . . Re-reading just now 'The Grave of Prometheus' from *One Foot in Eden* (1956) I was struck again by the relaxed-seeming skill with which Muir handles blank verse and applies to his mythological subject a diction at once aptly traditional and surprisingly fresh:

A mineral change made cool his fiery bed,
And made his burning body a quiet mound,
And his great face a vacant ring of daisies.

Muir's hatred of industrialism, which is refracted through these lines, used to seem to me fairly peevish. But now the heirs of Prometheus seem set to destroy the world completely. Muir's image in 'The Horses' of tractors abandoned in the fields after 'the old bad world' has 'swallowed its children quick' has acquired new resonance.

(1992)

15

Naomi Mitchison

As I finished reading Jill Benton's quite brief account[1] of ninety-three years of crowded life, I realised why Naomi Mitchison's story, unlike those of her friends Vera Brittain and Stevie Smith, could yield no neatly pointful TV bio-drama. At what stage has the 'central character' settled into definitive state? With resilience (and, I suppose, some luck) Naomi has moved on from each crisis in personal or working life to some new manifestation of 'Nou' (as family and intimates call her). Even yet, one feels, she might do or write something astonishing which would cause us all to rethink her place in history.

The televised story might have been this: a brilliant girl from a family of scientists, an amateur geneticist in her teens, whose first published work is an article about colour inheritance in rats, defeats her mother's attempt to make her a conventionally accomplished wife in a virtually arranged marriage, fulfils her promise with degrees and fellowships and wins (like Dorothy Hodgkin) a Nobel Prize, upstaging her renowned brother J. B. S. ('Jack') Haldane . . . Nope . . . Naomi let her marriage be arranged and submerged her scientific flair.

Try again. Her husband of a few months, Dick Mitchison, Jack's friend, is fighting in France. Word comes that he has been injured. His skull is fractured. He is unlikely to live. If he does, his mind will surely be impaired. Naomi dashes to the French hospital, finds him in pain and delirium. The widow will vow on his deathbed to dedicate her life to struggle against war . . . Well, Naomi has been a great peace campaigner, before, during and after the heyday of CND around 1960. But in fact Dick survived, passed his Bar exams a couple of months later and gave her, with his family's *rentier* wealth, a lifestyle of big houses, grand parties, nannies, butlers . . .

The young couple find that each feels a need for adventure outside marriage. In the era of 'Bloomsbury' they candidly seek multiple sexual relationships. For Naomi, at least one of hers, with a classical scholar called Wade Gery, becomes a serious, problematic affair . . . Could we make our drama out of the sad underside of high 'progressive' ideals – recrimination, alienation, suicide? Hardly, since Nou and Dick celebrate their golden wedding with five surviving children, and twenty grandchildren.

What about the crises of conscience of the 1930s, when slump and the rise of Fascism propel the Mitchisons into left-wing politics and all the dilemmas which those entail – 'class' issues versus feminist ones, armed resistance as against pacifism? What about Naomi's trips to the Soviet Union and to repressed Vienna, her flirtation with the Stalinist 'God That Failed'? Well, her scientist brother Jack eventually dramatised his break with the Communist Pary of Great Britain in 1957, after two decades as its most distinguished intellectual, by departing for Calcutta and taking out Indian citizenship. But Naomi somehow reconciled the middle-of-the-road Fabian Labourism to which Dick gravitated – he became an MP in 1945 – with her own interests in Marxism and, later, Scottish home rule. She never became an anti-Soviet Cold Warrior, though, or because, she had never been convinced by Stalinism – or by any male-devised creed.

What about the baffled creative talent? The writer of best-selling historical fiction in the 1920s produces, in 1931, *The Corn King and the Spring Queen*, set in the ancient Hellenic world, hailed as a masterpiece. But her next novel, about contemporary political and sexual life from a feminist viewpoint, is rejected by publishers, finally censored by the one who takes it, and then panned by reviewers from left and right. When she moves to Argyll, to an estate at Carradale, just before the new war, isn't she in a mood to agree with her friend Stevie Smith that the marginalisation and exclusion of women writers who step out of line is inevitable?

Certainly, Naomi published no novel for eight years. But meanwhile she refashioned her identity. With Dick mostly absent in London, she befriended the Kintyre fishermen, had perhaps her most remarkable relationship with one of them, Denny MacIntosh, poached on the estates of neighbouring land-owners, and taught herself how to farm competently – all this while mourning a last child who died just after birth in July 1940, that month of horror when France fell to the Nazis. Somehow, while maintaining virtually open house for local people, friends up from London and Free French servicemen, she kept a diary, which ran to a million words, for Mass Observation. She also became, for the first time, predominantly and blatantly 'Scottish', after an upbringing in Oxford and married life in London. The highly emotional poetry she wrote about Highland people was not published for decades, but she was publicly involved in John MacCormick's Scottish Convention, was elected, post war, to the County Council and appointed to the Government's Highland Panel. Her deeply researched novel *The Bull Calves* (1947) was about her eighteenth-century Haldane ancestors living through Union and Jacobite rebellion.

Another scenario? The tragedy – or tragi-comedy – of the rich socialist (*Lady* Mitchison, to boot, after Labour made Dick a peer) who tries to create a vital, just, and prosperous community in Carradale, runs into a mass of local jealousies and is finally diselected? But by the 1950s Naomi's interests were shifting to the 'Third World'. In 1962 a young African friend installed her as Mma – Queen Mother – of his clan in Botswana when he became chief. From getting a modern harbour for Carradale, Naomi moved to helping her new people, on her regular visits, to improve life in their arid and famine-prone environment. This labour continues.

So does the open house at Carradale, where 'dressing for dinner' has long been abandoned and stray great-grandchildren, bewildered foreign guests and inquisitive researchers into NM's works bump into each other unexpectedly in rooms where remarkable paintings by now-famous artist friends catch the eye above the arcane books and the discarded toys and games of generations.

Jill Benton, an American college professor who got to know Naomi well in her flourishing eighties, has responded with warmth and shrewd insight to her subject's personality. Her book sets up useful signposts for whoever will write the much, much longer biography which will one day be required. If she seems rather baffled by Naomi's strange relationship with her remarkable mother, she is illuminating about her unusual closeness to brother Jack, her affairs with Wade Gery and a communist academic, John Pilley, and her faithfulness, after her fashion, to Dick. (This stretched to presenting herself, inwardly rather bitter, as Candidate's Devoted Tea-making Wife when he stood for Parliament.)

It is good that the book foregrounds Naomi's feminism, obvious in her passionate advocacy of birth control, but ignored by reviewers of her early fiction, disdained as irrelevant to the class struggle by left-wing 'allies' in the thirties and disguised by asexual activities post war on behalf of world peace and the development of the Highlands. Naomi now rejects the label, but *Early in Orcadia*, that lovely novel published when she was ninety and crowning her lifelong, scholarly interest in archaeology, shows why 'feminist' still applies. It has to be said, though, that as biography this book is uneven and at times misleading. Professor Benton is consistently ill-attuned to the complexities of British politics – a pity, since these have always been in the forefront of her subject's mind. Scottish readers may be cynically unsurprised to find that a London-based publisher has let through one sentence with three howlers: 'Tom Johnson (sic) had been the first chairman of the Scottish National party (sic) and then Secretary of State for Scotland until 1942 (sic).' But they must boggle when told that in 1945 Naomi was asked to contest for Labour 'the Dundee seat in Aberdeen'.

I cannot resist a less grave correction. Jill Benton refers to Naomi still dancing at eighty. I saw her with my own eyes dancing vigorously with Roddie MacFarquhar at one of her *ninetieth* birthday celebrations.

Her seven decades of literary production have generated successive labels, of which '*doyenne* of Scottish writing' is only one. 'Historical novelist', 'left-wing publicist', 'Mass-Observer', 'children's writer', 'pioneer of feminist science fiction' – all of these have a marginalising effect. ('Important novelists' write about drunks in New York or fine feelings in NW3.) None suggests the aspects of Naomi – *almost* self-contradictory – which most awe me – her erudition (scientific as well as historical) and her quenchless appetite for people, life, travel, swimming, dancing ... Wyndham Lewis' powerful portrait on the front cover of his friend the writer, scowling over her work, hints at the former. The photograph on the back of a sturdy nonagenarian forking potatoes out of her Carradale garden captures her bodily toughness, but not the ageless, mischievous delight of her sudden smile.

(1990)

16

Morganmania

Heinrich Heine coined the term 'Lisztomania' to convey the excitement surrounding the virtuoso composer-pianist's tours in the 1840s, from Turkey to Ireland, Russia to Portugal: in 1840–41, Liszt played 45 concerts in 31 towns within 67 days, and travelled well over 2000 miles to do this, everywhere acclaimed with something not unlike 'Beatlemania'. The result? Hard to summarise, but, very probably, a distinct shift in European sensibility.

Edwin Morgan perhaps speaks Hungarian better than Liszt, who learnt the language of his native land only late in life, but whose name may well have inspired Morgan's 'Siesta of a Hungarian Snake'. The translator of Sandor Weores (and Heine) has also travelled to Turkey to perform, and the experiments of Portuguese-speaking Brazilian concrete poets inspired his own 'concrete' ventures (including 'Siesta'). He has an intensely Romantic sensibility and is, of course, a virtuoso performer. In 1990 the European Capital of Culture was gripped by Morganmania. The poet's seventieth birthday happily coincided with Glasgow's ceremonial marriage to the Muses. Newspaper articles and public occasions fumbled to assert Morgan's centrality (somehow) to Glasgow culture. The result? Well, a distinct shift in Scottish sensibility was, surely, being registered?

Morgan as culture hero of Nomeancity? A university professor? A come-out gay? A man interested in many, many things, but not in football? A friendly man, but systematically non-gregarious, neither a joiner of Parties nor a reveller at parties? And a constant, even aggressive opponent of the nostalgia for vanished tenements and rust-belt technology which suffused much of Glasgow 1990, as it has done so much recent writing about the city? Most improbable. But what good news – a flying fish, a swimming bird, a branched and breering contradiction, great fun: Edwin the Angle, King of Northumbria, spliced with Morgan, Welsh from British Strathclyde, to produce a wholly native graft bearing strange fruits. A makar alert to the whole of the long tradition of craftsmanship in Scots, who nevertheless writes primarily in English, or in languages of his own invention, whose favourite novel (it seems) is *Wuthering Heights* and who'd rather have Milton than Burns with him on a desert island.

No poet is so much 'taught' in Scottish schools, or so well known in person in those grim places: his travels to them under the SAC scheme must, year-in, year-out, though less spectacular, have equalled *in toto* Liszt's mileages noted above. Yet his most popular poems with young people are about a vicious gangster ('King Billy') and a blind hunchback peeing 'In the Snack Bar'. There is no poet more learned in ancient Latin and 1960s aesthetics, more 'academic' in his erudition: but who communicates better in public reading, who grabs the resistant tyro faster? And who has more contempt (albeit gently expressed) for those who would explain such paradoxes with big talk of Calvinist hangovers, 'English imperialism', crises in Scottish consciousness, antisyzygies . . .

Come to think of it, that Hungarian snake is an antisyzygy, surely? Harmless, serenely at rest, a creature tamed by Orpheus: s sz sz SZ sz SZ sz ZS zs ZS zs zs z

*

In 1990, for just under £85 (rather more than a boxed set of Wagner's *Ring* on cassette, but below the price of a flight to Amsterdam, a city not without special meaning for Morgan) one could suddenly purchase a Morgankit in four volumes, though not quite so complete as it looked at first sight.

The *Collected Poems*[1] omit quite a lot of work from earlier volumes, as well as those erotica which Morgan tantalisingly avers won't be published in his lifetime. (And one still has to seek his translations in many scattered places.) The rather limply titled *Crossing the Border*[2] (presumably, it evokes the Auden–Britten choochoo in the Grierson-Watt film *Night Mail*: but Morgan has lived in Scotland all his life, except for army service) collects the criticism of Scottish writers from Dunbar to Tom Leonard. For Morgan's critical thoughts on non-Caledonian makars, dramatists and novelists one

179

will have to turn to the volume of *Essays* which Carcanet published in 1974, or go to the National Library of Scotland for, for example, Morgan's 1977 Warton Lecture on ' "Sublime and Alarming" Images in Poetry' – I haven't had time to do this yet, but learn of it through the bibliography of works by and about Morgan constructed by Hamish Whyte for Edinburgh University Press's festschrift, where it takes up 115 pages, and nearly half the volume – despite which, Whyte has to admit that it is not comprehensive.

About Edwin Morgan[3] is the best edited of the three prose volumes: a book which will be of very practical use not only to future critics but to mere readers of poetry anxious to understand Morgan better (though E. M. himself, quoting Coleridge, would warn the latter that 'when no criticism is pretended to . . . the poetry gives most pleasure when only generally and not perfectly understood'). Besides searching scholarly contributions, there is an acute biographical introduction by Kevin McCarra, there are essays of special interest by Iain Crichton Smith and Douglas Dunn, a sensible piece about 'teaching' Morgan in schools by Geddes Thomson, and a modest and vivid account by Robin Hamilton of his experiences as Morgan's student at Glasgow University in the 1960s: the prime of Mr E. M., but even in this happy period the master did not drop his guard, his self-effacing reticence about his own life and work.

That guard is dropped, with a very loud noise, in *Nothing Not Giving Messages*,[4] an odd but fascinating volume which begins with an inventory of objects, books, records in Morgan's flat in Anniesland, taken by the editor Hamish Whyte on 4 July 1989 (was the Transatlantic resonance fortuitous?) and ends with a list kept by 'E. M.' himself of books read between 1927 and May 1940, an odyssey from G. A. Henty and Percy Westerman to T. S. Eliot, V. Woolf and the great nineteenth-century Russians. In between, Part 1 reprints nine interviews with Morgan conducted in the 1970s and 1980s by various persons and Part II collects articles, statements, lectures, etc. in which the poet talks about his craft and his life: 'The Lion as Poet . . . the Poet's Working Day . . . What it Feels Like to be a Scottish Poet . . . Poets in Schools . . . Poet in Person . . .' etc., etc.

The 1988 interview conducted by Christopher Whyte suddenly transforms everything – lighting up with an almost livid flash the cagey responses to questions printed before it, in this volume, and illuminating the wary attitude towards 'Scottish tradition' found in the essays in *Crossing the Border*. It's not just that Morgan talks about being gay explicitly for the first time in 'prose' (one could have deduced that from certain poems long since). It's the gusto with which he recalls his gay life, along with the candour with which he recognises that his attitudes, including his inhibitions, belong to his own generation, born unluckily long pre-Wolfenden, but, luckily, matured before AIDS. References elsewhere to writer's block in the 1930s, unhappiness in the 1940s, can now be specifically related to his sexuality – but Morgan allows for historical contingencies as well, refuses to let his own gayness dominate his perspective on society and history.

It's not just being gay which counts, it's where you're gay (Glasgow, Scotland, middle class) and what's happening around you. The 1930s, Morgan remarks in an essay on 'MacDiarmid's Later Poetry' (1978) were not truly a 'political and socio-economic decade':

In terms of the life of mind . . . it was a decade when other things were more central: in particular, biology and time, the link between these being probably the idea of evolution, though there was also much interest in dreams and precognition. There was a new attempt to see man in the round, in a cosmic rather than social setting . . .

Behind Morgan we must clearly see not just Mayakovsky, Pound, Ginsberg, Carlos Williams and so on but the fiction of Wells and Jules Verne and the popular 'science-writing' of the decade in which that category of journalism was invented. However, it is important to know, from the Whyte interview, that Morgan learnt much about art and life from a gay student whom his parents, with endearing incaution, employed to teach him piano and Latin in his teens. Lex Allan was full of news about gay poets – Auden, Spender, Lorca. He was also, like these poets, 'political'. And it was Morgan's infatuation with a young, alas heterosexual, Communist which led him to Russian classes at Glasgow University . . .

Just so, there is no doubt that Morgan's belated surge of mature creativity which brought him national and international recognition in the 1960s was energised by his first wholly successful romance, with a Catholic storeman, John Scott. But which came first – the widespread feeling from the outset of that decade that everything new was possible, and everything possible new, the verse of the Beats, the music of the Beatles? Or was it that his 'second life' prime of sexual fulfilment − 'joy' is a word he uses with telling effect − enabled him to sort himself out in relation to the general, new cultural influences, to seize a moment of history which was *his* as much as it was J. F. K.'s, Ian Hamilton Finlay's, Richard Demarco's, John Cage's, Holub's, Vosznesensky's?

Such questions intrigue Morgan himself. He tells Christopher Whyte:

If you're of my generation your power is in some way linked with the fact that there are these undeclared feelings and, if they were fully declared, you might lose some of your power.

Even in the 1960s, Morgan couldn't 'come out'. But what 'came out' of Morgan was new power, charging experiments based on radically different, even incompatible formal aesthetics. 'In the Snack Bar', as 'social realism', stands about half way between the impersonality of concrete poetry and the quivering Romantic sensualism of 'Strawberries'. Morgan also produced collage poems; 'instamatic' poems attempting to 'document' bizarre episodes found in newspapers (very much in the spirit of Surrealism, another influence on the poet); 'sound poems'; 'computer poems'; sonnets; 'science fiction' space-poems; and I wot not what − a whole department-store with toys for kiddies, leisure-wear for young lovers and useful wares for responsible adults ('Approved by the Matthew Arnold Good Housekeeping Institute' or 'Made in Europe: Guaranteed Socially Relevant').

*

Enough of this flippancy. Morgan is one of our major writers. 'In spite of all temptations to belong to other nations', he remains Glaswegian − and, as Robin Hamilton's memoir shows clearly, was quietly central to the emergence from the 1960s of Glasgow's first-ever identifiable 'school' of writers. He regrets the exile of W. S. Graham, the first poet whom he knew personally − 'someone who came from Greenock and Glasgow ought not to have lived so long in a telephoneless cottage in the wilds of Cornwall.' And for all Morgan's healthy insistence that present and future are what matter − past and tradition be damned − his critical essays make it easy for us to relate him to earlier Scottish writers.

In an important early essay on Dunbar (1952) he writes of that makar's 'agility . . . virtuosity in tempo and momentum . . . glancing and headlong jugglery'. The author of 'Cinquevalli' connives in the old poet's delight in 'words with no matter' at the expense of serious Chaucerian moralising. He writes with gusto about Robert Garioch's meeting with Houdini – his Edinburgh friend too was a great 'escapologist'. 'The quickness with which Byron sees the potential of a new word' is one of the many aspects of *Don Juan* which Morgan praises in a wonderfully observant essay: he revels also in Carlyle's 'barbarous' neologisms and the 'heady pleasures of excess' generated by MacDiarmid's 'enormous risks with vocabulary'. And he can quote a poem by William Fowler, one of James VI's Castalian Band, which already, in the late sixteenth century, looks like something which only Morgan could have written:

> my sight aux vents, mes pleurs unto the seas
> my flames to feu, mes gazings unto your ees.

Repressed sexual energy is common enough: addiction to languages and dictionaries is not. But here is another paradox. *Nothing Not Giving Messages* looks like the title of a Barthesian tract in post-structuralist semiotics, perhaps by one of those tricksy theoretical critics who aver that authors are written by texts and that the vaunted subjectivities of the former are merely ideological constructions. Of this kind of 'criticism', Morgan will have none. Even the sculpture-poems of Finlay, striving for semiotic absoluteness, he relates to the personality of the artist. Revelling in the surfaces and interfaces of discourses, registers, genres, structures, Morgan still challenges us, hopefully, to find Morgan himself, his true biography, in his multifarious poetic output.

*

Well, what of the man? Everything in these new volumes combines to confirm one's impression of him in person, at readings, in those brief but pointful conversations which this friendliest yet most reserved of men indulges us with before whizzing off as fast as he decently can back to base, back to the dictionaries, the omnivorous reading, the restless writing, the Beatles records, the newspaper cuttings, the videos of *Star Wars*, at home in Anniesland. Morgan is balanced, humane, almost incapable of uttering a cliché, yet never

one to flaunt intellectualism. He is always *clear*: he is clear even
about the 'mystery' which he insists is there at the core of aesthetic
experience, of poetic inspiration and achievement. He has no time
for gods or dogmas, credits no afterlife, delights in the immediate,
the material and the mundane, and preserves intact the Wellsian
faith of his youth, that science and technology are good things in
themselves and in no way alien to poetry. Above all, he values
energy: that quality manifested when mild Professor Morgan suddenly launches out on the platform as Loch Ness Monster or Mummy
or Mercurian, juggles with words like Cinquevalli, plucks his lexical
guitar with Little Blue Blue, invades Heaven with Jack London or
grumbles in a Glasgow video box near the close where the shilpit
dog fucks grimly. Even that dog, *such* energy ... like the trio in
'Trio', like the hard man on Glasgow Green.

In his conversation with Christopher Whyte, dizzying speculation
is joyfully unleashed. 'Glasgow's said to be the bisexual centre of the
universe', remarks Morgan – and goes on to exemplify this from his
own experience: for instance, that the Glasgow hard man can be very
gay indeed after his fashion. He agrees with Whyte that a theme
linking the 'Glasgow school', found in Leonard's and Lochhead's
work, is an 'interest in what it means to be male or female.'

Perhaps the instant appeal of Morgan's varied verse has most to
do with the uncensorious, compassionate curiosity with which he
projects human vitalities, joyful, vicious, ambiguous, male, female
('Goddesses' is one of his best sequences). Perhaps that is 'it'. Is 'it'
especially Scottish? If so, we are other than we have thought. History
and tradition must be reconstructed. One might start by reconsidering
that remarkable love, borne by the Douglas towards the Bruce,
which led the former to heroics and death in Spain. We might also
ask why our local monster is 'Nessie' and why, alone in western
Europe, our men wear skirts ...

I was about to write 'to conclude with a serious point' ... But I
think that my last point is not-un-serious. 'Morganmania' does bring
with it a re-examination of ourselves – in the context of forward-
looking optimism, a merry view of Scotland, and shared laughter.
We cannot all be gay but we can all try to be gayer. Morgan, as
Geddes Thomson writes, 'is, first of all, a poet of the present, of the
headline in today's newspaper, of things that are happening here and

now.' And, here and now, he is a wonderful antidote to over-solemn broodings – about, for instance, our 'relations with England' and 'relations with Europe' both of which, as Morgan exemplifies, can be great fun. The more languages, dialects and idiolects we can use, the less Standard English will bother us. Behind all, as Morgan reminds us, quoting Walter Benjamin, is the 'true language' in which all poetry is written, existing independently of all particular tongues awaiting release by original writer and then by translator alike . . . 'At times', Morgan writes, 'when states are anxious to establish their national identity and to prove the virtues of their language, they have very often in history indulged in widespread translation from other cultures; yet in the process of doing this they subtly alter their own language, joining it in many unforeseen ways to a greater continent of almost undefined and non-specific human expression.'

(1991)

17

Paul Edwards

The Gaelic records refer to the Africans landed as slaves in Ireland by Vikings as 'blue men', *fir gorma*. But they were the same colour as Elen, one of the 'blak leidis' at the court of James IV, perhaps the person sneered at by Dunbar in his poem, 'Ane Black Moir', about 'My ladye with the mekle lippis'. We know such things from the work of Paul Edwards.*

Muffled, wry, laughter greeted, in some knowledgeable quarters, the announcement during the recent furore over the Scottish History professorship at Edinburgh University that one of thirty currently unfilled chairs in that institution was in 'English and African Literature'. There is probably no other chair with that title anywhere in the world. It was created as a one-off, 'personal' appointment for Edwards not long before he retired last year after more than a quarter of a century's teaching in the English Literature department. It marked, but incompletely, Edwards' most original contribution to scholarship: his part in the rediscovery of Olaudah Equiano, the first important African writer in English.

Equiano (*c.* 1745–97) was an Igbo from what is now eastern Nigeria, kidnapped by African slavers as a child and sold in the New World colonies. Acquired by an English officer, he served in the Royal Navy. Resold to a Quaker merchant, he managed, by trading on his own account, to buy his freedom. Eventually he became the first notable leader of black people in Britain, and an important figure in the campaign against the slave trade. His autobiography,

---

* This was written just before Paul Edwards died in May 1992. I give it here with tenses unchanged.

published in 1789, was a best-seller. But from the mid-nineteenth to mid-twentieth centuries it was forgotten. Edwards has done more than anyone to give it 'classic' status, editing not only a facsimile reprint but also two paperback abridgements now used in universities all over the world.

Working on Equiano drew Edwards into wider study of the history of blacks in Britain. Together with David Dabydeen, a Guyanese literary critic and art historian based at Warwick University, Edwards now edits a series, Early Black Writers, for Edinburgh University Press. The first two volumes appeared in the autumn of 1991. One, *Black Writers in Britain, 1760–1890*, is an anthology full of surprises. The other contains letters from black settlers in Sierra Leone edited by Christopher Fyfe, himself recently retired from teaching African history at Edinburgh.

In these emaciated post-Thatcher days in higher education, young people may find it hard to believe that during the 1970s and early 1980s Edinburgh was a pioneering centre of black studies. Besides Edwards and Fyfe (whose *History of Sierra Leone* is definitive) research students sought out Professor George ('Sam') Shepperson, with his legendary out-of-the-way erudition about the history of Africa and the black diaspora. V. G. Kiernan was a famous authority on the histories of race relations and European imperialism. Younger scholars were inspired to work on previously obscure pan-Africanists and on the influence of the Scottish Enlightenment on anti-slavery thought. It was not unknown for a black scholar based in London to come to Edinburgh in search of insight. Now, alas, that creative base has been ravaged. Shepperson's chair in Commonwealth American History has long since been unfilled.

But Paul Edwards' interests gave him also seminal connections with the resurgence, from the 1950s, of creative writing by black people in English. After taking his first at Cambridge in Early Celtic and Icelandic Languages and Literatures, frightened, he jokes, of becoming a mediaevalist, he went on to teach in Ghana, then at the University in Sierra Leone. His earliest publications were textbook anthologies of African narrative. After his arrival in Edinburgh in 1963 (initially as teacher of English as a foreign language), he connected the city to the explosion of new writing by African and Caribbean blacks. The major Guyanese novelist, Wilson Harris (whose wife comes from Edinburgh), was his good friend. Younger writers sojourning in the city – such as Kole Omotoso from Nigeria – joined in the multi-racial *salon* which Edwards created in University space and time. He helped Caryl Phillips from St Kitts greatly with his novel *Cambridge*. David Dabydeen – poet and novelist as well as scholar – is the aptest conceivable collaborator in Edwards' latest venture.

Like Scott's Counsellor Pleydell, Edwards worked out how to combine professional excellence with incessant conviviality. Sober morning tutorials in his office have been confronted by the remarkable collection of kitschy and obscene ashtrays and nicknacks adorning his table: in the afternoon, the fridge would open, wine would appear, and initially bemused first-year students would find themselves laughing and arguing with tipsy lecturers, visiting Africans and whoever else cared to poke his or her head in.

Meanwhile, Edwards sustained his arcane scholarly labours not only in black history but in Icelandic scholarship. Together with Hermann Palsson he has translated nearly a score of sagas, ten of them available as Penguin classics. His more obscure scholarly contributions range from articles on such topics as 'Jamaican-Scots Radicals in Regency London' to a book on *Vikings in Russia* and an essay on 'Drink and Poetry in Old Icelandic and Anglo Saxon'.

But between these apparent extremes he has written a lot on the great tradition of English poetry. Whatever topic arose at his *salon*, he would find some way of relating it to Wordsworth. His favourite party trick is a recitation from memory of Shakespeare translated into Sierra Leonean creole. He yields to no one in his love of Byron and Matthew Arnold. And it was his delight in mainstream English literature which made him, in turn, a vastly loved teacher for several generations of Edinburgh undergraduates.

A native of the English Midlands, he has never lost his demotic Brummie irreverence. He could not be politically correct. He has been seen, can of beer in hand, declaiming from the platform of an academic conference that Edward Wilmot Blyden, the major nineteenth-century black African scholar, was 'just as shitty as the rest of us'. (Blyden did indeed hold silly racist opinions typical of his own day.) Applied to Eng. Lit., Edwards' combination of affection and familiarity delighted students elsewhere encouraged to revere the likes of Wordsworth as gods whose very eructations reeked of perfume.

His health has not been good in recent years. Over telephones between London and Denmark, Edinburgh and Singapore, word has too often travelled, 'Paul's in hospital again.' Scholars from Scotland visiting Canada and Uganda have been asked, 'And how is Paul . . .?' Edwards' unique combination of interests has certainly helped to save Scotland's current cultural resurgence from the blight of parochialism.

His heroes, however, are such as may appeal to the compatriots of Hugh MacDiarmid. He has an especially soft spot for Robert Wedderburn, author of *The Horrors of Slavery* (1824), now edited by Ian McCalman for the Edwards-Dabydeen Edinburgh University Press series. Wedderburn was the mulatto son of a wealthy Scots-Jamaican planter and one of his slaves, whom he sold when she was five months pregnant with Robert. He was brought up by his grandmother, Talkee Amy, nurturing a deep resentment against that 'mean Scotch rascal'. He became Royal Navy sailor, Unitarian preacher and, in London, founder of a sect of 'Christian Diabolists'. He was jailed for blasphemy in 1820 and in his late sixties did two years' hard labour 'not simply for running a brothel, but for brawling in the street outside it'. He has aspects in common with the hero of *Egil's Saga* (*c.* 1230). 'The ruthless Viking is also the poet of his own grief: he is a sorcerer, yet his mastery of runes can cure sickness; he is an ingenious lawyer and a raging drunk, a wanderer on the face of the earth and a settled farmer.' Like Edwards himself, both Wedderburn and Egil were highly versatile. And neither was capable of being dull.

(1992)

18

Karl Miller

Some time in the 1940s, Hector MacIver, who taught English at Edinburgh's Royal High, showed the school magazine to his friend Norman MacCaig. The poet remembers exclaiming, 'What's it like to have a genius in your class?' Both in prose and verse one pupil, Karl Miller, displayed extraordinary promise.

In Miller's *Authors* (1989) [1] he writes passionately about two other poets to whom MacIver introduced him personally. Both MacDiarmid and Dylan Thomas lived in 'humble dwellings' a long way from London. 'Both men suffered and broke down, both were described by gossips as mischievous, as egotistical misbehavers.' But from both the boy Miller 'received nothing but kindness'. It may be that the vastly admired Laird of Bloomsbury, editor of that unique institution, the *London Review of Books*, at heart still worships and envies those Celtic scapegraces.

Miller left his native land four decades ago. But in his own contribution to *Memoirs of a Modern Scotland*, [2] which he edited in 1970 – someone should republish this book, with its starry team of writers, including MacDiarmid, Muriel Spark and Sorley MacLean – he calls Edinburgh his 'Romantic Town', quoting Scott, a former pupil of his beloved *alma mater*. Not even Mrs Thatcher seems to have roused Miller's ire more than the removal of the Royal High from its buildings on Calton Hill, now earmarked for a Scottish Parliament, to new premises in a mere suburb. Its classical grace, paradoxically, derived from the heyday of Romanticism. Miller's writings constantly hark back to that Scottish dichotomy and to related ones.

If Miller is, as his old friend Neal Ascherson claims, 'the best

190

editor' of recent times, he rivals Francis Jeffrey, master of the *Edinburgh Review* and ally of Miller's arch-hero the memorialist Cockburn. Both were Royal High former pupils. In *Cockburn's Millennium* (1975),[3] Miller lavished erudition on 'Cocky' while brooding rather weirdly over the psychic division between the stiff male geometry of the New Town where the lawyer lived on business days and the maternal clefts and bosoms of the Pentlands where he had his country retreat. Miller's most ambitious book, *Doubles* (1985),[4] makes a long march, as it were, from Cockburn's territory round world literature, only to come back to the Royal High.

The theme isn't eccentric – countless critics have commented on the significance of 'doubles' and the allied topic of orphans, not just in *Jekyll and Hyde* but in Dostoevsky. Miller's handling, though is most idiosyncratic. *Doubles* starts with Hogg and his *Justified Sinner*, published in Edinburgh when the great *Review* was slugging it out against *Blackwood's* and reeking of that epic arena of controversy. Close to his conclusion, Miller produces, after Dickens and Pope, Yeats and Wilde, Frost and Lowell (*etcetera*), the unexpected example of Sandy Brown, acoustician-architect by day, jazz clarinettist by night, half-Indian, orphaned – and a contemporary of Miller's at school . . .

After working all night with MacIver on the school magazine, Miller would walk at dawn back to his 'village', Gilmerton, then a mining community more distinct from Edinburgh proper than it is today. Cockburn had not approved of the uncouth inhabitants of such places. Miller grew up on the wrong side of the tracks, having been born quite near the wrong side of the blanket. 'When I went to school at the age of 5,' he has said, 'I didn't know who my father was . . . When I came to be registered I was by myself and unable to answer the questions.'

In Karl Fergus Connor Miller's full name, romantic echoes of *Ossian* clash with a Marxist monosyllable. He was born at the height of the last depression, in 1931. His father, a gifted expressionist painter, split from his mother before his birth. Miller was reared by grandmother and aunts. He knew his mother well, admired her fighting spirit, and after his marriage his father, a loner in London, would come to see the grandchildren. But, as he has acknowledged in *Cockburn's Millennium*, his childhood was very close, socially as well as geographically, to the proletarian nightmare projected in Bill Douglas's great autobiographical film. He has always emphasised his common origins, and his attachment to Scots language. (One of his objections to the Scottish National Party seems to be that it confuses class attitudes with national ones. Burns, he says, spoke out for the people, not for the lairds.) He greatly admires the writing of James Kelman. He is devout in the ethnic religion, football.

Inevitably, he features in the *Faber Book of Soccer*.[5] This is with a fervent defence of Paul Gascoigne against obtuse detractors. Miller likes bad boys. He likes outsiders. And he found nothing stranger in the behaviour of his 'double' friend Sandy Brown than the clarinettist's advice, after seeing him play, that he was getting too old and should give soccer up. 'You don't say that lightly to a Sunday footballer.'

But who can be free of duality, Miller wonders in *Doubles* – 'who isn't *a pluribus*, who isn't the polity of multifarious denizens that Stevenson predicted?' This is a very Scottish question, familiar to Boswell and others who wrestled with the dangerous thought of Hume when it was still fresh. Miller won't concede that he himself is 'Scottishly forked . . . tartanly cleft'. He claims to have 'a very robust sense of having been one and the same from the start'. But he acknowledges that this may be based on illusion. And for London admirers he remains an enigma.

He arrived at Cambridge University with a capacity both to awe people and to bind their loyalties to him which has never left him. For the poet Thom Gunn, his senior there by a year, 'His very abrasiveness was part of his charm . . . He matured my mind amazingly, and I learned from his habit of questioning, of questioning everything.' When Gunn brought him poems, Miller would pin them on the wall above his desk and hand down a verdict after several days. He himself was under the spell of his tutor in English at Downing, F. R. Leavis. His Calvinistic intellectualism met a double in Leavis's English Puritanism. It seems probable that his poetic talent, like that of other students of Leavis, was strangled by the Master's hyper-critical habits.

But Ascherson, a Cambridge contemporary, recalls that Miller was lured at times from the rigours of Downing to the 'easy friendship and good cheer' of King's, a college anathema to Leavis. His direction in life may well have been settled by what a gifted Kingsman, Mark

Boxer, did to *Granta*, a hoary student magazine of gossip and skits. 'Marc', later a famous cartoonist, brought graceful distinction to the layout and introduced intellectual weight. Then he made the magazine nationally notorious when he was sent down for publishing blasphemy. Miller, already a *Granta* regular, was editor when the magazine, after some months, reappeared.

Contributors to *Granta* look as select as any group recruited for literary pages Miller edited later. Beside such undergraduate notabilities as Gunn, Ascherson, Tam Dalyell and Miller's namesake Jonathan, *Granta* called on the dons Hobsbawm and Daiches, the novelist Angus Wilson, the architectural historian Pevsner. After brief false starts as Treasury civil servant and BBC producer, Miller, in 1958, went to the *Spectator* as literary editor.

Ascherson remembers a seismic shock for literary London. One suspects that Miller, a kindly, generous, modest man emphasised his Scotch carapace for purposes of defence as well as offence. One of the younger English writers for the *London Review of Books* relates how, after he'd printed three or four pieces, Miller said over the phone, 'Must meet you. Come to the office. We can talk for seven minutes.' Deeply impressed by such Calvinistic precision, the young man arrived on the dot to find Miller clamped to a phone, unable to talk. Yet what seemed like offhandedness could have been shyness. Ascherson, at home with Miller's manner, delights to recall a meeting when Miller said, 'I'd offer you a cigar, Neal, but I've only got eight left,' yet concedes that even now 'no one can deal with Karl conversationally.'

Moving away from strict Leavis-ism, Miller still emanated a critical rigour which terrified reviewers used to the 'boozy upper-class sodality' (Ascherson's phrase) of the Connollys and Mortimers. They were asked to *rewrite*. Here was an editor paying 'punctilious attention to *every bloody word*'.

Aloof? MacCaig contributed reviews and poems to the *New Statesman*, whither Miller went as literary editor in 1961, and to the *Listener*, which he edited from 1967 to 1973. He thinks he has met Miller only twice, more or less by chance, in the four decades since he left Edinburgh. Miller's is not a pubbable personality. He is so private that few associate him with his wife since the mid-1950s, Jane, a distinguished writer herself on feminist and multicultural matters. The tales are all of a man working hard in his editor's den, grunting curtly through a big cigar.

At the *NS* his repertoire of contributors now seems dazzling. Reviews by A. J. P. Taylor aborded poems by Graves and MacIver's friend MacNeice. Hobsbawm wrote on history as himself and on jazz as 'Francis Newton'. ('An agreeable bunch of kids' was his 1963 verdict on the Beatles. 'In 20 years' time nothing of them will survive.') However, the *NS*, though now under John Freeman, still glittered in the shadow of its great long-time editor Kingsley Martin (1930–60). Miller left when Paul Johnson took over; he didn't like him. At the *Listener* he had overall control. Stuart Hood and Raymond Williams wrote on the media, the music critic Hans Keller and Spurs hero Danny Blanchflower wrote on football. Seven new poems by Heaney appeared at once. The layout was truly beautiful. But Auntie Beeb owned the weekly, and Miller couldn't change its rather bland, Establishment, image.

Miller's next move was improbable. With no record as scholar or teacher, he won a chair in English at University College London, on the strength, it is said, of a superb interview. In academic life, abrasiveness and shyness are not remarkable, and colleagues have enjoyed his decency, wit and love of literature. Blake Morrison, a graduate student of Miller's, remembers his minute supervision with gratitude. From this friendly base, in 1979, as the Thatcher era dawned, Miller sallied to set up his very own magazine, with Mary Kay Willmers and Susannah Clapp as his coadjutors.

The *London Review of Books* sells about 17 500 copies twice a month, much less than the *Spectator* or the *NS*, though much more than Auberon Waugh's *Literary Review*. But to speak of 'rivals' is beside the point. *LRB* is *sui generis*. It doesn't pretend to provide a comprehensive reviewing service for dons and librarians like the *TLS* – the latest issue notices a rather random selection of just twenty books. *LRB* is funded by the Arts Council on the same basis as *London Magazine* and a few other 'national' literary journals. But it isn't like these, either. It devotes much space to political issues. When Tory MPs and others query state subsidies for anti-Government views, Alastair Niven, the Arts Council Literature Director, can point out that there are just as many complaints from the left.

These must relate to Miller's adherence to the old notion that novels and poems are written by people, to wit *Authors* (the provocative title of his latest book). This proposition outrages post-structuralist and deconstructionist 'new theorists', who regard themselves as left-wing and see in the idea of 'authorship' an insidious tool of white, male, heterosexual, bourgeois hegemony. Miller gives new theorists and the like space in *LRB* – he positively approves of new feminist theory. In a recent issue a Young Turk appears to insinuate that Shakespeare, 'The Teflon Bard', was an elitist reactionary complicit in state suppression of dissident poets . . . But when, in *LRB* in 1991, the distinguished Professor Rawson came close to libelling trendy Professor Fish in an *ad hominem* attack of astonishing violence, no constant reader can have imagined that Miller disapproved.

LRB is said to be vastly influential in south-east England, where most of the copies purchased in the United Kingdom are read. The remaining three-sevenths go overseas and it may be that in Harvard and Vancouver, Sydney and Wellington, commonrooms echo with laughter and rage as sides are taken for and against Fish and Rawson. But *LRB* isn't a 'learned journal'. And it pays well below NUJ (National Union of Journalists) rates. Neither lucre nor useful additions to academic c.vs. explain why it attracts as contributors high-flying dons and well-known newspaper columnists.

The secret seems to be simple. A mellowed Miller allows his reviewers freedom to write at whatever length they like. So Paul Foot gladly takes time off from *Mirror* tabloidese, Ian Aitken springs from the Procrustean bed of his *Guardian* political column, and both prove in *LRB*, to themselves as well others, how well they can write given the chance. Academics can abscond from the conventions of the professional journals. Wild ideas escape from the pendants' zoo. Personal digressions are encouraged . . .

There is an *LRB* agenda – anti-monetarist, in favour of the NHS, state schools, constitutional reform and the humane teaching of arts subjects in well-funded universities. But Miller, except in rare cases like the space he strangely gives to silly poems by Fiona Pitt Kethley about sex, doesn't show his hand directly.

Scotland remains ever in his thoughts. He hopes for much from the Scottish Labour front-benchers Smith, Cook and Brown. Books about Scottish history get reviewed, and important new Scottish creative writing. But *LRB* has steered well clear of debates over devolution and independence. Has Gilmerton's lad o' pairts, Mac-Iver's prodigy, sold out to Bloomsbury? A recent interview suggests that he is sceptical about the concept of metropolitan centres of excellence. 'Peru could turn out to be more important than Paris.' His obsession with doubles and dualism recurs in this context. 'You can't give up the idea of there being centres. Equally, you can't give up the other idea, that centres are an illusion, or purely an oppression.'[6]

(1992)

19

Kenneth White's Orient

In Mahler's wonderful *Lied von der Erde*, texts translated from Chinese were used to express to the utmost Romantic loneliness, sense of loss and distance. Arthur Waley's translations provided for Bloomsbury a delicious vision of scholar poets getting drunk under the moon. As Yeats and Pound pointed to special wisdoms to be found in Japanese *No* drama and Chinese *shih* poems, the East was packaged into Twenties Modernism.

One of the good things which happened in that much-maligned decade the 1960s was a reassessment, led by post-Poundian poets, of the significance of East for West. It went along with a new interest in 'tribal' cultures, notably native American ones. Boring anthropologists earlier in the century had gone around asking folk how they related to their uncles. Now interest fastened on how 'primitives' related to horses and seals, whales and crows and spirits. Ways were found of putting this together with what could be learnt of Taoism, Zen, Shintoism. And Penguin, in 1966, provided beginners with a seductive translation of *The Narrow Road to the Deep North* and other travel writings by the seventeenth-century *haiku* poet Basho.

A major American poet, Gary Snyder, who pioneered this new Orientalism, has acclaimed the work of Kenneth White – 'poetry of the one world appearing and disappearing as we paddle through the sky-sea of eternity.' Reviewing Snyder's own verse, way back, C. B. Cox wrote, 'There is no anxious forcing of nature to serve a romantic sensibility, but a serene acceptance of physical life so joyful that it becomes like a vision.' One could say exactly the same of White's *Pilgrim of the Void*.[1] His use of the East is diametrically opposite to Mahler's. He strives to be fully there, to live, as it were, with Basho.

Mainstream have produced White's book beautifully. There are no illustrations, but as it falls open vivid images spring from wide-margined pages. It is tempting to dip in for snack after snack. However, though originally published in French as two separate books (1980 and 1990), *Pilgrim of the Void* repays reading from start to finish – from its humorous enjoyment of busy Hong Kong, washed-out Macao, surprisingly wild Taiwan, through the Thailand of tourism and prostitution and vast denatured Tokyo, to the northern island of Hokkaido, home of the enigmatic Ainu people, where, after four days' wait by a remote lake, White sees the annual arrival of wild swans from Siberia. Homage to Yeats implicitly rendered, White explicitly concludes with tribute to Basho. The book ends at the site of the villa near Kyoto to which the weary poet retired in 1692, in a garden where *haiku* have been inscribed on rocks.

A *haiku* is damnably easy to write: three lines, seventeen syllables. Basho's distinction, in fact, was to make the form subtler, harder to practise. Even so, in English at least, it is a puzzle to say where profound beauty shades into utter banality. And this, as it happens, is the problem we have with White's much-acclaimed writing.

All travel writers select out. Some will emphasise frustration, nausea, struggle. White never has the trots, doesn't get robbed. He can take or leave the prostitutes on offer. (His explicit descriptions of Thai night-life are one reason why this book, for all its charm, won't be a suitable present for Aunt Effie.) Money only once seems a problem: when a typhoon blocks roads in Taiwan, White regrets having to fly. He travels light but his backpack has room, when he goes to Hokkaido, for a 'heavy blue book of Ainu songs published by the University of Tokyo', as well as photocopies of remarks on the swan by the eighteenth-century French naturalist Buffon.

What goes on throughout the book is an interplay between body submerging itself, as a rule comfortably, in the stream of existence and an intellect informed by deep reading, from early youth, in Oriental philosophy and literature. There is a lot of vivid writing to enjoy, including amusing conversations in pidgin (for all his erudition, White isn't at all fluent in spoken Chinese or Japanese). There is also much to be learnt, about Buddhism, 'primitive tribes', Basho and other interesting topics. But . . .

White does not discourage his admirers from claiming that he

198

reaches important truths. Sometimes, 'truths' are expressed in ways which disconcertingly recall Wodehouse's Madeleine Bassett, as when he remarks 'The sea and I never get tired of each other.' But even when he is writing sharply, a worry persists that this very clever man, who deliberately denies himself recourse to irony, is performing an exquisite con-trick.

Consider a climactic passage in the Thailand section. White has gone to the hills to ground with the 'tribes'. In a village of the Blue Meo, he visits a 'famous old opium-smoker'. There is a green cockatoo on a perch in the corner. Opium or hemp? White chooses hemp. 'So the old opium-smoker lies on his side and puff-puff-puffs, sucking like an infant. I smoke my pipe of grass. The guide smokes a cigarette smeared with opium. Every man his pleasure . . . The blue smoke curls up the shafts of sunlight, curls-up-the-shafts-of-sunlight, blue in blue. The green cockatoo, I really understand the life and presence of the green cockatoo. I fact I *am* the green cockatoo. But if I change my point of view I'm also the fire. I am so many things neither "I" nor "am" has meaning any more.'

Yes. Well. Um . . . Very nice. Two problems though, Professor White.

First, as you know very well, and have amply shown in your other prose and verse, such transcendental states are also available to the meditative poet in, shall we say, a car park in Cowdenbeath. So why go in for what you must know is a crude polarisation of East (spirit) and West (matter)? Your Preface insists that the East–West 'split' must be 'healed'. What 'split'? As Joseph Needham's mighty labours have shown, the origins of 'Western' technology and science lie in China. Japanese spirituality seems to be less incompatible with an avid materialism than, say, Spanish mariolatry.

Second, East–West technologies are ravaging the natural world you celebrate. Bye-bye whales. This has to be a political problem. But the negative side of that 1960s exploration of alternative visions of the world, despite all these disavowals of 'I', is its intense, anti-political, individualism. Long before Thatcher, it presumed to abolish society. You boast that you read no newspapers. Your meetings with Orientals are discrete. That is, they exist, all these girls with pretty tits and bums, these men with their comic English, even the sage old opium-smoker, only to service, with sex and jokes and insights, the pilgrim, whose philosophy prohibits him from giving a damn about the social crises they inhabit.

I like the Japan section best because you're up against a society so energetic that you have to acknowledge its ambiguous vitality, and a literary culture so dense as to defy instant understanding. You even talk about one Oriental you meet here, a writer, as if he were your equal. You're a humbler pilgrim here, just a bit worried at times.

(1992)

20

Alasdair Gray's *Lanark*

A few weeks ago I gave an Open University tutorial in Glasgow and afterwards strolled across to a pub with one of the students. We'd gone on overtime talking about Wordsworth, and the student's wife had had a fair wait – she was sitting, with an empty glass in front of her, deep in a book of strangely distinctive appearance – one couldn't fail to recognise *Unlikely Stories Mostly*. I said, 'I see you're reading Alasdair Gray.' She looked at me in wonderment and gratitude. 'Have *you* read him?' she said. 'I've never met any one else who's read him. I was thinking it was just me, first *Lanark*, then this.'[1]

You will recall that *Lanark*, when first published, carried a warning that one might catch *Lanark*, and added 'Because it is widely regarded as a social disease, those infected may be reluctant to confide in even distant relatives . . . The important thing is to drink heavily and not to worry.' I am afraid that I early on became a dangerous carrier – I have now lost count of the number of copies I've given as presents. I was able to reassure my fellow sufferer in that Glasgow pub that our condition was far from unusual. She explained that as a victim of asthma and eczema she felt that Duncan Thaw's story was somehow about her. I could have replied that while reading it I've often felt it's about me, or about anyone who's ever felt shy at a party and dreadful the morning after.

Lanark is full of homely observations which might make any reader think, gosh, life's just like that. But adjectives such as 'intimate' and 'sensitive' capture only a fraction of Alasdair Gray's achievement. For a start, *Lanark* is often a very *funny* book indeed. Secondly *Lanark* is a beautiful book in a way both old-fashioned and starkly original, and this is because Alasdair Gray is a remarkable graphic artist as well as being a monstrously versatile writer. Our sense of what the people in *Lanark* are like and what the author's cosmic vision consists of must be conditioned at every point by the designs which beautify it. The effect is old fashioned because it evokes past artworks as various as the illuminated manuscripts of the Middle Ages, the enigmatic fantasies of such Renaissance painters as Piero di Cosimo and Hieronymus Bosch, the moralising and allegorical plates found in printed books of the sixteenth and seventeenth centuries, the intricately coded yet vividly lifelike pictures of Hogarth, the illuminations of William Blake, the work of Pre-Raphaelites and their influence on book design, the erotic teasings of Aubrey Beardsley and the semi-surrealist watercolours of Edward Burra. Furthermore, they are fun for us overgrown kids, who furtively miss the pictures we used to find in children's books. The novelty of the designs comes from a new combination of sheer playfulness with learned allusion and serious ethical and political intent.

Lanark was some thirty years in the making and the text, like the designs, digests half a lifetime's thought and feeling about art and life. Alasdair Gray in his 'epilogue' to the novel is wittily explicit about *some* of the many literary influences he has felt. But I think the effect of such allusions as we can spot is very different, not only from straight plagiarism – stealing – such as Sholokhov, for instance seems to have stooped to in *Quiet Flows the Don* – but also from the specific, localised parodies deployed by David Lodge in *The British Museum Is Falling Down*. I hope I shall be forgiven for evoking once again T. S. Eliot's old but I think still sprightly perception about Tradition and the Individual Talent – I do so briefly because *Lanark* gives Eliot's bright idea some validity, since it is the work of someone who has digested the entire tradition of fictional narrative and made something quite new which rearranges our sense of that tradition.

I said *entire* tradition. I have worried over the magnitude of this claim, yet see no reason to retract the adjective. What is missing? We have epic, beginning *in medias res*, just where *Lanark* begins and covering large sweeps of action involving many characters. We have saga and folktale and romance – Lanark fights a dragon, rescues a girl, goes on quests. Gray's book evokes also Spenser and Bunyan and the development of allegory by Protestant polemicists. The cry of Bunyan's Christian – 'What shall I do to be saved?' – rings through Gray's book. *Pilgrim's Progress* can be seen as the start of the novel in English. And Lanark packs in allusions to, makes new *use* of, every later development in the genre. We meet again the documentary realism of Defoe and Richardson as revived in spirit by late nineteenth-century naturalism, and this is astonishingly combined with the satirical fantasy of Swift and all its S.F. progeny. Like Fielding in *Tom Jones*, Gray mixes low life with erudition, and I cannot forbear to point out that one of the characters is called, partly, Smollett. But Sterne is surely more significant, the grandfather of all modernist fiction, and he is evoked by typographic shifts, by teasing our conventional notions of time, by forcing us to recognise that fiction is different from all other forms of life.

It now seems almost superfluous to add that Goethe and Melville, Dickens, Joyce and Kafka are all strongly evoked or to note that Thaw-Lanark is much like a cross between Pierre in *War and Peace* and Raskolnikov in *Crime and Punishment*. I want to dwell for a moment on the contribution of a writer who does not figure in *Lanark*'s epilogue – Walter Scott. Anthony Burgess has said that Gray is the best Scottish novelist since Scott. I think this may be true in that he resumes, as no other novelist save Grassic Gibbon has done, two of Scott's projects. First, Scott vivified through fiction a recently invented conception of history, seen as man's development by stages from primitive hunting and gathering to the industrialised 'civilisation' which was emerging in Europe in his own day. *Lanark* is an historical novel in that three different but overlapping constructions of Glasgow are used to illuminate the progress of twentieth-century man from barbarism to barbarism via the application of new technologies. Second, Scott, struck by Maria Edgeworth's construction of a plausible Ireland, 'felt (I quote him) that something might be attempted for my own country, of the same kind ... something which might introduce her natives to those of her sister kingdom in a more favourable light than they had been placed hitherto ...'[2] By 'sister kingdom' Scott meant 'England'. Substitute 'the world' for England, and Gray's project is analogous. He sets out to put Glasgow, the centre of modern Scottish life, 'on the map', as we say – and few maps are as thought-provoking as Gray's design, used on the cover of *Lanark* in paperback, which shows a minuscule Gray in the foreground of an aerial vista of Lowland Scotland, from west to east, with a sad, scowling replica of a seventeenth-century depiction of Hobbes' *Leviathian*, man as state and giant, king and dragon, looming up behind, from the North Sea where the oil is.

In chapter 22 of *Lanark*, its hero, in his first emanation as Thaw, explains to his art-school friend McAlpin:

'Glasgow is a magnificent city,' said McAlpin. 'Why do we hardly ever notice that?' 'Because nobody imagines living here,' said Thaw. McAlpin lit a cigarette and said, 'If you want to explain that I'll certainly listen.'

'Then think of Florence, Paris, London, New York. Nobody visiting them for the first time is a stranger because he's already visited them in paintings, novels, history books and films. But if a city hasn't been used by an artist not even the inhabitants live there imaginatively. What is Glasgow to most of us? A house, the place we work, a football park or golf course, some pubs and connecting streets. That's all. No, I'm wrong, there's also the cinema and library. And when our imagination needs exercise we use these to visit London, Paris, Rome under the Caesars, the American West at the turn of the century, anywhere but here and now. Imaginatively Glasgow exists as a music-hall song and a few bad novels. That's all we've given to the world outside. It's all we've given to ourselves.'

Giving Glasgow to its own people, and to the world, Gray has been conscious of fellow-workers in the project. The names of Archie Hind and James Kelman figure in the epilogue to *Lanark*, as do those of other living writers in these parts, and they remind us that *Lanark* is not only a beautiful book, not only an *ambitious* book which directly, with astonishing courage, challenges comparison with *Paradise Lost*, *Faust* and *Moby Dick*, it is also a very *Scottish* book and a *topical* book about Scotland here and now. It treats with sad respect the Scottish past of mediaeval Catholicism, eighteenth-century Enlightenment (as evoked by the name and ideas of the fictional Monboddos), inventive industrialisation, aborted socialist revolution, and waste. It wrestles with Knox and with Knox's god and is a profoundly *religious* work if that word still has any meaning and purpose. But *Lanark*'s prime concern is with present and future. I am both glad and sorry to recognise that the book has become *more* topical since it first appeared three years ago. Glad, because this confirms our impression that it is a book of enduring significance. Sorry, because the onslaught on human values by these forces which

Alasdair Gray represents by the Council, the Institute and the Creature, has manifestly intensified. As the *Sun* newspaper invites us to worship heroic policemen fighting against men whose aim is to halt the destruction of Britain's productive capacity, as a leading liberal newspaper cynically betrays a confidential informant and lets Sarah Tisdall go to prison, as certain naval and military events of 1982 are deliberately obfuscated by the imposition of new evasions upon discredited lies, the vision of Apocalypse with which *Lanark* ends seems horrifically close. If you think that I am exaggerating, go back and re-read the book thinking about these things and about the implications of the coming *Garden* festival in Liverpool, a city devastated by planners, and now blighted by unemployment, where politicians of left and right seem on the brink of echoing the words of Scougal in Unthank's Chapterhouse, chapter 36: 'I'm sorry if my remarks upset people. I apologise. But blood will have to flow, I see no other way.'

There is so much more to be said, not only about *Lanark* but about *1982 Janine*,[3] a book as extraordinary in its different way, which I hope everyone has already bought, and which carries forward and makes in the end explicit Gray's faith, implicit in *Lanark*, that Scotland has the potential to be a just, well-fed and happy country. It is marvellously appropriate that the last Frederick Niven Award should be given to a book unique in Scottish literary history, yet summative of many abiding concerns, which will surely inspire other writers, in verse and drama as well as in fiction, to try to emulate its intellectual daring, its artistic and political commitment, its stylistic wit and virtuosity, and its deep compassion.

(1984)

21

Devolving English Literature

Publication of Robert Crawford's splendid book *Devolving English Literature* is a wonderful moment for those of us who have persisted, against recent taste, in acclaiming Walter Scott as a master writer. No one in their senses has ever denied that Scott was vastly influential. What Crawford shows is that Scott's teasing, delightful experiments in verse and fiction point forward not only to the fustian nationalisms of nineteenth-century Europe (in print, opera and paintings) but to the energies of Yeats, Joyce and Eliot.

Crawford surveys the effects of Scottish writers, from Thomson of *The Seasons* onwards, on what now sometimes goes by the clumsy appellation of 'world literature written in English'. Marginalised within the canon of English literature – a university subject which, Crawford argues, itself originated in the Scottish Enlightenment – Ossian, Burns, Scott and Carlyle had exemplary, inspirational force in the development of American writing and, almost as directly, on the Modernist movement.

The key figures in English-language Modernism were 'provincials' – Irish Yeats and Joyce, US-born Pound and Eliot, working-class Lawrence, Polish Conrad, Scots MacDiarmid. Behind their attempts to relate modern life to ancient and 'primitive' mythologies lay the presentation of cultural relativities by Scots, under the 1707 Union, aware of their nation's inward cultural divisions and outward dominance by the Standard English culture of London. So Pound's comprehensive ambitions in *The Cantos* are in descent from Adam Smith's review of the French *Encyclopédie* in the 1750s, and the subsequent creation of *Britannica* in Edinburgh.

The Modernists' snook-cocking use of demotic speech has its antecedents in the achievements of Burns, and of Carlyle:

When Carlyle's work was attacked by his friend Sterling for its 'positively barbarous' style, Carlyle looked towards Scott as the first of a number of linguistic precursors of his own inventive, eclectic, non-Standard English diction, relishing an age 'with whole ragged battalions of Scott's-Novel Scotch, with Irish, German, French and even Newspaper Cockney ... storming in on us, and the whole structure of our Johnsonian English breaking up from its foundations . . .'[1]

Although it is a safe bet that no previous critic has ever compared Pound's erudition with that of the comic Bradwardine in *Waverley*, the components of Crawford's revision of literary history are rarely unexpected. The creation of a British identity to include themselves, and so of a new 'British Literature', by writers from Thomson through Scott – epitomised by Boswell's invention of his 'Dr Johnson' – has been widely noticed. No one could miss the influence of Scott on Fennimore Cooper and of Carlyle on Emerson (though I must confess that Crawford's discussion of Whitman's debt to the verse of Scott and Burns was a revelation to me: 'Walt' Whitman created a 'bardship' clearly akin to 'Rabbie' Burns' – local, demotic yet universal). The impact of *The Golden Bough*, by the Scots anthropologist Frazer, on Eliot, in particular, has attracted much comment. And Crawford is not the only critic to point to affinities between the Irishmen Heaney and Paulin, the Scots Morgan, Dunn and Leonard, the St Lucian Walcott and the Australian Murray, in their cultivation of the status of 'barbarians' fluent in Standard English but affirming local loyalties against the ex-imperial metropolis, London.

But it is Crawford who has had the erudition and imagination to bring these matters together in a reconstruction of the story of literature over the last two and a half centuries. And, praise be, he writes with infectious gusto about the books which he is repositioning. He make me want to re-read Smollett and Carlyle, to look again at Stevenson and Davidson. His pages on Burns at least equal the most perceptive criticism of that much-misrepresented and undervalued poet ever published.

Best of all, now that Crawford has put his argument together, it has the ring of self-evident truth. He will be delighted, I think, to read the parody of parodistic Carlyle in *A Night at the Opera*, just published in Canada by the Scots-Canadian novelist Ray Smith.[2]

My only reservation is that the authority which this brilliant study will rightly exercise may create among us a limiting, chauvinistic, new critical orthodoxy. Dickens, admittedly Carlyle's disciple, was, as Crawford doesn't acknowledge, a potency behind Eliot's demotic. Larkin may have been more of a Modernist than he cared to admit, but that doesn't mean that old English Hardy wasn't the great exemplar behind his writing. And it is a pity that Crawford, rightly paying tribute to the most fashionable West Indian, Walcott, ignores the more violently 'barbarian' work in 'nation-language' (creole) of Edward Kamau Brathwaite and underplays the impact of jazz on and through African-American performance and writing. We Scots invented much in modern culture, but not the drums and *griots* of West Africa.

(1992)

22

Jackie Kay's *Adoption Papers*

Ma mammy bot me oot a shop
Ma mammy says I was a luvly baby

Ma mammy picked me (I wiz the best)
Your Mammy had to take you (she'd no choice) . . .

Jackie Kay's 'Adoption' sequence was famous before its appearance in book form, and its publication raises issues of interest about genre (as between poetry printed, verse performed, and drama versified) and about text (and its instability: c.f. Shakespeare).[1]

Most people buying the book *The Adoption Papers* will probably know already that the sequence relates to the adoption of Kay herself, the child of a Scottish woman by a Nigerian father, and her upbringing in Glasgow by white parents. Her adoptive brother, also black, does not feature in the sequence as printed by Bloodaxe, though he was mentioned in the radio dramatisation broadcast by the BBC in August 1990. Her adoptive father was industrial organiser for the Communist Party. She herself is now the 'single parent' of a son by a black father and is publicly lesbian. Aged 30 when this book appeared, she is probably the most publicised British poet of her generation, though ironically she is better known in London, where she lives, than in her native Scotland.

As Kay was establishing her reputation, sections of 'The Adoption Papers' were published as free-standing individual poems. Such sections represent her, for instance, in Carole Rumens' anthology *New Women Poets* (Bloodaxe, 1990). Kay is an extremely effective reader, able to hold her own with black performance poets and with such Scottish virtuosi as Morgan and Lochhead. Like many others, I first admired her quality when I heard her read texts I hadn't seen, including some 'Adoption Papers'. The text of the broadcast dramatisation differs largely from that in the Bloodaxe volume, both in overall arrangement and in verbal detail. Kay's words were enhanced on radio by music evoking Scotland and Africa. They were divided between actresses representing the natural mother, the adoptive mother and the child – who was performed with charm and conviction by an up-and-coming white actress, Kathryn Howden. The new Bloodaxe text marks shifts between three voices by using three different typefaces, though Kay as her own reader can contain all three within one voice.

How a reader wholly ignorant about Kay herself and about the complex textual history of the 'papers' would respond to the sequence I can barely guess. From where I am it seems that, as with the young Auden, as with Stevie Smith, and as with older Scottish contemporaries of Kay's who are also very strong public performers (even Sorley MacLean, even 'late' MacCaig), an unstated subject of the printed verse is the personality of the author known from readings. Even on radio, the text evokes 'Jackie'.

Kay is historically not altogether unique. Maud Sulter's *As a Black Woman* (London: Akira Press, 1985) was the first book by a black female brought up in Scotland. But compared to Kay's, Sulter's verse seemed predictable in its feminist and black agenda – for instance:

> I want to rejoice
> in the blackness
> of the skin . . .
>
> I want to match
> the power
> of expression
>
> With the unity
> of history
> and herstory.

When Sulter moves, on one occasion, into Scots, the result is an interesting but uneasy mixture of demotic mimicry and feminist sermonising.[2] Kay's voice, whether the spelling is Scots or (as is far more usual) English, is distinctive, relaxed, fresh. Yet part of 'Jackie's appeal is her capacity to represent an astonishing compound of marginalised and problematic existences. She is black, of mixed origin, adopted, gay, an unmarried mother: these marks alone would seem hard enough for your average English person to accept. But on top of all that, she has never disavowed her adoptive parents' communism. There is a piece about her in the third issue of *New Times* (25 January 1992), journal of the Democratic Left, the successor-party to the CPGB. 'Kay', writes Margaretta Jolly, 'tells me with a grin that her first poem was published in the *Morning Star.*'

Thirty years ago, her obvious 'Scottishness' might, in the metropolis, have seemed a further oddity or even stigma (contempt for 'Lallans-mongers' was commonplace). Now the position is much more complex. Scottish poets read with Afro-Caribbean writers and black and Asian performance poets with northern English accents at, for instance, the admirable Apples and Snakes cabaret in Covent Garden. Tony Harrison's 'School of Eloquence' sequence presented the political implications of the vernacular so strongly that many younger English critics have taken the point. Among Scottish poets, Liz Lochhead, warm, funny, feminist, has proved especially attractive to English audiences. Despite continuing prejudice and obtuseness in the metropolis, the prestige of Scottish culture in all its aspects – literary, artistic, musical, political – was rising through the 1980s as Kay established herself. (It is a happy fact that Alastair Niven, the Literature Director of the Arts Council of Great Britain by which Kay is currently employed, is a Scot with a specialist interest in black writing.)

So it may be that Kay's warm, positive, witty Scottishness is precisely what permits her to charm audiences with an identity compounded of aspects which even singly might embarrass them. Scottishness does not demote or override her feminists concerns – there is not a trace of 'the national question', let alone of nationalism in *The Adoption Papers*, and the bitterest passages in the title sequence deal with racial prejudice encountered in a Scottish school. But, rather as the bizarre West of Scotland humour of John Byrne's TV series *Tutti Frutti* and *Your Cheating Heart* rendered somehow acceptable strong presences of madness and sadism in the scripts, so Kay, like Lochhead, can take extremely disturbing subject-matter and make it poignant and heartening.

211

Kay, like Lochhead, is dramatist as well as poet. Lochhead, to judge from her latest book, is now a writer for the stage rather than the armchair. *Bagpipe Muzak* (London: Penguin, 1991) collects four of her hilarious character sketches in prose for cabaret with a score of verse items several of which are labelled 'recitations' – that is, they are cabaret pieces in verse, some of which spin off directly from her work on a dramatisation of *Dracula*, almost all of which can be called 'occasional'. It is a strength of Scottish culture that intercourse between literary tradition and the forms of music hall, pantomime and popular song is commonplace. But, granted that 'Adoption Papers' was so very effective as broadcast, it make sense to ask whether Kay's artistry, like some of Lochhead's, will come to seem dependent on public performance.

On the evidence of this book, the answer may be 'No'. The verse of 'Adoption Papers' is informal-seeming, and is given, dramatically, to contrasting voices. Yet its full effect is not instantaneous, as in *pur sang* performance poetry. In particular its shifts between history and dream/nightmare make its narrative enigmatic.

The story, overall, is straightforward. A student goes back to Nigeria leaving a woman working as a waitress in Aberdeen pregnant. She leaves her child in the hospital in Edinburgh whence it is adopted by a Glaswegian communist couple. Many years later, the child, now in her twenties, seeks out her natural mother. The sequence offers complete sympathy to all three women. Reading it (and listening to it) its dominant theme is not race but consanguinity and affinity between women absorbed in the painful, wonderful processes of child-bearing and child-rearing.

> I always wanted to give birth
> do that incredible natural thing
> that women do . . .

The next voice is the child's, reporting how as she struggled for life, her adoptive mother

> came faithful
> from Glasgow to Edinburgh
> and peered through the glass
> I must have felt someone willing me to survive:

she would not pick another baby.

Then the natural mother reflects:

> She is twenty-six today
> My hair is grey
>
> The skin around my neck is wrinkling
> Does she imagine me this way . . .

Thus far, 'history'. But midway through the poem we are in the land of dreams. The natural mother remembers going home after the birth:

> I went out into the garden –
> the frost bit my old brown boots –
> and dug a hole the size of my baby
> and buried the clothes I'd bought anyway . . .

A week later she sees 'the ground move and swell', the baby starts crying:

> I gave her a service then, sang
> Ye banks and braes, planted
> a bush of roses, read the Book of Job . . .
> Late that same night
> she came in by the window
> my baby Lazarus
> and suckled at my breast.

The reference to Lazarus establishes intertextuality with the terrifying world of Sylvia Plath. Discomfort is increased in the next passage, 'The Tweed Hat Dream', in which the adoptive mother reports the arrival of the natural mother in a tweed hat: she leaves her alone with the baby:

> . . . suddenly I'm pounding the stairs
> like thunder. Her tweed hat
> is in the cot. That is all.

Neither episode 'happened'. Yet both episodes happen.

In 'The Adoption Papers', warmth, fellow-feeling, good sense, those Burnsian virtues within Scottish life, hold in check delusion, obsession, desperation. The eventual encounter between natural mother and child is suspended between 'The Meeting Dream' and history: it is not unproblematically clear that the meeting actually takes place. The sequence ends with the dark calm of the natural mother:

> I wrapped her up in purple wrapping paper
> And threw her down the old well near here . . .

(another dream?) and the muted expectancy of her daughter awaiting a letter from her:

> Fantasising the colour of her paper
> whether she'll underline *First Class*
> or have a large circle over her 'i's . . .

A similar tension between warmth and horror, charm and anguish characterises other poems in the collection. 'Severe Gale 8' is a nightmare sequence about Thatcher's Britain. 'My Grandmother's Houses' is packed with witty observation of working-class Glasgow life, but begins with a view of the cemetery and ends with 'ambulances/screaming their way to the Royal Infirmary'.

'Pounding Rain' and 'In the Seventh Year' are affirmative poems of lesbian love:

> We are turquoise and clear some days
> still as breeze; others stormy like stones
> you are in deep stroking my bones
> my love an ache, the early light . . .

but other poems deal vividly with the situation of gay male AIDS sufferers.

Perhaps the most significant of the 'gay' poems here confront the apparent paradox that men from the preposterously *macho* culture of the West of Scotland working class can be homosexual. This interest aligns Kay with the 'Glasgow school' of Scottish writing which became famous in the 1980s. Lochhead's fascination with the wilder aspects of sexuality (*Dracula*) is matched by the sometimes anguished concern about what men do to and with women in the fiction of Gray and Kelman and the recent poetry ('Nora's Place') of Tom Leonard. In different ways, all these proudly 'West' writers question the romanticisation of the strong men of the mines and shipyards which still figures in the plays of Bryden and the fiction of McIlvanney.

In 'Close Shave', Kay impersonates a married miner obsessed with his secret relationship with a male fellow-worker. In 'Dressing Up', a young transvestite revels in his escape from tenement conformity.

> My family's all so squalid
> I'm trying to put it behind
> me – real typical working class
> Scottish: Da beats Ma drinks it off . . .
>
> . . . See at Christmas I had
> on black stockings Santa would kill
> for and even Quentin Crisp would
> look drab beside my beautiful
> feather boa – bright fucking red.
>
> Ma ma didn't touch her turkey
> Finally she said What did I do
> I know what they call you, transvite
> You look a bloody mess you do.
> She had a black eye, a navy dress.

The last line there epitomises the strength of Kay's technique. She can draw her lively details, her conversational voices, into sharp punchlines, deftly 'timed' throwaways. I am reminded of the best poetry of Charlotte Mew.

Consanguinity, affinity, terror . . . In Kay's book flesh seems, as it were, interchangeable between woman and woman, man and man, woman and man, child and adult: in intimacy, in bed, in craving for attention and reassurance, we are all Eve Tamson's bairns. And the fragile preciousness of flesh is always under threat. A poem here, 'Summer Storm Capolona', describes generous fellow-feeling: Italian peasants take the speaker and her child in its buggy into their home during a thunderstorm. But this is a refuge from fierce fear:

> Didn't somebody say more people die
> of lightning than aeroplane crashes.

The absence of a question mark is characteristic: a possibly unreliable statement is thus turned by apprehension into a kind of fact, the fact of apprehension:

> The skin around my neck is wrinkling
> Does she imagine me this way . . .

Four

Revolving Culture

23

Losing the Traverse?

Towards the end of the 1988 Edinburgh Festival, I spent the best part of one Sunday watching in succession the four plays presented Upstairs in the Traverse. I'd been rather apprehensive in advance. Seats in the Traverse can be uncomfortable, yet it's also quite easy to doze off in the muggy atmosphere which its small spaces can generate. But, despite this reservation and that, about one or other aspect of the shows, I stayed alert and thoroughly enjoyed myself.

Each performance was packed out. Charming and efficient staff found ingenious ways to squeeze in more and more bodies. Each audience in turn, though, was responsive. The bill of fare was piquantly varied, though Scots accents prevailed throughout.

Stephen Mulrine's translation, lightly Scotticised, of Alexander Gelman's *glasnost* smash-hit from Moscow, *A Man with Connections*, was heartily performed by Bill Paterson as a corrupt manager and Marty Cruickshank as his *en effet bourgeois* wife. Jenny Killick, directing, faced, I felt, almost insoluble problems with the pernickety business and cumbersome naturalistic set which the script called for. It's an old-fashioned, 'stagey' drama, a bit like squeezed-down late Ibsen, cameo *Eyolf* or *Borkman*. But worth trying, meaty, interesting. Killick had still more to contend with in *Prickly Heat* by Simon Donald, who has featured so brilliantly as actor in so many recent Traverse productions. A London reviewer had compared this play, set in a condemned tenement in Glasgow during a heatwave, to a cross between Tennessee Williams and Ian Heggie. I thought this was rather cute till Donald himself told me that he had never seen a Heggie play and had caught only one Williams, on TV. *Prickly Heat* is an episodic, at times surreal, succession of scenes involving bizarre fantasists. Some episodes are funny, some disturbing, some pall. The author took part as a wholly enigmatic character who ended up in the large fridge which contributed much to the fun throughout. Superheated Chekhov? Beckett with context? Good, anyway, to see a new Scottish play performed to a full and enthusiastic house.

About *The Conquest of the South Pole* by Manfred Karge, translated into a gritty Scots idiom by Tich Minter and Antony Vivis, I shall have something to say later. Like *Dead Dad Dog*, which rounded off my day, it gave Killick's Assistant Director, Stephen Unwin, a chance to display considerable virtuosity. Sam Graham, who had played a rather dowdy role in Karge's play, transformed himself to render John Mackay's conception of Eck, a bright young Scottish intellectual doomed to move to London in despair over his inability to get good work at home. He is haunted for a day by the ghost of his Tory father, delightfully played by Ralph Riach. Four chairs served as a set, juggled at times between the two men, once swung alarmingly about in an effect which Unwin admits to copying from Brook's *Mahabharata*. The show moved very fast, at times quite fiercely satirical, at times almost sentimentally touching. Mackay first surfaced a few years ago as a member of Merry Mac Fun Co, a team of Edinburgh University students whose cheeky anti-Unionist satire won a wide Fringe following. The sad fact that he himself has moved to London enhances the impact of *Dead Dad Dog*'s attack on Scotland's English and Anglicised cultural establishment, blocking the prospects of young Scots.

It is ironic, therefore, that Unwin, like Killick, is English. But then, the Traverse, in twenty-five years, has never had a Scottish Artistic Director. The Scottish flourish with which Killick and Unwin chose to precede their own departure to London, making way for another English director, Ian Brown of TAG, can be seen as a tribute to the vigour with which Scottish culture has latterly sold itself to, or imposed itself on, gifted English people working here.

Joyce McMillan has made a remarkably good job of telling *The Traverse Theatre Story*,[1] without fear or favour but with generous appreciation of the positive qualities displayed in turn by nine artistic directors. Up to a point, it's a tale of success which she tells. In a city of which the primly bourgeois cultural bleakness had latterly been relieved for a bare three weeks a year by an International Festival of

Music and Drama, a club was founded which, through the swinging sixties, became identified more than any other British institution with experiment and internationalism in drama. It has survived as an arena for new plays, long unique in Scotland, despite the fact that it was always inherently uneconomic and has become increasingly so. Several of its young directors moved on to fame in the South and beyond. One of these, Gordon McDougall, (1966–8 – 35 world premières in 19 months) looks back on his time at the Traverse as the happiest of his life. It is doubtful if Max Stafford Clark (1868–9) now in charge of London's Royal Court, Michael Rudman (1970–73), likewise renowned in The Smoke, or Mike Ockrent (1973–5), smashingly successful on Broadway, have any spare time in which to reflect nostalgically. As McMillan points out, it is Scottish playwrights who remember glowingly the regime of Chris Parr (1975–80) which ended in a 'flurry of acrimonious letters', after this Oxford graduate had expressed his 'strong antipathy to the British establishment and its metropolitan values' by trying to bring new local writers to a broader-based audience. Tom McGrath, Tom Gallacher, Hector Macmillan, Donald Campbell, Marcella Evaristi, and, perhaps most momentously, John Byrne were among the Scottish beneficiaries of this sea-change.

Sea-change, because the Traverse had been founded in reaction *against* the Scottish cultural and theatrical scene as it appeared in 1963. McMillan does full justice to the enthusiasm and imagination with which a mixed clique of incomers and dissident Edimbourgeois created a little theatre with a club drinks licence in a 'crumbling former doss-house and brothel' on the Lawnmarket, as a centre of emancipation from the 'lace curtain limitations' on the city's cultural life; also, of unbashed internationalism. The dominant incomer was Jim Haynes, from Louisiana, the most picturesque of the locals was Richard Demarco. What they had in common was expansive sociability and an almost whorish readiness to accept anything from any part of the world which looked experimental. Neither, I think it is fair to say, has ever had any strongly defined 'taste' in the usual sense of that word, nor has either been inhibited by any substantial political commitments. The 'come all ye' ethos of improvisation and amateur enthusiasm which, for good and ill, became associated with the Traverse, owed much to both men – though in practical terms, as

McMillan shows, it was a professional actor, John Malcolm, who fished up the idea which was floating around of a permanent 'fringe' centre and with the help of a director, Terry Lane, then Stage Manager at Pitlochry, ensured that it would take the form not of a bookshop cum gallery but of a professional theatre. Haynes wasn't even in Britain when the club opened, with sixty theatre seats and a vastly ambitious first year's programme which included British premières of plays by Arrabal, Mishima and Jarry and the world première of *The Balachites* by an Edinburgh University philosopher, Stanley Eveling.

Fortuitously, the actress Colette O'Neill was stabbed with a paper knife on stage on the second night and nearly bled to death. Advance bookings soared with the publicity which this engendered. The atmosphere of shock and scandal on which the Traverse – and its supporters – thrived was thickened as Haynes, with John Calder, organised a Drama Conference in the 1963 Festival during which a naked girl fleetingly appeared in the gallery of the McEwan Hall. When Lane left after just a year – he remains, McMillan reports, 'understandably bitter' about the way in which he was forced out – Haynes followed him as Artistic Director and was for a time indisputably dominant, though as *Traverse Theatre Story* shrewdly notes, it was that 'unsung' hero Callum Mill who sustained professional standards as director and actor, under Haynes' aegis, for eight crucial months – 'one of the few periods in the history of the Traverse when it fully acknowledged and exploited its roots in Edinburgh and in Scotland . . . offering a real interface between Scotland and the wider world, between Scottish actors and directors and the international theatre scene.' It was top-flight Scottish performers playing in avant garde classics who worked on that interface. But in fairness to Haynes it was his commitment to *new* writing which gave the Traverse what proved to be its permanent role, and a basis for Arts Council subsidies.

Haynes departed amid rows and tears in June 1966 – his support for Demarco's idea that the latter's new Gallery should come under the Traverse banner was one factor in his breach with the committee. Yet his long shadow remains. He was there in person, friendly as ever, at the theatre's farewell party for Jenny Killick in August 1988. More significantly, Killick herself had maintained with enthusiasm his emphasis on brand-new writing.

As McMillan sees it, Haynes' 'irresponsible defiance of "the rational calculation of economic means" has been proved right and right again.' The Traverse has to take risks to be true to itself. Moving, for the 1969 Festival, into larger premises in the Grassmarket, with a flexible modular 100-seat theatre, increased the financial risks. The conversion of an unsuccessful bar area into the 60-seat Downstairs Theatre in May 1984 by Killick's predecessor, the quiet Canadian Peter Lichtenfels, was 'an extraordinary gamble to maximise income and expand against the trend.' It has to be said that such gambles have latterly involved a colossal degree of subsidy from the Arts Council and from local government – the 'real' price of a seat at the Traverse could buy a very good seat indeed at Covent Garden rather than a precarious perch on a foam-rubber bench in a sweaty but austere space where an actor's spit might hit you at full velocity. How much has Scotland's investment in this extraordinary institution which was, till the end of 1987, still a private club, in fact benefited the country's culture?

Who can say? Theatre is an ephemeral art form. God knows how quaintly dated some of the Traverse's boldest productions of the heady days might seem now. Playscripts, at least those by Scottish authors, are rarely published. I recall, of productions of works by Stanley Eveling and C. P. Taylor, who through the 1960s and 1970s provided so many Traverse premières, an aura of intelligence and moral concern – and an atmosphere of slight embarrassment. Intimate theatre can be shy-making for a rather gentle, squeamish soul, like myself.

I suppose I was a natural sucker for the light 'feminine' touch which Jenny Killick brought to the Traverse. Writing about the 1986 Traverse Festival for the *New Statesman*, I was moved to quote Ian McEwan's phrase, 'womanly times', and to praise the 'warm, open feel' of the premises.

In retrospect, Killick's first year as Artistic Director was indeed a good one. She had felt her way into the Traverse, and the local cultural scene, under Lichtenfels. In 1986 she produced two out of three new plays from Scotland with her characteristic light, affectionate touch. Tom McGrath's *Kora*, a 'documentary' play about the struggle by tenants and social workers to improve conditions on a Dundee housing estate, was warmly uncondescending and unsentimental. *Lucy's Play* by John Clifford followed the same author's Festival triumph with *Losing Venice* – also directed by Killick – in the previous year. But the best of the three, I thought, was Chris Hannan's *The Orphan's Comedy*, which fell to Stephen Unwin.

Hannan had also featured in 1985 with *Elizabeth Gordon Quinn*, an extremely impressive piece of writing, set against the 1915 women's Rent Strike in Glasgow, and so bulging with life and ideas that one cried for it to burst out of the little Traverse auditorium. Now he came up with a play with 'classic' features which fitted Traverse Upstairs perfectly. I may as well quote my own review:

How does one describe its flavour? W. S. Gilbert with political bite? Ben Jonson bang up to date? Brecht with Glaswegian warmth and compassion? It is brilliantly written, in a non-naturalistic style. Characters and situations are all over the top, larger than life. This aspect suggests Dario Fo, while the futuristic but here-and-now plot recalls Alasdair Gray's novel, *Lanark* . . . [*see* pp. 201 ff, above]. But the central idea is all Hannan's own. We are in a fertility clinic in a country where the government, commited to the Low Unit Cost society, encourages childbirth so as to maximise the number of consumers. The place is dominated by the outrageous Salmon, MCP *par excellence*, compulsive gambler . . . As a way to repair his gambling losses, his imagination seizes upon condoms, of which his clinic has a secret supply. With the local crime queen, he sets up a market in condom futures. The logic of capitalism, as he expounds it, means that condoms, being rare, will cease to be a commodity and can become an abstract concept. Rubber can be turned into gold! Why shouldn't people wear condoms like jewellery? But his secretary and mistress . . . spurned, expecting his child and intent on revenge, also understands capitalism. She releases his store of condoms on to the open market. Residents of a deprived housing scheme snap them up and make fortunes reselling them . . . The climax comes when Salmon learns that the bottom has fallen out of contraceptive futures and kneels front stage lamenting and pouring condoms in handfuls over his head.

Hannan had moved on. Clifford, alas, had not. McMillan writes appreciatively on the values which Killick shared with the group of new writers with whom she had become particularly associated – besides Hannan and Clifford, Peter Arnott and Simon Donald. They were frustrated with the small-scale, quiet, detailed, personalised, social-observational drama into which the Traverse had been drifting since the end of the 1970s. To a man (for initially they were all men) these playwrights were obsessed, at different levels, with large, sweeping, political and social themes, with parables, allegories, epics, and historical parallels; and Killick was determined to release the Traverse space from its black box appearance and its literal sets, and to make theatrical life flow through it as if it represented the world itself.

So *Losing Venice* burst deliciously upon us with its spirited young actors, bright clever set, and highly intelligent, not to say erudite, script making light but effective points against militarism and macho values in a fabricated early-modern Mediterranean world. But the formula very quickly produced its own clichés. Of ten Traverse Festival productions of new plays by British writers during the three Killick years, five were oppressively close to each other in themes and methods. Clifford followed *Lucy's Play* with *Playing with Fire* in 1987, when the highly promising young Amy Hardie floundered with *Noah's Wife* and Peter Jukes arrived from England with *Abel Barebones*. Then in 1988 Theatre Downstairs offered Jukes' *Shadowing the Conqueror*. All these were loosely episodic, quest-based in structure, all used historical anachronisms as a way of generating humour and also of pointing to present-day relevance in imagined, folktale-like situations attributed to prehistory, classical times or mediaeval Europe.

The interesting but unsuccessful *Barebones* can be taken as typical of this, presumably transient, genre. Jukes could be a significant writer in future, but I suspect that he is less gifted as a dramatist than the others – his wordy texts suggest that he might come into his own as a travel-writer *à la* Theroux. Cain's murdered brother turns up as a tramp in the North Riding of Yorkshire in the mid-fourteenth century after the Black Death, and gathers a 'humble company, from the ranks of the wretches' to quest for the land 'West of the Sun, East of the Moon' where nobody ever dies. As usual, space is found for a Scots-speaker, in this case a comic blacksmith discovered beating ploughshares into swords. As usual, there is a semi-feminist element, provided by sensible Winnie who mocks the idea of the Humble Company, but (please enjoy this anachronism) joins it disguised as Roger Bacon, 'father of British empiricism', complete with spectacles and telescope. Like *Losing Venice* and *Shadowing the Conqueror*, this script self-consciously includes a writer, Friar

Meekly, who records the Humble Company's story. When a 'rogue knight' peruses this text and finds that the Friar has slept with his wife, he draws a sword to kill him:

'I've no choice. I'm just a victim of literary convention.'

To which Meekly responds:

'But you can't do this. It's an epic not a romance. You're mixing genres.'

Erudition and anachronism are accompanied by rather portentous aphorisms such as 'it's not the people's power keeps the cart of progress going, but the fear of the people and their power.' Horseplay and moments of mini-spectacle helped to drag the heavy cart of this play forward just fast enough for it to be endurable.

So the phase of Traverse history characterised by the Killick–Clifford collaboration gave opportunities for young writers, directors and actors to tease audiences with pantomimic epics until the law of diminishing returns prevailed. In retrospect, I am pretty sure that it will be the emergence of Hannan, for which both Killick and Unwin take vast credit, and the memory of Peter Arnott's stunning *White Rose*, about a Soviet woman flying fighter planes over Stalingrad, produced by Unwin in Lichtenfels' last season, which will seem to have had enduring significance for the development of Scottish theatre.

But what of Traverse's inheritance of internationalism? This has been sustained partly by importing productions from abroad – South Africa, Canada, France, Japan, Ireland – of varying type and uneven distinction, and by in-house production of translated plays. The Peruvian Vargas Llosa's *Kathie and the Hippopotamus* (1986) was clever and glossily enjoyable. Enzo Cormann's *The Prowler* (1987) was a strange French one-hander – or rather two-hander, since a live hawk was on stage throughout – about a violent psychopath, brilliantly rendered by James Kelman into bitter Glaswegian. The Gelman of 1988, I have mentioned. That leaves us with the German connection – sustained, in part, by Goethe Institute sponsorship. After plays by Kroetze and Jandl in Lichtenfels' last year, and a feebler offering by Kusz (again, translated into Scots speech) in 1986, came the sensational Karge. In *Man to Man* (1987) Tilda Swinton, an English actress who has emerged to deservedly wide fame during several years' involvement with the Traverse, acted alone, as a woman who, after her crane-driver husband's death, takes over his job, lives as a man, and under Hitler serves in the SA, then works postwar as a farmhand and in a plastics factory. The language, in Antony Vivis' translation, was heavily charged. earthy, densely allusive, and I must confess that I couldn't always understand it. But one had to admire its energy, on which Swinton founded a performance of overwhelming commitment.

I went to Karge's *Conquest of the South Pole* in 1988 with mixed reports buzzing in my ears – one critic I respected had praised its projection of the plight of unemployed youth, another had complained that Karge had earned no right to project working-class life as he did. I found that, by accident rather than foreplanning, it was a play which encapsulated the positive features of the Killick phase in Traverse history. Thus, it involved a quest, during which a group of characters on stage, so to speak, wrote their own script. It had comic horseplay, an episodic structure, and made it serious, topical points, about unemployment and yuppification, with a lighter touch than Jukes but a sharper cutting edge than Clifford. I thought it displayed at its most impressive the recent Traverse ethos, in which youthful vitality and charm have fused with oppositional politics.

Braukman, Slupianek and Buescher burst on stage chorusing 'Why can't a camel ride a bicycle? Because it has no hands to ring the bell'. Seiffert, *alias* The Moose, is revealed to be hanging himself in a box on stage behind curtains. These are jobless youths in a German mining town, but the atmosphere is already charged with fantasy, which takes over as Slupianek (wonderfully acted by Alan Cumming) persuades the others to join him in re-enacting Amundsen's journey. He seduces Braukman's wife so as to get the use of 'her' attic. Braukman, as the fantasy proceeds, leads a revolt; Shackleton, who never reached the Pole, was greater. We should, as people, as unemployed, identify with *failures*. The climax comes at a birthday celebration where Rudi, a friend of the group who has Yupped, describes an 'adventure holiday' which he and his wife have enjoyed at the Pole. Enraged at being patronised, Slupianek summons up a Faithful Dog ('in fact', a teenage boy), the group chase Rudi off stage and then march the remaining 178 and nearly-a-half steps (degrees) to the Pole (the dinner table) in a wonderful conga which brings the house down. You think it's over but no. We end with the lonely Amundsen-Slupianek at the Pole, consoled by the sound of childbirth. His child, though Braukman's child – a co-operative effort.

The play very firmly sets individualism in tension with co-operation. Its socialistic class animus is evident enough from the savaging of Rudi. But simple-minded agitprop *Conquest* isn't. The language is stylised, often choric. Imagination, theatre, over against intolerable reality, hope wrested out of despair, are issues dominating the agenda. The play is funny, at times touching in quite a prosaic way, at the climax epically moving. Lowland Scots voices sustain it perfectly. Now it has gone to London. Will it ever be seen in Scotland again?

The end of the club status alone would have meant that the Traverse entered a new era in 1988. Still more momentously, a change of directorship is accompanied by plans to end the long Grassmarket experiment and move the Traverse, in three years time, into a custom-built theatre in the financial centre which will plug the famous Castle Terrace 'hole in the ground'.

The Traverse fought for and won this prospective new home (in the gift of the District Council) against competition from the Royal Lyceum, which will lose its own Studio Theatre in the new development. It is noteworthy that Killick, Unwin, Ian Brown and the Traverse chair, Sheena Macdonald, all favour the move. It is not surprising that Jim Haynes has spoken loudly against it.

I seem to recall that Joyce McMillan once described Traverse Upstairs as one of the most beautiful theatrical spaces in Europe. But she clearly now believes that the proposed move would be a desirable gamble within the Traverse tradition. I remain to be convinced. The Traverse will be in danger of being overshadowed by the Lyceum, which has recently achieved soaring subscription rates, which has its own exciting small-scale experimental company in Communicado, and possesses a restaurant and bar which can rival in attraction the Traverse's present facilities, let alone whatever product of architectural ingenuity fits the theatre into Castle Terrace.

I suppose the counter-argument is that two lively theatres close together will help to advertise each other and will build up at last the year-round public for good, gutsy drama which so signally didn't exist in 1963 and hasn't fully emerged even now. But that in turn implies that the uniqueness of the Traverse will be less apparent. Its name, we learn from Joyce McMillan, derived from a slip of memory. Lane thought that 'Traverse' described the kind of layout used in the original Lawnmarket theatre. He realised that the correct technical term was 'Transverse' only after the misnomer had become famous. That name, in twenty years' time, might stand for no more than a routine 'Little Theatre' and nostalgic twinges in the minds of old and middle-aged people.

(1988)

24

Worker's Culture – Popular Culture – Defining Our Terms

It recently fell to me to welcome to Glasgow a very distinguished Indian writer – an elderly former diplomat, a man of the world, who had come to take part in discussions with other writers in an event under the Glasgow 1990 umbrella. He expressed his concern to me, after a day or two, that he had not been able to find a book with the words of our 'traditional Scottish songs' in it. It emerged that what he was after were such items as 'I Love a Lassie', 'Loch Lomond', 'Roamin' in the Gloamin'' and 'I Belong to Glasgow' – twentieth-century music-hall songs but identified in his mind with Scottish tradition. Somewhat embarrassed, I could only suggest that he tried a music shop rather than a bookshop. I was even less disposed to be effusively helpful when he mentioned a wish to see Scottish country dancing . . .

In his seminal book *The Break-Up of Britain*, first published in 1977, Tom Nairn included passages as mischievous and memorable as Orwell's famous assault on the trendy Left in *The Road to Wigan Pier*. Nairn denounced

that prodigious array of *Kitsch* symbols, slogans, ornaments, banners, war-cries, knick-knacks, music-hall heroes, icons, conventional sayings and senti-ments (not a few of them 'pithy') which have for so long resolutely defended the name of 'Scotland' to the world. Annie S. Swan and Cronin provided no more than the relatively decent outer garb for this vast tartan monster. In their work the thing trots along doucely enough, on a lead. But it is something else to be with it (e.g.) in a London pub on International night, or in the crowd at the annual Military Tattoo in front of Edinburgh Castle. How intolerably vulgar! What unbearable, crass, mindless philistinism! One knows that *Kitsch* is a large constituent of mass popular culture in every land, but this is ridiculous![1]

Nairn's assault on 'tartanry' and the legacy of the 'kailyard' was accompanied in the same year by *The DC Thomson Bumper Fun Book*, published by Paul Harris, in which various serious-minded people discussed the output of the most powerful indigenous Scottish publisher still, then, at the height of its dominance. The *Sunday Post*, George Rosie pointed out, was 'arguably the most successful newspaper in the world', featuring in *The Guinness Book of Records* as the paper coming closest to saturation of its market: in 1971 its estimated readership of 2 947 000 represented more than 79 per cent of the entire population of Scotland aged 15 and over.[2]

Then, in 1981, Barbara and Murray Grigor mounted in St Andrews and Edinburgh an exhibition, *Scotch Myths*, which provided, as Colin McArthur recorded, 'a massive exposure and deconstruction of Tartanry and Kailyard as manifested in postcards, whisky bottle labels, shortbread tins, tea cloths, and music hall songs.' Fragments of this vomit-inducing display can currently [in 1990] be seen somewhere in the labyrinth of the *Glasgow's Glasgow* exposition in the new 'Arches' venue of the City of Culture: bumped into there, they might just inspire nostalgia, not for the kailyard, but for those heady days in the early 1980s when the local intelligentsia fell like hyenas on Nairn's Great Tartan Monster. McArthur himself followed up *Scotch Myths* with an event in the Edinburgh Film Festival at the capital's new Film House. *Scotch Reels*[3] confronted Walt Disney's *Rob Roy* Scotland and Ealing Studios' *Whisky Galore* Highlands, but also raised awkward questions about recent Scottish traditions of depiction of the urban working class: at that event I first heard the term 'Clydesidism' applied to such material as Bill Bryden's *Willie Rough*. From the point of view of a present-day Scottish woman, how could one excuse the nostalgic idealisation of the working class in heavy industries now on the verge of extinction and the associated all-male culture in which class bitterness was combined with football, drink and gambling? Such questions will be asked all over again this year when the film of William McIlvanney's *The Big Man* appears; in the novel, the *machismo* of the screen Western is enacted in Strathclyde.

There are signs that Nairn, George Rosie, the Grigors, McArthur and those who worked with them and their ideas in the early 1980s have had some effect, or, at least, that they represented a powerful wave already in motion. Billie Connolly's rejection of kilts in favour of wellies was by then world famous. 7:84 Scotland had assailed Tourist Board and *Brigadoon* notions of Highland history in *The Cheviot, the Stag and the Black Black Oil*, a landmark in the history not only of Scottish theatre but of Scottish entertainment in the broadest sense – even if John McGrath's later work has tended to substitute a Gaelic proletarian pastoral for the older *Whisky Galore* stereotype. Since 1982, however, there has been heightened awareness in the media of the treacherous nature of Scottish stereotypes. And the successful production of *Jock Tamson's Bairns* at the Glasgow Tramway, opening the 1990 jollifications, revealed a very earnest attempt by highly gifted actors, dancers, musicians, responding to the ideas of the producer Gerry Mulgrew, the script-writer Liz Lochhead, and the painter Keith McIntyre, to deconstruct tartanry, the Burns cult, and Scottish *machismo* all at once. Lochhead's role followed up her establishment, with Elaine C. Smith, of a powerful new style of socialist, feminist cabaret: McIntyre's savage representation of Burns Night which appeared on the posters for *Jock Tamson's Bairns* could be read as an oblique comment on the populist depictions of heroic dossers by Peter Howson and the epic manner in which Ken Currie, according Diego Rivera and Léger the sincerest form of flattery, has elegised – see his murals in the People's Palace – the Clydeside working-class tradition.

'Wait a moment,' I hear you muttering, 'Why is this guy rubbishing the Scottish labour tradition? What's wrong with Burns Night, anyway? Wasn't Burns a working-class democrat? Isn't it good that Scotland still shows pride in working-class traditions of struggle?'

I have two ripostes to make, if that is what you're thinking. First, has Labour's electoral dominance in Lowland Scotland over the last decade actually done much for Labour's working-class voters? Did the Attlee, Wilson and Callaghan administrations have more than a few good effects, short term, on the situation within our class-divided capitalist society? The *nostalgia* characteristic of the artistic products favoured by the labour movement in Scotland has apparently not helped in any way to inspire a successful socialist practice.

231

It is very good that we should remember the bleacher lassie of Kelvinhaugh and the heroes of the Donibristle Moss Moran mine disaster. It is not at all rotten that local Labour parties in Scotland join their Nationalist and Tory counterparts in mounting Burns Suppers – Burns was actually a very good writer indeed. I suppose John McGrath's fantasies about a primordial Gaelic communalism constantly cheated and bullied by wicked Sassenachs do no more than reinforce the characteristic ruefulness and paranoia of the *Gaeltacht*. I don't mind people singing 'Flower of Scotland', in which our spacious country is reduced to a 'wee bit hill and glen' (c.f. 'butt and ben') so long as that helps us to beat England at Rugby and get into the World Cup final. As it happens, I find Ken Currie's paintings very moving and not in the least unintelligent. But even if you throw in a few anti-apartheid songs and musical contributions from Chile and Nicaragua, what have the *uses* of popular culture which have been *made* by the labour movement in Scotland helped to achieve? Total Labour Party dominance in Lowland Scotland voting patterns and the yuppification of central Glasgow and the Old Town of Edinburgh, that's what, if anything, they have helped to achieve – there is a gulf between mandate and proclaimed ideology on the one hand, and practical results on the other, which yawns as widely as the familiar gap between Bonnie Scotland myths on tea-towels and telly and the realities of life in Easterhouse and Pilton.

My second riposte, a facetious one, is this: if I sound snooty about Scottish popular culture, I am merely continuing the august tradition of our beloved movement's high-minded heroes. Imagine John Maclean enjoying what John McGrath calls 'A Good Night Out'. William Knox's biographical dictionary of *Scottish Labour Leaders* between the wars shows beyond contradiction how they generally distanced themselves from the cultural forms – using 'cultural' in its broadest sense – favoured by their working-class constituency. It is not in itself to their discredit that over three-fifths, at least, were abstainers from alcohol: Scottish pub culture, among other effects, has donated vast profits to the Tory brewing dynasties. But along with a taste for cups of tea went a self-improving mistrust of more vital elements in the culture which enabled the Scottish working class to maintain morale in very bad times. Knox links their attitude to the Victorian cult of 'respectability'. Music and art should be used to elevate the moral status of the proletariat. The great Orpheus Choir was a very positive result of this ambition: but the unsuccessful promotion of a Glasgow Socialist Music Festival was accompanied by an unwise contempt for jazz. One writer in *Forward* in 1928 managed to combine racism and élitism with misdirected class feeling and temperance propaganda in his assault on the new music. Jazz, he claimed,

brings the *jungle* within the reach of the poorest person . . . it has its greatest power to impress after a *seven course dinner*, and some *uncorked bottles* . . . It has the creative power of a bull in a china shop . . . There is such a wonderful sadness about it that the *least intellectual* may quickly grasp it. [Emphases added]

Glasgow's Socialist Art Circle, founded in 1921, seems to have produced exhibitions between the wars of dire conventionality – working-class people depicted, as one critic put it, nothing more revolutionary than 'Elizabethan cottages and lambs frisking in the meadows'. In the 1930s support for these exhibitions ebbed away.[4]

It was left to people associated with Marxism and the Communist Party to attempt to generate up-to-date socialist cultural products aiming at popular appeal. Douglas Allen has written about 'Scotland's Hidden Film Culture' of the 1920–40s. He sees it as one component in a complete 'socialist counter culture' which included 'a network of clubs and institutions engaged in drama, literature, music, field sports, swimming and even rambling'. The Workers' Film Societies screened the best of world socialist cinema and developed the use of cinema as propaganda at public rallies and fundraising events. The Glasgow Kino Group, emerging in 1935, went further, creating films itself, with help from two very talented graduates of Glasgow School of Art – Helen Biggar and Norman McLaren. *Hell Unlimited*, made in 1936, rejected documentary realism, as Allen points out, in favour of a 'montage of fantasy, surrealism and agit prop' – anticipating methods advocated by the Grigors and Colin McArthur in the 1980s.[5] Biggar went on to design sets for Unity Theatre which emerged during the Second World War as an amalgamation of the city's leading left-wing theatre groups. The aim, as one of its producers put it, was to create 'a native theatre, something which is essentially *reflecting* the lives of the ordinary people of Scotland' [emphasis added]. Previously only Joe Corrie's plays had given working-class experience back to working-class audiences. (It is useful at this point to be aware that Corrie's plays were very popular *outside* the labour movement, in the network of amateur theatrical clubs which was very strong in Scotland in the 1930s and thereafter.) Unity put on plays by James Barke, John Kincaid, Ena Lamont Stewart, and George Munro which dealt with industrial militancy, the blitz, the lives of working-class women, and even football. Their work reached a peak of 'popularity' (please note inverted commas around that word) with *The Gorbals Story*, by Robert McLeish, produced in 1946 and addressed to the acute postwar problem of working-class homelessness: a leader of the Glasgow squatters was allowed on stage at the first night to harangue the Lord Provost and other dignitaries there assembled. Unity was now a professional company. The play's success as a touring vehicle made it bread and butter for the actors. As the Cold War froze, and public funding was withdrawn, the invitation of a run in London's West End was irresistible. But that preceded the company's disintegration. A play about Glasgow roots was deracinated: and the commercial film which spun-off from its metropolitan recognition was arguably distorted so as to neutralise Unity's original political message.[6]

But what, in any case, are the implications of *reflection* as an aim in socialist cultural interventions? Granted that *The Gorbals Story* was 'popular', that the film was part of 'popular culture', what value in a capitalist, consumerist society, does one attribute to 'popularity'? Should it be the aim of socialists to 'reflect' life in such a way as to get across to the widest possible audience under the conditions provided by capitalist 'market forces' on the one hand and funding from state, local government and business sponsors on the other? Or should the labour movement encourage 'proactive' rather than 'reactive' cultural expression: supporting and initiating challenging work which, because of innovative form and new ideas, may to begin with puzzle audiences and be, in one sense, 'unpopular'? Let us go back to the debates of the early 1980s and see what theoretical perspectives have been on offer.

To begin with, we need to define 'culture'. As used in the phrase 'Glasgow City of Culture' the word is usually taken to imply what can be called 'high culture': classical music rather than rock, ballet rather than football, Shakespeare rather than Jeffrey Archer. According to certain long-influential writers, in Marxist as well as liberal traditions, the 'mass culture' of industrialised society offers no more than debased, commercialised, crude variants of the high forms: Jeffrey Archer gives readers and play-goers a simplified and distorted experience compared to what they might get from George Eliot's novels or Ben Jonson's plays.

Such views are now very unfashionable. The worship of 'high culture' was inevitably associated with the traditional belief that in aesthetic matters there were eternal and universal laws, governing proportion in form, truth to nature and so on. But within the 'high cultural' forms revolution upon revolution has apparently flouted these laws. Very few people still believe that poems have to be in regular metre, that strict conventions should govern the depiction of human figures by painters, that music should ideally be controlled by sonata form, or that Shakespeare has to be presented reverentially. Furthermore, it takes very little knowledge and thought to expose the fact that forms supposed to be high have been modified by 'popular' influences, and in most cases even originated in the 'popular' arena. Until quite late in the nineteenth century, the novel was generally regarded as popular escapist stuff. People of all classes, in Elizabethan London, flocking to Shakespeare's plays, clearly thought of them as sheer fun. The most widely esteemed twentieth-century 'art' composer, Stravinsky, did more than just flirt with jazz idioms. Opera, in Italy, is part of popular culture, and it seems to be heading in that direction in Britain. The narrow definition of 'culture' is, in fact, useless.

Unfortunately, the broader alternative is so capacious that it includes everything. When we speak of the 'culture' of an Amerindian – sorry 'native American' – people we normally give the word this broad sense: it covers traditional agricultural practices, styles of riding and dress, ideas about kinship, and so on, as well as visual, verbal and musical arts. 'Scottish culture' can be discussed equally broadly, with our sweet tooth and our savage drinking customs set alongside our poetry and architecture. And within such a broad definition, the limits of 'popular culture' are very hard to define. Habitually – whether discussing Renaissance Europe or present-day Glasgow – one tends to eliminate certain art forms and customs which clearly belong to the élite. Yet even these may have a 'popular' aspect. It is possible to think of only a very few sports, for instance, which attract no 'popular' participation: polo, 'real tennis', what else? Just as jousts and public ceremonials in the sixteenth century appealed to large crowds, so the life of the British royal family today is of absorbing interest to enormous numbers of people. What about chess? It is not in Britain, particularly 'popular'. Yet when, as I have seen in one English city, it is played with large pieces in a public open-air space, it clearly belongs to the realm of 'popular culture'.

Which brings us to this slippery word 'popular'. In discussion of 'popular culture' today, the adjective doesn't refer solely to things which are very 'popular' in the usual sense. Few people in Scotland play cricket or go curling compared to those who watch or take part in football matches. But neither curling nor cricket are exclusive, élite practices. Jazz is a 'minority' art form compared to rock or country-and-western, and since the 1940s some of the best players have been highly sophisticated, even cerebral, musicians. But the fact that a ration of jazz is provided on Radio 3 doesn't mean that it is an élite preserve.

One of Britain's best jazz critics has been Eric Hobsbawm, who used the pseudonym 'Francis Newton', borrowing the name of a fine black trumpeter of the swing era, Frankie Newton, who was a Communist. Which brings me to the matter of 'workers' culture'. Though jazz originated as proletarian music with elements of protest, Newton's class consciousness was exceptional. Coal-mining and whaling ballads are freely sung nowadays by people who've never been down a pit or stepped on to a fishing boat, let alone a whaler. This illustrates the general point that while the culture, in the broad sense, of a workplace and the families associated with it is very specific to that community, its expression in words, song, paint, on stage or in a novel gives it a currency potentially as wide as the whole nation, the whole world. In the larger arena such expression becomes subject to the aesthetic criteria, ideological factors, and even market forces, which apply to artistic products generally. Ewan McColl's radio ballads represented 'workers' culture', both in their substance and in their expression: but the medium which they used literally occupied the airwaves of the whole of Britain.

Another point: 'worker' tends still to summon up the image of a strong man engaged in manual labour in a large, heavily capitalised, workplace: women are associated with this image only in cases where they, too, work in factories. The term 'worker's culture' doesn't seem to refer to shop assistants, local government officers, or secretaries, still less to computer operators. Finally, there would probably be widespread reluctance within the labour movement to apply the term 'worker's culture' to certain practices undeniably popular among those classified as 'workers' by the Marxist test of relation to the means of production – gambling, for instance, or watching *EastEnders*. Because the term relates to Ken Currie's haunting image of the thinking working man reading Gramsci it actually tends to assimilate 'worker's culture' with 'high culture', adding such elements as industrial and political songs, trade union banners and Joe Corrie plays to the canon of suitably serious left-wing art.

Back now to the period around 1980, when the Open University was producing what proved to be a very successful course on 'popular culture' to which I contributed in a small way myself ... This drew on the work of the famous Centre for Contemporary Cultural Studies at Birmingham University. The Centre was set up in the 1960s as a spin-off from the concerns of the 'Old New Left', as we must now call it. Up to that time, serious discussion of 'popular culture' had been very scanty. The Old New Left was inspired to turn in that direction partly by the influence of George Orwell's political discussion of boy's comics, James Hadley Chase and other 'popular' items, more decisively by the perception that the so-called 'mass media' – tabloid newspapers, radio, TV – were extremely important factors in contemporary politics. The Birmingham Centre's first Director, Richard Hoggart, was famous for his book *The Uses of Literacy* (London: Chatto, 1957), which drew on his own experiences as a working-class boy. But at that point such academic work as existed on 'mass culture' was generally by outsiders who took, from Leavisite or Marxist positions, the pessimistic view that popular music, pulp fiction, TV soap opera and so on were essentially debased.

Hoggart was succeeded before long by Stuart Hall. The work of Hall and his coadjutors was influenced by the explosion of interest in continental Marxist, structuralist and post-structuralist theory associated with the abortive revolutions of 1968. Oddly enough, Herbert Marcuse, thought by many to be a major inspiration of the student revolt, almost vanished from sight under a welter of European names ritually cited in article after article, book after book. There were the four Bs – Brecht, Benjamin, Borges and Barthes. There was Althusser, the guru of post-structuralist Marxism and his disciple, the literary theorist Pierre Macherey. The post-structuralist psychology of Lacan triggered many theses of mind-numbing opacity. There was Jacques Derrida's 'deconstruction'. But beside – or against – the heavy new jargon from Paris lovingly satirised by Posy Simmonds in her *Guardian* strips about the Weber family, there was the clear relationship between Marxist thought and political practice inscribed in the writing of Antonio Gramsci, whose concept of 'hegemony' became extremely potent in the discussion of popular culture both through history and in the present day. First translated into English in the late 1940s by Hamish Henderson, Gramsci's thought has been especially influential in Scotland, where, either because we are provincial and out of date, or, as I like to think, because we are too canny, the ideas of Althusser and other French thinkers have been much less discussed.

I annoyed some high-minded colleagues in the early 1980s by questioning whether some of the theoretical Emperors were actually wearing any, or many, clothes. It seemed to me then – and subsequent developments appear to have borne out my hunch – that the debate over popular culture in English left-wing circles represented a compound of displacements. First, terms were imported from France which rang very oddly in English. Second, very heavy theoretical superstructures were, with comic solemnity, imposed on discussions of such matters as Sherlock Holmes stories, James Bond films, and *Coronation Street*. Third, at a time when left-wing politics in Britain were in deep crisis, it seemed to me that some fellow academics were using theoretical argument over popular culture as a substitute for genuine political practice. As the 1980s wore on, the pessimism implicit in much cultural analysis deepened, until it came to seem as axiomatic in the writings of pundits in London and Birmingham as in the political rhetoric of the SNP that the whole of English culture was irreversibly warped by 'Thatcherism'. In one extreme example, published as recently as 1988, an able English writer actually appeared to argue that popular paperback memoirs of working-class childhood were intrinsically Thatcherite because they were by *individuals* about *themselves*.[7]

Nevertheless, a great deal of value has come out of all that theoretical anguish. Discussion of gender and its construction and projection in cultural forms has a greatly improved focus: the issue of race can be illuminated in the same way. The Gramscian concept of hegemony has generated a great deal of very useful historical debate, helping to show, for instance, how the development of professional sport was articulated with class and politics in Victorian Britain. Above all, no one has any excuse any more to be dismissive of discussion of 'culture' on the grounds that bread-and-butter issues should be paramount. It should now seem essential that the labour movement takes account of the ideological and political implications of culture, achieves – as Ken Livingstone's Greater London Council valiantly tried to do – a generous and coherent cultural policy, and recognises – as rhetoric associated with Glasgow 1990 has often done – that in some of its manifestations 'culture' can be economically vital, generating good, interesting jobs.

I'll finish by summing up what I seem to have learnt myself over the past few years both from the academic study of popular culture and from practical involvement in various arts organisations struggling for survival in Thatcher's Britain.

First, I think it can be liberating to use 'culture' and 'popular culture' in the broadest possible sense: that is, without any implicit value judgements. Serious theatre is a cultural activity – but so is pantomime. Ballet does not necessarily represent something intrinsically finer than football. The art of Dudley Watkins, creator of the Broons, deserves as much intelligent consideration as the paintings of William Johnstone. Nothing need be either applauded or dismissed because it is 'popular' in the sense of 'watched by millions', 'bestseller', 'top of the charts'.

A second point emerging from where discussion of culture was in the 1980s is that the term 'ideology' is one which needs to be handled with care. In Britain, it is generally taken to refer to a particular set of political or perhaps religious views – 'Thatcherism', 'Trotskyism', 'Islamic fundamentalism' – which the person using the word doesn't like. The broader alternative usage imported with the theories of Althusser suggests that 'ideology' is dominant in all the thoughts and actions of the vast preponderance of humankind, who misconceive reality and behave accordingly. Only 'scientific' thinkers armed with correct – that is Marxist – ideas, and to a lesser extent, writers or artists, stand outside, can challenge, this hideous miasma of falsity. Since any bright child, confronted with Emperor Althusser, is likely to ask how on earth these few elect persons manage to escape from the general affliction, the abyss of total despair yawns behind his argumentation. To return to Tom Nairn's Great Tartan Monster – aren't we all, as Nairn himself suggests, helplessly implicated in its writhings, simply because we are Scots? Isn't 'ideology', false consciousness, simply an ineradicable part of the human condition? Can any political argument, any course of action, have validity?

One can avoid Althusserian extremes, I think, and still usefully employ 'ideology' to embrace the entire arena of 'culture', with both terms defined at their broadest. The question is whether, being the ideological creatures we are, we can use whatever 'freedom' we have to change, remould, the thinking of others in the direction of social justice. Here, Gramsci's concept of hegemony can help us. (Though we cannot agree how to pronounce the word in this country – a Glaswegian colleague once suggested Hey Jimmy as a popular alternative.)

Gramsci had no time for the liberal-idealist tradition which conceived of culture as having nothing to do with politics, as a spiritual matter. But he was equally critical of fellow-Marxists who saw culture as merely 'reflecting' – that word again – the economic base. He anticipated the tendency which finally emerged on the British New Left to discard the base/superstructure dichotomy of 'orthodox' Marxism. The working class, Gramsci argues, when it achieves power, must dominate not only economically, but morally and intellectually. Hegemony – domination – implies *cultural* domination.

We have seen in Eastern Europe recently how dismally a party purporting to dictate on behalf of the proletariat, and equipping itself lavishly with publishing facilities, TV stations, opera houses, sporting facilities, concert halls and not least censorship, can fail to establish genuine ideological, moral or intellectual ascendancy. I trust that no one in Britain believes any more that the establishment of a socialist government with lasting power to determine what goes on culturally would somehow produce automatically a nation of socialists. We have also seen, I think, how Thatcherism has failed, despite the sycophancy of most of the popular press and overt and tacit restraint placed on broadcasters, to Thatcherise the British mentality over ten dogmatic years. But I still think that we can derive wisdom from Gramsci.

The labour movement has to assert itself in dialogue over the whole range of issues which could be called 'cultural' rather than economic: and has to be ready to listen to what people outside it say, and learn from them. Only in this way can it begin to work out a socialism which is harmonious with the ideas, wishes and felt needs of people in general. We should not abandon ourselves to such thoughts as '*Neighbours* is terribly popular, therefore it's a good thing'; but nor should we think on the lines of using the same format, inserting preconceived socialist ideas and producing an equally popular left-wing soap opera.

A key term from Gramsci is *leadership*. The labour movement should take the lead in pressing open, and keeping open, spaces – in the media, in theatre, in print – where cultural issues can be fully and responsibly discussed. On these issues – I'm thinking of gender, race, nationalism, and, indeed, cultural policy itself – the movement is not united. No preconceived solution can be put across on its behalf. 'Leadership' involves an insistence that certain issues be frankly and intelligently confronted, not arrogant indoctrination. The arts offer many ways of opening up and extending debate. The participation of subtle West African musicians alongside Euro-American rock stars in the great Mandela concert at Wembley did more to counter negative stereotypes of savage niggers just down from the trees than even the words of Mandela himself.

While writing this, I happened to see and buy a volume of new Scottish plays edited by Alasdair Cameron for an enterprising English publisher: four originally produced at the Traverse, one from Wildcat, two from 7:84's *Long Story Short* presentation, on tour, of brief sketches by young, or youngish, writers, praised by Cameron as 'a courageous experiment in raising issues and asking questions which are usually ignored or swept under the carpet', which got a warm response from audiences in the Highlands. Cameron's analysis of the features of present-day Scottish drama which differentiate it from English is very intelligent and well focused. He notes, for instance, the dominance of 'serio-comic naturalism', all the way from Joe Corrie to John Byrne. 'Perhaps', he says, this mongrelism stems from the debt which the mainstream Scottish theatre owes to the variety stage and its cheerful mixing of genres. From the late nineteenth century, the variety and pantomime stage was for many years the only place where Scots was spoken as a matter of course in the theatre. For the same reason, Scottish drama assumes a much greater degree of audience involvement than is usual in most English plays ... There is a further possible debt to the variety stage in the sentimental streak which runs through an overwhelming majority of Scottish plays ... Even the political plays of Wildcat rely on plentiful helpings of sugar to sweeten their message.[8]

Granted the frequent cross-overs between Scottish theatre and prime-time TV – so that Gerard Kelly and Elaine C. Smith may be seen in *City Lights* by a vast audience at the same time as they're performing in socialist or feminist theatre somewhere in Lowland Scotland – one might deduce that there are especially good opportunities here for the development of cultural forms which are both 'popular' in every sense and 'political' in the sense that they provide leadership in the discussion of difficult issues. Both Hamish Henderson and John McGrath have rightly emphasised in recent years that artists in various media are closer to popular life in Scotland than is common south of the Border. It is a source of delight, and even awe, for instance, that our great poets – Sorley MacLean, MacCaig, Morgan – regularly attract large audiences who come prepared to enjoy themselves in easy rapport with the writers concerned: perhaps we owe it to Burns that poetry in Scotland isn't always associated with pure elocution, strenuous intellectualism and genteel boredom.

But let us not deceive ourselves into easy optimism. Consumerist values weigh more in everyday life here than nostalgia for *The Steamie* and a lost working-class urban kailyard. The *Sunday Post* remains reactionary and the *Sun* sells lots of copies in Scotland. More disturbingly still, there is the tendency to package, distort and politically neutralise Scottish culture as saleable 'heritage'. This is an area where Scottish Labour Historians need to be particularly vigilant, and I can suitably finish here.

(1990)

25

Art for a New Scotland?

By August 1987, when an exhibition called *The Vigorous Imagination: New Scottish Art* opened in the Edinburgh Festival, there was a consensus, internationally, within the United Kingdom, and even within Scotland itself, that some rather remarkable painting was happening in the homeland of Raeburn and Charles Rennie Mackintosh. It wasn't eccentric of Edward Lucie Smith to devote a chapter to Scotland in his survey of *Art in the Eighties*.[1] Several Scottish artists born between 1953 (Steven Campbell) and 1964 (Stephen Conroy) had stormed the art market amid talk of a 'New Glasgow School'.

'*The Vigorous Imagination* was the death-knell of Scottish art in the eighties – that was when it was all over as far I was concerned', said Ken Currie in March 1992, fingering an empty coffee cup in the bar of Glasgow's Tron Theatre. That, he went on, was when he personally decided to distance himself from any 'Glasgow School', 'Movement', or 'Renaissance'. There is no doubt that the most interviewed and controversial of the young Scottish figurative painters is very much his own man. Yet it has to be the case that he gained, however reluctantly, from being reviewed, on first appearance, as part of a 'movement'.

There are three stories to tell about 'Scottish art in the eighties'. The first relates to packaging, to marketing, and to the creation of instant 'art history' by Lucie Smith and others. The second concerns the perceptions and aspirations of certain very gifted young painters, some trained in Dundee and Edinburgh rather than Glasgow, who were conscripted willy-nilly behind the banner 'New Glasgow Boys'.

In the third story, the intervention of gallery-owners and critical trend-merchants on the Scottish scene is gratuitous, almost irrelevant. It tells of a revival of Scottish cultural self-confidence which can be traced back to the experiments in Scots writing conducted by MacDiarmid and Grassic Gibbon in the 1920s and 1930s; to the 'revival' of Scottish folk music in the 1950s associated with Hamish Henderson, Norman Buchan and Ewan McColl; to the rise of the SNP in the 1960s; and to the stirrings around the same time of a new *avant garde* attitude to writing in Glasgow, with Edwin Morgan the poet as its senior eminence and Alasdair Gray the novelist at its head and centre. Above all, the third story involves a re-siting of Scottish cultural consciousness: an increasing sense of distance from the United Kingdom's south-eastern metropolis which turned, during the Thatcher years, into something not far from contempt, and a corresponding urge to relate art, music and literature in Scotland to non-insular tendencies, to what had been going on in Europe, in the New World, and in the South ('Third World'). In the words of MacDiarmid (from *To Circumjack Cencrastus*, 1930) quoted in 1979 as an epigraph to the first issue of *Cencrastus*, a magazine which went on to typify the new conjunction of nationalist and internationalist visions:

> If there is ocht in Scotland that's worth ha'en
> There is nae distance to which it's unattached . . .

That issue contained an essay on 'The Tradition of Painting in Scotland' by Duncan MacMillan, whose monumental volume *Scottish Art: 1480–1990*[2] would issue from a decade of comprehensive revaluation. Also, an apocalyptic statement by Eduardo Paolozzi, on 'Junk and the New Arts and Crafts Movement':

Modernism is the acceptance of the concrete landscape and the destruction of the human soul.
Modernism is the process where plagiarism and pastiche become indistinguishable, like images blurred and corroded by sea water.[3]

The self-exile of Paolozzi, born in Leith, represented the characteristic movement of major Scottish artistic talent since the days of the Colourists: *out*. MacDiarmid's friend William Johnstone had brought in Paolozzi to teach alongside Grangemouth-born Alan Davie in the Central School in London . . .

Art for a New Scotland?

1979 was the year when the politicians' wagon rolling towards Scottish home rule broke its axle on a large rock. In the referendum of March that year, a majority of Scots *who voted* supported the devolved Assembly proposed by the Labour Government, but were thwarted by a rule devised at Westminster that over 40 per cent of the *total electorate* should be in favour. The outcome, in retrospect, seems to have been a renewed, angry determination by people involved in the arts to assert Scotland's capacity for cultural independence. To a greater or lesser extent this can be seen in the careers and pronouncements of leading young figurative painters in the decade which followed.

Locally based heroes and heroines for these young people were not conspicuous. The better painters resident in Scotland, including the preponderance of art college teachers, were content, however estimably, to work in the cautious, reliable spirt of the native bourgeoisie: it was painting for lawyers and bankers with good taste. Davie and Paolozzi still lived in south-east England. Joan Eardley, who had travelled in the other direction, from England to Glasgow, had died young. In 1962, John Bellany and Sandy Moffat had met MacDiarmid through their friend Alan Bold the poet, and had been powerfully affected. As Moffat put it, they 'rejected the prevailing watered-down traditions of French painting as unsuitable for a modern Scottish painter.' They had mounted unofficial open-air exhibitions in the Edinburgh Festival, seeking to popularise a more vital art. But they had both found London 'a breath of fresh air', after 'narrow minded and moribund' Scottish art circles.[4] Bellany, from 1968, had taught in southern English art schools. Moffat's contrary decision, which had taken him to Glasgow School of Art, was of much importance in the second of our stories, and, by knock-on effect, in the first.

*

'How did it all start?' asked a triumphant Clare Henry, art critic of the *Glasgow Herald*, introducing a catalogue of *The Vigorous Imagination*.[5] She says it began for her at the New 57 Gallery in Edinburgh in 1981. 'A group of students organised by Sandy Moffatt were having a show.' Here, she met Steven Campbell. About the same time, at a little exhibition in Ayr, she encountered sketches of boxers, prostitutes, drunks and dance hall fights . . . 'I enquired after

245

the unknown artist and was informed that he was working in a supermarket stacking shelves. I wrote a rave review. Peter Howson stopped stacking shelves and began to paint again in real earnest . . .' And so, rather like Yul Brynner in *The Magnificent Seven*, Henry went on finding new stars. *The Vigorous Imagination* jubilantly displayed the incredibly young virtuoso, Stephen Conroy, as the latest 'discovery'. Meanwhile, metropolitan critics were lured to behold the work of the 'Glasgow Pups', and they had begun to attract the attention of the big-time art market. When considering the international success of these young painters, it is worth recalling the trends spotted by Lucie Smith. He points to a 1981 exhibition at the Royal Academy, *A New Spirit in Painting*, which, he says, marked a rejection of the previous trend to assimilate painting with sculpture, re-positioned Picasso, Bacon, Hockney and others at the head of tendencies interested in figuration, and brought into the limelight the German neo-expressionists. The Ecole de Paris was long since clapped out, New York was faltering – North European art was 'in', British artists were trying to be more British, Latin American 'magic realism' was lurking in the wings, and post-modernist pastiche classicism – as in Italian *Pittura Colta* – was brazening itself forth. In their diverse ways, the new Scottish painters seemed to be in step with current trends, above all in their devotion to figuration and their allusiveness with it.

Campbell's chosen route is of symptomatic interest. Born in Glasgow, he worked as a maintenance engineer before going to Glasgow School of Art in his mid-twenties in 1978. When he left in 1982, he headed for New York, and his earliest solo exhibitions were seen in that city, in Chicago and in Munich. In 1985 he returned to Scotland briefly for a major exhibition in the Fruitmarket Gallery, Edinburgh, then, next year, came back to live in his native city. His prole-to-riches transit almost bypassed London completely, though his characteristic paintings sent up besuited English persons from the oeuvres of Wodehouse and Conan Doyle, entangled in strange incidents amid English rusticity.

However, Campbell was not involved with the core group of younger students fostered by Moffat at the Glasgow School. To Currie, Howson and others, the only students at the time who were interested in producing figurative work, Moffat introduced his own

246

repertoire of interests, in art history, cinema, literature and philosophy. 'We were united in our heroes,' Currie has recalled. 'Picasso, Léger, Beckmann, Kollwitz, Grosz, Heartfield, Masareel, Dix, Rodchenko, Lissitsky, Mayakovsky, Rivera, Eisenstein,' and, he ends significantly, 'Brecht, MacDiarmid.' [6]

Currie and Howson were set beside Campbell, Mario Rossi (Glasgow School of Art 1975–9), Stephen Barclay (GSA 1979–83) and Adrian Wiszniewski (GSA 1979–83) in an exhibition called *New Image Glasgow* in August 1985 which toured to London, Milton Keynes and Nottingham. Moffat, almost inevitably, introduced the catalogue. He noted the return to figurative imagery as 'the most significant artistic revolution of the past five years . . . extravagantly promoted in the Biennales, museums and art markets of Western Europe and America.' He quoted the *Guardian*'s art critic, Waldemar Januszczak, reviewing an exhibition by Rossi earlier that year, to the effect that the new Glaswegians currently made up 'the most coherent group of young artists in Britain', though noting himself that at the Glasgow School they had 'contrived to work in comparative isolation from each other.' There had been, he said, a 'strong tradition of figurative and expressive painting in Glasgow (Colquhoun, MacBryde, Eardley and Crozier) but all that survived of this tradition had become, by the late seventies, lifeless and respectable, destroyed by an admixture of middle-class taste and banal abstraction.' He quoted an essay by Currie in a School of Art magazine: 'There are no great issues . . . no convictions . . . there is only paint, formless masses of paint.' Though Campbell was still in New York, Rossi lived in London, and Wiszniewski now exhibited exclusively in London, Moffat concluded that 'Scotland is now a livelier place for artists than at any time since 1945.' [7]

The exhibition did indeed reveal current or latent congruities between its six young male painters. The strong Scottish tradition of draughtsmanship appeared to advantage. While Rossi and Wiszniewski were into cryptic allegorisation of their own experience, the rather fey charm and Légerity of the latter's figures related not only to Campbell's parodied pastoral but also to the prominent melancholy eyes which were to dominate Currie's projections of working-class humanity. Barclay, palpably influenced by both Campbell and Wiszniewski, worked, as he put it, under 'war's permanent shadow' and in this way also anticipated later Currie.

247

But Currie's exasperation with *The Vigorous Imagination* as displayed in Edinburgh two years later, was echoed by local critics. Januszczak had hailed the *New Image* exhibition in a big *Guardian* piece called 'The Glow that came from Glasgow', and he and Henry had been aided in their promotion by Marina Vaizey and Bill Packer of the *Sunday Times* and *Financial Times*. A new wave of Glasgow Girls from Glasgow School of Arts were acclaimed in the wake of the Glasgow Boys. The male Glasgow painters dominated *The Vigorous Imagination* physically. To quote my own review in the *New Statesman* (14 August 1987):

Newcastle-product Sam Ainsley's feminist banners are brushed past in stairways. Dundee-trained Keith McIntyre's re-workings of ancient myths as modern pastoral are cramped into a dingy corridor. Conroy, Campbell and Peter Howson and Ken Currie . . . command the big spaces which the casual dropper-in won't miss. I concede that Howson's whopping pictures of male workers and dossers need space, much as I still distrust his transactions with machismo. And I still find Currie's depictions of sad people hoping amidst industrial decay very moving indeed. But why must men overwhelm? Has Gwen Hardie been punished for choosing to live in Germany or is it that, like Redfern, she's an Edinburgh alumnus?

*

The city of Glasgow itself was in transition. In the 1980s, while its heavy industries remained in terminal decline, its Labour-dominated local authority devised the 'Glasgow's Miles Better' slogan. The city had long had art galleries to equal and, in some respects, surpass, Edinburgh's. More music of every kind was made there, month in, month out. Theatre throve, notably at the internationally famous Citizens. Charles Rennie Mackintosh's reputation, literally embodied in his School of Art's masonry, was a stimulus to those concerned to rescue Glasgow from stereotypes dominated by knife-wielding gangs, sectarian football supporters, and weekend drunks. What Bill Hare has called 'the Burrellification process'[8] had begun, involving not only the opening of the glossy new Burrell Collection premises, but the drive which secured Glasgow the status of 'European City of Culture for 1990', entailing a year of festival events to put Edinburgh's three weeks firmly in their place.

As the 'New Glasgow Boys' moved on in their increasingly divergent artistic directions, they could be seen as representing deep and painful contradictions. Campbell, Conroy and Wiszniewski could be typed as aesthetes turning their backs on rustbelt blight and mass unemployment, unconcerned with the 'national question' highlighted by Jim Sillar's famous by-election victory for the SNP over Labour in Govan in 1988. ('An Art for Art's Sake atmosphere prevails over the whole project', wrote Stuart Morgan in a generally incomprehensible essay introducing Campbell's Third Eye Centre installation in 1990. 'In Campbell's painting styles meet *without* mixing.')[9] Howson's horrible yet heroic (male) proletarians connected with the cult of *The Big Man* as reworked by William McIlvanney, the West of Scotland's most popular 'serious' fiction writer, in a novel of 1985, later filmed. Currie was always, and has remained, harder to place.

He received a remarkable commission, in 1985, to produce murals for the upper floor of the People's Palace, a museum of local history on Glasgow Green. A communist by conviction, he depicted Glasgow's working-class history in a style obviously influenced by Léger and, still more, by Diego Rivera, but also by trade-union banners. The content was largely determined by urban folk-song. This was History Painting deserving capital letters. Did it show Currie to be, as Hare patriotically put it, 'the finest genre/history painter that Scotland has produced since David Wilkie'?[10] (The elevation of Wilkie is crucial in the recasting of Scottish art history by Hare's colleague Duncan Macmillan.) Was Januszczak to the point when he called the People's Palace works 'perhaps the most impressive British murals since Stanley Spencer's Glasgow shipyard scheme'?[11] Or were left-wing critics versed in post-structuralist theory right to attack Currie for unintended complicity with bourgeois values?

Paul Wood in *Edinburgh Review* quoted Walter Benjamin – better that writing should be 'consumable by no one than by the enemy'. Currie's reworking of realistic conventions meant that his work 'foreclosed rather than raised' political questions. If public responses had been positive, this was because of 'admiration of the dexterity and magical skills of the artist in being able . . . to conjure illusions of life out of paint and canvas.' Wood took grave issue with Currie's lengthy explanations of the allegorical content of his murals. 'The meanings have to be recoverable from the pictures, otherwise the whole enterprise turns turtle, the captions become the works, and the works their secondary illustrations.' Currie's invocation of a peculiarly Scottish popular culture seemed to Wood to open the 'Pandora's Box of nationalism'.[12]

Ian Spring was also worried by the salience of 'verbal commentary' in Currie's murals, but on opposite grounds: where Wood saw a truckling to popular taste, Spring discerned a subtle élitism. In Currie's quotations from Marx or from socialist songs, the words were 'often obscured so that some extra cultural knowledge or an effort of interpretation is required. There is ... an extra dimension that the cognoscenti will read and understand.' Furthermore, with the decline of the mass movement depicted in them, 'Currie's paintings work as nostalgia pieces ... but have no political clout.'[13]

Yet it was hard to taint Currie with opportunism, sentimentality or complacency. For a start, he is an exceptionally articulate man well equipped to reply to intelligent critics. I myself believe that Allan Harkness was right, *pace* Wood, to detect a Brechtian practice in Currie's work, including the famous murals.[14] The conventions used relate to public displays – to May Day demonstrations and the like – in which workers displayed the tools of their crafts and the slogans of their aspirations. Quotations from folk-song likewise relate not to the unmediated conditions of working class life, but to their transmutation into art. Even the body tattoos which adorn Currie figures are invoked by him, as he told Harkness, as 'popular culture, believe it or not. Self-organised things by working class people like fêtes and carnivals.'[15]

The murals exploit illusionist space rather less, in fact, than Spencer's. In them, what Spring accurately describes as 'a common colour scheme – the red/orange of molten steel – and the chiaroscuro of directional lighting'[16] – evoke theatrical tableau effects creating a critical distance as in Brecht's drama. Noting this gives me basis for relating Currie's work to that of Keith McIntyre (Edinburgh born, Dundee-trained), who now has his studio in the same building as Currie's in the east of Glasgow. McIntyre is deeply interested in the performing arts.

Ironically, around the turn of 1991–2, Currie's latest exhibition of massively public history paintings was on display (December) in *Edinburgh* University's Talbot Rice Gallery, while McIntyre's equally monumental sequence inspired by the Lockerbie air disaster was shown (January) in Glasgow's much-visited Kelvingrove Museum.

It was interesting to compare both with the huge New Year retrospectives of Alan Davie – a hundred paintings in the McLellan Gallery in Sauchiehall Street, Glasgow, forty-seven works on paper and eleven canvases following Currie into the Talbot Rice. Davie has hardly been short of ambition. 'Sometimes I think I paint simply to find enlightenment and revelation, I do not practise painting as an art', Davie said in 1958: he has ransacked world culture for images to express humankind's 'inner and commonly shared emotions', whether in his thirties splashing away like Pollock, or, latterly, appropriating the totemic symbolism of the Hopi.[17] His work is commonly spacious in scale. Yet it has always, irresistibly, implied a private purchaser. Cleverly composed, colourful, witty, it is often the kind of art which people with large means and large houses might favour as appealing to the kids. When it is more passionate and erotic, it strives to give sublime status to individual pulsings and throbbings. Its seriousness is that of private psychotherapy. I like it (who wouldn't?) but don't find it moving at all.

*

Currie and McIntyre, in contrast, are civic artists. They paint for a community, albeit it may exist only in their imaginations. When I first met McIntyre in 1986, he spoke of the effect of Alasdair Gray's writings on him. Gray – himself a striking portraitist, muralist and allegorist, trained at the Glasgow School in the 1950s – had a favourite saying in those days to the effect that we should live and work *as if* in the early days of a new and better nation. Currie, in 1992, in the Tron Theatre bar, flicks away my point that the Talbot Rice is rather a private place for his public paintings to be shown. 'You shouldn't not do something because you're limited from doing it – my job is to produce big pictures.' McIntyre is delighted to have learnt that over 100 000 people saw his Lockerbie work (even if it was only the massive picture displayed in the museum's entrance hall – the sequence was actually tucked away, not very well sign-posted, in a room upstairs). Currie is happy to admit that he has done pretty well out of the art market, but deprecates the buying of big houses and big cars by other Glasgow ex-'Boys' and when we part heads off to take a bus home. McIntyre simply lost money over Lockerbie: he worked for a year on an overdraft. His dad thinks he's daft not to paint small things he can sell.

Like Currie, McIntyre (b. 1959) started in revolt against the lack of human relevance in the colourist tradition favoured by teachers, in his case at Duncan of Jordanstone's College, Dundee. He too was drawn to images of work – the fishing industry of eastern Scotland. Then he moved to Moffat in the Borders, where he excavated images of ancient communal ritual, such as the 'crowning' of shepherd lad and lass, from old photographs. He had worked close to Lockerbie, and was transfixed by the horror which descended on the town when the Pan Am 'Clipper' flight 103 exploded above it.

The central figure in his Lockerbie cycle is a calm, sad, androgynous angel. McIntyre is interested in the 'magical realism' of writers such as Márquez and Calvino. When a child at Lockerbie asked her father what had happened, he told her an angel had fallen from the sky. Corpses draped on the rafters of a building from which slates had slid looked from below, someone told McIntyre, 'like angels'. His sequence is in a very straightforward, easily explained way, allegorical. There are no directly shocking images. The angel's face broods over rafters, over the streets of a city such as flight 103 had left, such as it would have gone on to, over a seascape with bright birds (McIntyre has the originals, stuffed, in his studio).

Though there is a hint here of John Bellany's obsession with marine imagery, McIntyre hastens to invoke a different inspiration, James Ensor – 'a major hero of mine. He pulled together many European characteristics – involving political satire, social comment, religious comment, the macabre – in a presbyterian sort of environment.' Ensor's ray-fish lurks behind the ghastly humanoid masks of figures in the work which McIntyre did in relation to *Jock Tamson's Bairns*, devised by Communicado Theatre Company as the launching event of 'Glasgow 1990', and involving a nightmarish parody of a Burns Supper in its critique of macho, couthie Scottish 'culture'.

McIntyre had signalled his interest in performance arts well before this. His gripe about *The Vigorous Imagination* is not that his work was obscurely hung compared to Conroy's but that the gallery didn't properly publicise the theatrical event connected with his rustic images and performed within its walls, involving dancers, a piper, a ballad-singer and the artist himself. In *Jock Tamson's Bairns* his imagery came to play a larger part than the words scripted by the increasingly exasperated dramatist, Liz Lochhead. He remained very close to the show's director, Gerry Mulgrew. While he was working on Lockerbie, Communicado's composer, Karen Wimshurst, moved into his studio to write beside him: the result is a cantata designed to be heard where the paintings are shown, with words by a poet from the Lockerbie area.

All this synaesthetic activity expresses McIntyre's belief that 'the indigenous history of the arts is not in painting in Scotland', rather in literature and music. Performance events, however, will attract the 'captive audience' which McIntyre wants for his public art. Pressed for an analogy for what he's up to, he refers to the way artists in Poland, short of oil paints, turned to the theatre to realise their images.

'If someone had said to me seven or eight years ago that I'd be living in Glasgow with two sons born here I wouldn't have believed them', McIntyre remarks with typical absence of affectation. Glasgow, he has come to concede, is indeed more exciting culturally, all the year round, than Edinburgh. It is good that Glasgow has the gallusness to create exciting new architecture, while Edinburgh is bogged down in conservation. 'That kind of confidence helps the arts enormously.' But his dominant allegiance, unproblematically, is to Scottish culture as a whole. 'I've always believed firmly in a kind of cultural national-ism.' When I interviewed him in March 1992, he was involved, running up to the general election, in meetings of Artists for an Independent Scotland. So was Currie, the same day. Unlike McIntyre, who is quietly reflective and generous, Currie is a man who talks swiftly, incisively, annihilating his bugbears with pithy wit. In the early 1980s, no messing about, he committed himself very explicitly, joining the now-defunct CPGB. Critics have seen in his latest work symptoms of disillusionment after the fall of the Berlin Wall and the collapse of communism. Yet pessimism about human nature was always there in Currie's work. In the People's Palace, his hunger marchers *Wandering Through The Thirties* are melancholy, at best dogged. His famous image of the *Self-Taught Man* reading Gramsci has in the background the neon lights which typify the Glasgow night culture of pubs, boxing and gambling which Currie (who, without sectarianism, sees virtues in the Calvinist tradition) holds in moral contempt.

He does not mind it when I say that entering his latest exhibition one might imagine it was the seventeenth-century room of a National Gallery. He is 'interested in what Giotto and Rembrandt brought as artists to aspects of the human situation'. The content of painting is what matters to him, involving the physicality of flesh, the sense of light. His new work he says, doesn't 'illustrate' what's happened in Eastern Europe, nor in Belfast (despite clear references to the Troubles there), nor even in Glasgow alone. In his huge *Troubled City* he is trying to make a 'universal statement'. Types representing 'human distinctiveness' – the Idiot, the Xenophobe, the Demagogue – jostle in a mêlée which recalls nightmarish Netherlandish and German crucifixions. *Wailing Women*, another large canvas, evokes Rembrandt. The ulcerated legs of one of Currie's hideous *Scottish Stoics* come from Grünewald, perhaps via Otto Dix. Currie is still an allusive painter and still strews his canvases with verbal signs – books, tattoos, slogans. But he is not implicated in that mode of modernism, where, according to Paolozzi in *Cencrastus 1*, 'plagiarism and pastiche become indistinguishable.'

Clearly, Currie has no truck with what Paolozzi calls 'acceptance of the concrete landscape and the destruction of the human soul'. As with McIntyre, one could describe Currie's project as 'humanist'. Neither is squeamish about the word 'universal'. Both stand unashamedly in the tradition of mediaeval fresco-painters, Renaissance muralists, Bosch's allegories, Rembrandt's *Night Watch* and the *Neue Sachlichkeit* of Brecht's Weimar contemporaries, a tradition not of 'northern expressionism' but of European public art. Such art depends for both men on what Currie calls a 'sense of community', a sense of people watching us'. And it implies public patronage. Currie has sold one of his big new triptychs to Cleveland Council. The Raab Gallery, which acts as his agent, attempts to find for him private buyers committed to public exhibition of their purchases.

*

How do Currie and McIntyre now perceive all that early acclamation in the 1980s? What happened in Scotland came along, McIntyre muses, at a 'convenient time'. Committed Scottish artists (as well as slick post-modernist ones) arrived when the art market was booming, there was money about, and the hype offered by Januszczak and others meant that they made contacts which secured them exhibitions abroad. Crucially, it became possible for the first time since the days of McTaggart for an ambitious painter to live in Scotland. Campbell's return after brief exile exemplifies this.

Currie, like McIntyre, denies that there is a 'national tradition of the visual arts in Scotland'.[18] Both, in its absence, look towards Europe, not to the United States, and certainly not to England. Though Currie has acknowledged Francis Bacon as an exemplar, he is notably silent about Spencer, whose Clydeside shipworkers, now monumentally displayed at London's Imperial War Museum, might have seemed an obvious precedent for his own large works. 'Bacon, Beckett, Brecht, Kafka and Shostakovich', Currie says, are united 'by an almost visceral concern for human beings in chaotic and incomprehensible situations'.[19] So the Scottish artist would ideally form part of battalion of cultural workers in various media seeking to change society through expression of the plight of persons.

Is Bellany, then, the Scottish precedent? Only up to a point. Currie never saw Bellany's work before he himself left art school. The big Edinburgh Festival Bellany retrospective in 1986 was indeed exciting. Here was a figurative painter of unquestionable integrity. But his quest had by then become personal, his recent painting since his health crisis is rather pretty. Out of all the hype surrounding *The Vigorous Imagination* and 'Glasgow 1990' have emerged two very impressive painters, Currie and McIntyre, very different in skills and temperament, linked by their matter-of-fact ways of living with the enormous ambition to create public, humanist, popular, serious paintings.

The title of this article, though – 'Art for a New Scotland?' – carries the burden of a question-mark. In the wake of the April 1992 election result, optimism about Scottish cultural resurgence is harder to sustain. The result was almost identical to that of 1987, when the Conservatives were reduced to only 10 parliamentary seats out of Scotland's 72 and Labour had 50. In 1992, the score was 11–49. Nevertheless, the fact that the Tories had not *lost* another half-dozen seats, as had been widely predicted, meant that they thought they could talk of having a 'mandate' to rule Scotland and maintain the Union (rather as if a football manager whose team had been tipped to lose 5–1 were to claim a victory after a 5–2 defeat). And the SNP's heady hopes of taking over half Scotland's seats proved to be sheer fantasy.

Over thirteen years, Conservative policies for the arts have contributed to an atmosphere of gloom and crisis affecting precisely the
public spaces which Currie and McIntyre need for their work. In
1991, both the Fruitmarket Gallery in Edinburgh and the Third Eye
Centre in Glasgow collapsed with six-figure debts – that is, they
were bankrupted. Whatever mismanagement contributed to these
disasters, chronic underfunding of visual arts by the Scottish Arts
Council, itself woefully short of funds, made them virtually inevitable. Both spaces are being resuscitated, but their new directors will
not be in a position to take risks.

Currie's reputation is now such that the sub-editor framing a two
page interview with him in the successful broadsheet *Scotland on
Sunday* had no inhibitions about writing that 'many rate him
Scotland's most important living painter.' The interviewer, Ajay
Close, clearly enjoyed his dark wit:

He describes a meeting of the pressure group Artists for an Independent
Scotland, where the right-on showbiz folk offered to donate their talents to
the cause ... Suddenly the pop star Ricky Ross [Deacon Blue] turned to
Currie: 'Ken, you could do a poster.' The founder of the school of Rational
Despair had to explain that the images he turned out weren't really appropri-
ate to a movement intended to engender national confidence.[20]

The question-mark applies, therefore, not just to the maintenance of
public spaces for innovative arts in Scotland, but also to the nature
of Currie's art itself. Both he and McIntyre are painting, on the scale
of Tintoretto and Veronese, images which connect not with the
rituals and self-images of Church and State but with the doubts and
despairs of a Scottish population which may be on the verge of mass
retreat into private bitterness and apathy, may be about to throw up,
from the hopeless lives of young unemployed people, very nasty,
quasi-fascist, or actually fascist, forms of blind revolt. Their latest
painting is not such as to appeal to Strathclyde Labour councillors
committed to attracting foreign investors to Glasgow, or to Edinburgh finance men cherishing in lush New Town flats and offices
choice examples of Alan Davie. Currie, Ajay Close points out, has
'never been interested in bread and butter politics: for him socialism
means intellectual enlightenment.' So the new Scotland towards
which he now projects 'Rational Despair' might prove to be a

country only of the mind, a land existing in little magazines and small galleries. That doesn't mean his art is bogus or unimportant: just that it offers questions, not answers.

(1993)

Notes

1. Introductory: Culture, Republic and Carnival

1. E. S. Sharratt, 'Reading the Texts: Archaeology and the Homer Question', C. Emlyn Jones, L. Hardwick and J. Purkis (eds.), *Homer: Readings and Images*, London: Duckworth (1992), 145–65.
2. Anna Grimshaw (ed.), *C. L. R. James Reader*, Oxford: Blackwell (1992), 286.
3. Thom Gunn, *Collected Poems*, London: Faber (1993), 399–402. I am grateful to Thom Gunn for permitting me to see a copy of this poem before publication, after I heard him read it on Radio 3.

2. Scotland in the Eighteenth Century

1. T. C. Smout, *A History of the Scottish People 1560–1830*, London: Fontana (1972), 241–5.
2. See Richard B. Sher, *Church and University in the Scottish Enlightenment: The Moderate Literati of Edinburgh*, Edinburgh: Edinburgh University Press (1985).
3. A. C. Chitnis, *The Scottish Enlightenment and Early Victorian Society*, London: Croom Helm (1986), 35.
4. A. Broadie, *The Tradition of Scottish Philosophy*, Edinburgh: Polygon (1990), 3.
5. D. Allan, *Virtue, Learning and the Scottish Enlightenment*, Edinburgh: Edinburgh University Press (1993).
6. D. Forbes (ed.), *Adam Ferguson's An Essay on the History of Civil Society*, Edinburgh: Edinburgh University Press (1966), xxvi.
7. Ibid., 84.
8. J. Macpherson, *Poems of Ossian* (facsimile reprint), Edinburgh: James Thin (1971). See F. Stafford, *The Sublime Savage: James Macpherson and the Poems of Ossian*, Edinburgh: Edinburgh University Press (1988).

3. Scotch Myths: The Patriot, the Manager and the Rebel

1. I am grateful to Professor Mackenzie for a printed copy of this lecture.
2. P. H. Scott, *Towards Independence*, Edinburgh: Polygon (1991), 49–53.
3. Ibid., 53, 58, 65–6.
4. P. H. Scott, *Andrew Fletcher and the Treaty of Union*, Edinburgh: John Donald (1992).

5. H. T. Dickinson, *Liberty and Property*, London: Methuen (1977), 105.
6. Scott, *Fletcher*, 101; Andrew Fletcher, *Selected Political Writings and Speeches*, ed. D. Daiches, Edinburgh: Scottish Academic Press (1979), 127 ff.
7. M. Fry, *The Dundas Despotism*, Edinburgh: Edinburgh University Press (1992).
8. Maclean papers in the National Library of Scotland.
9. J. Barke, *The Land of the Leal*, London: Collins (1939), 474.
10. D. Kirkwood, *My Life of Revolt*, London: Harrap (1935), 114.
11. James D. Young, *John Maclean: Clydeside Socialist*, Glasgow: Clydeside Press (1992).
12. Ibid., 115.

4. Rewriting Scottish History: The Arnold History of Scotland

1. The *Gill History of Ireland*, ed. J. Lydon and M. MacCurtain, appeared from Gill and Macmillan, Dublin, between 1972 and 1975.
2. G. Donaldson, general ed., *The Edinburgh History of Scotland*, 4 vols., Edinburgh: Oliver and Boyd (1965–75).
3. A. Grant, *Independence and Nationhood: Scotland 1306–1469*, London: Edward Arnold (1984), 170. The other titles in the series are: Alfred P. Smith, *Warlords and Holy Men: Scotland AD 80–1000* (1984); G. W. S. Barrow, *Kingship and Unity: Scotland 1000–1306* (1981); J. Wormald, *Court, Kirk and Community: Scotland 1470–1625* (1981); R. Mitchison, *Lordship to Patronage: Scotland 1603–1745* (1983); B. Lenman, *Integration, Enlightenment and Industrialisation: Scotland 1746–1832* (1981); S. and O. Checkland, *Industry and Ethos: Scotland 1832–1914* (1984); C. Harvie, *No Gods and Precious Few Heroes: Scotland 1914–1980* (1981).
4. J. Prebble, *The Lion in the North: A Personal View of Scotland's History*, London: Secker and Warburg (1971), 131, 133.
5. Barrow, op. cit., 83.
6. See P. Miller, *The New England Mind: The Seventeenth Century*, Cambridge, MA: Harvard University Press (1983; originally New York 1939), and numerous related titles by Miller.
7. Lenman, op. cit., 147.
8. R. Mitchison, *History of Scotland*, London: Methuen (1982, 2nd edn.).
9. Mitchison (1983).
10. Ibid., 131–2.
11. Ibid., 162.
12. Lenman, op. cit., 58.
13. Smyth, op. cit., 181.
14. Grant, op. cit., 34
15. J. Walvin, *The People's Game*, London: Allen Lane (1975), 70–4.

5. Burns, Scott and the French Revolution

1. B. Lenman, *Integration, Enlightenment and Industrialisation: Scotland 1746–1832*, London: Edward Arnold (1981), 99.
2. A. Ferguson, *The Honourable Henry Erskine*, Edinburgh: Blackwoods (1883), 280–85.
3. J. G. Fyfe (ed.), *Scottish Diaries and Memoirs, 1746–1843*, Stirling: Eneas Mackay (1942), 300.
4. Lord. Cockburn, *Memorials of His Time*, Edinburgh: A. & C. Black (1856), 80–83, 91.
5. E. Fletcher, *Autobiography*, Edinburgh: Edmonton and Douglas (1876), 64–6.
6. Ferguson, op. cit., 342.
7. T. Crawford, *Burns*, Edinburgh: James Thin (1978), 242–8.
8. K. Miller, *Cockburn's Millennium*, London: Duckworth (1975), 135.

6. Scott and Goethe: Romanticism and Classicism

1. O. G. Sonneck (ed.), *Beethoven: Impressions by His Contemporaries*, New York: Dover (1967), 169.
2. E. Johnson, *Sir Walter Scott: The Great Unknown*, vol. 1, London: Hamish Hamilton (1970), 282.
3. J. W. von Goethe, *Elective Affinities*, trans. R. J. Hollingdale, Harmondsworth: Penguin (1971), 54.

7. Tartanry

1. J. Prebble, *The King's Jaunt: George IV in Scotland, 1822*, London: Collins (1988).
2. T. Nairn, *The Enchanted Glass*, London: Radius (1988).
3. Prebble, op. cit., 22.
4. Ibid., 246.
5. Ibid., 358.
6. Ibid., 355.
7. Ibid., 364.
8. H. Cockburn, *Memorials of His Time*, Edinburgh: A. & C. Black (1856), 375–7.
9. Prebble, op. cit., 272.

8. Social Centuries

1. T. C. Smout, *A Century of the Scottish People, 1830–1950*, London: Collins (1986).
2. T. C. Smout, *A History of the Scottish People, 1560–1830*, London: Collins (1969).
3. L. Leneman, *Living in Atholl: A Social History of the Estate, 1685–1785*, Edinburgh: Edinburgh University Press (1986), 66–7.
4. Ibid., 222–3.
5. Ibid., 122–4.
6. Ibid., 201–2.
7. T. C. Smout (1986), 275.
8. Ibid., 2.
9. Ibid., 218.
10. Ibid.
11. Ibid., 229.
12. T. Leonard, *Intimate Voices*, Newcastle: Galloping Dog Press (1984), 124.
13. Smout (1986), 2.
14. Ibid., 33–5.
15. Ibid., 33.
16. Ibid., 54–5.
17. Ibid., 59.

9. Thomas Campbell's Liberalism

1. William Beattie, *Life and Letters of Thomas Campbell*, London (1850), vol. 3, 442–5.
2. 'The Pleasures of Hope' in *Complete Poetical Works of Thomas Campbell*, ed. J. Logie Robertson, Oxford: Oxford University Press (1907), 13–14.
3. Editorial, prefacing *The Metropolitan*, vol. 1, May to August 1831, iv.
4. *Metropolitan*, vol. 2, September to December 1831, 213.
5. Beattie, op. cit., vol. 3, 75.
6. Ibid., 81, 87, 110–12, 119.
7. Ibid., 124, 130–31; Cyrus Redding, *Literary Reminiscences and Memoirs of Thomas Campbell*, London (1860), vol. 2, 337–9.
8. *Inaugural Discourse of Thomas Campbell, Esq. on Being Installed Lord Rector of the University of Glasgow, Thursday, April 12th, 1827*, Glasgow (1827), 8.
9. Redding, op. cit., vol. 2, 8–22.
10. Anand C. Chitnis, *The Scottish Enlightenment and Early Victorian English Society*, London: Croom Helm (1986), 169.
11. Redding, op. cit., vol. 2, 106–7.
12. E. J. Hobsbawm, *The Age of Revolution: Europe 1789–1848*, London: Weidenfeld and Nicolson (1962), 103–4.
13. Redding, op. cit., vol. 2, 171.

14. Lord Byron, *Letters and Journals*, ed. Leslie A. Marchand, London: John Murray (1973–82), vol. 2, 140–41; vol. 3, 219–20, 232; vol. 4, 164; vol. 8, 219.
15. Mary Ruth Miller, *Thomas Campbell*, Boston: Twayne (1978), 161; *Letters of Percy Bysshe Shelley*, ed. F. L. Jones, Oxford: Oxford University Press (1964), vol. 1, 340–41.
16. Miller, op. cit., 23.
17. Thomas Campbell, 'Letter to [a] Mohawk Chief . . .' *New Monthly Magazine*, vol. 4, London (1822), 100.
18. Chitnis, op. cit., 15–20.
19. Ibid., 23–4.
20. Beattie, op. cit., vol. 1, 370, 387; vol. 3, 362; Redding, op. cit., vol. 2, 76.
21. Miller, op. cit., 119–22.
22. *Complete Poetical Works*, ed. Robertson, 189–91.
23. Ibid., 200–201.
24. Beattie, op. cit., vol. 1, 267–8.
25. Redding, op. cit., vol. 2, 123–4, 136–7: c.f. Miller, op. cit., 143–4.
26. Angus Calder, 'Thomas Campbell's *Gertrude of Wyoming*' in *Romanticism and Wild Places*, ed. Paul Hullah, in preparation.

10. Samuel Smiles: The Unexpurgated Version

1. V. G. Kiernan, *Marxism and Imperialism*, London: Zed Books (1974), 61.
2. S. Smiles, *Self-Help* (1859). The passage about Caesarism was not in the first edition, but added later. See, e.g. Penguin edition (1986), 21.
3. K. Fielden, 'Samuel Smiles and Self Help', *Victorian Studies*, xii, 2 (1968), 167.
4. S. Smiles, *Thrift* (1875), 235–7.
5. S. Smiles, *Autobiography* (1905), 66.
6. Ibid., 78–9.
7. Ibid., 72.
8. Ibid., 103.
9. Ibid., 103–4.
10. Ibid., 131–3.
11. Ibid., 127.
12. W. S. Shepperson, *British Emigration to North America*, Oxford: Blackwell (1957), 259.
13. J. McAskill, 'The Chartist Land Plan', in A. Briggs (ed.), *Chartist Studies*, London: Macmillan (1959), 304–41.
14. S. Smiles, *History of Ireland* (1844), 47, 55, 65, 257, 340, 427, 481, 484.
15. H. House, *The Dickens World*, London: Oxford University Press (1941), 83.
16. S. Smiles, *Self-Help*, 210.
17. Ibid., 22.
18. Ibid., 3–4.
19. A. Calder in Open University Course A312, *The Nineteenth Century Novel and Its Legacy*, Milton Keynes (1982), Unit 11, 26–32 and Unit 26, 27–32.

20. S. Smiles, *Self-Help*, 7.

21. Ibid., 21, 164–5, 330–31.

22. J. Ridley, *Lord Palmerston*, London: Constable (1970), 441.

23. S. Smiles, *Self-Help*.

24. S. Smiles, *Self-Help* (Penguin edition, abridged by G. Bull, 1986). Keith Joseph's introduction, while extolling Smiles' 'understanding' of the 'entrepreneurial function', does allow that for Smiles 'self culture' was its own reward.

11. 'A Mania for Self-Reliance': Grassic Gibbon's *Scots Quair*

1. Lewis Grassic Gibbon and Hugh MacDiarmid, *Scottish Scene*, London: Jarrolds (1934), 295.

2. Roy Johnson however approves of Young Ewan telling a 'big lie' for political ends, in his militant essay, 'Lewis Grassic Gibbon and *A Scots Quair*', in *The 1930s: A Challenge to Orthodoxy*, edited by John Lucas, Hassocks: Harvester, (1978), 55.

3. *Grey Granite*, London: Pan (1973), 119.

4. See Graham Trengove, 'Who is You? Grammar and Grassic Gibbon', *Scottish Literary Journal*, vol. 2, no. 1 (1975), 47–61. Quotations from *Sunset Song*, London: Longman (1971), 30–31.

5. See J. K. A. Thomaneck, '*A Scots Quair* in East Germany', *Scottish Literary Journal*, vol. 3, no. 1 (1976), 65.

6. Ian S. Munro, *Leslie Mitchell: Lewis Grassic Gibbon*, Edinburgh: Oliver and Boyd (1966), 151.

7. Gibbon and MacDiarmid, op. cit., 154.

8. Ibid., 19–36, 139.

9. John Stevenson and Chris Cook, *The Slump*, London: Quartet (1979), 5, 286.

10. Peter Keating, 'A Miners' Library', *Times Literary Supplement*, 6 January 1976, 16–17.

11. 'Inside every engineering craftsman lay the ideal type, derived from the old millwright, of the man who is hired to do a job, and to do it from start to finish without interference from his employer.' James Hinton, *The First Shop Stewards Movement*, London: Allen and Unwin (1973), 96.

12. Arthur Marwick, *The Deluge*, London: Bodley Head (1965), 70, calls Kirkwood 'the prototype of the hard-headed Lowland Scot'. My quotations from Kirkwood and Churchill come from David Kirkwood, *My Life of Revolt*, London: Harrap (1935), vi, 11. On 101, writing about the Munitions of War Act of 1915, Kirkwood exclaims, 'I was happy in Beardmore's as a free man. I resented being in Beardmore's as a slave.'

13. Kurt Wittig, *The Scottish Tradition in Literature*, Edinburgh: Oliver and Boyd (1958), 330–3.

14. Francis R. Hart, *The Scottish Novel*, London: Murray (1978), 233–41.

15. David Craig, *Scottish Literature and the Scottish People*, London: Chatto and Windus (1961), 292; David Craig, 'Novels of Peasant Crisis', *Journal of Peasant Studies*, vol. 2, no. 1 (1974), 52–3.
16. Cairns Craig, 'The Body in the Kitbag: History and the Scottish Novel', *Cencrastus*, no. 1 (1979), 18–22.
17. Munro, op. cit., 176.
18. Gibbon and MacDiarmid, op. cit., 146.
19. Raymond Williams, *The Country and the City*, London: Chatto and Windus (1973), 268–71.
20. Ian Carter, 'The Peasantry of Northeast Scotland', *Journal of Peasant Studies*, vol. 3 (1975–6), 151–91.
21. See Sheila Rowbotham, Lynne Segal and Hilary Wainwright, *Beyond the Fragments: Feminism and the Making of Socialism*, London: Merlin (1979).

12. Miss Jean Brodie and Kaledonian Klan

1. Muriel Spark, *The Prime of Miss Jean Brodie*, Harmondsworth: Penguin (1965), 36.
2. Ibid., 120.
3. Ibid., 85.
4. Ibid.
5. S. Bruce, *No Pope of Rome: Anti-Catholicism in Modern Scotland*, Edinburgh: Mainstream (1985), 82–101.
6. Spark, op. cit., 97.
7. Spark's *Curriculum Vitae*, London: Constable (1992), all we have of her memoirs so far, sheds no light on this matter.
8. K. Miller (ed.), *Memoirs of a Modern Scotland*, London: Faber (1970), 151–3.
9. Spark, op. cit., 109.
10. Ibid., 85.

13. Labour and Scotland

1. C. Ponting, *Breach of Promise: Labour in Power, 1964–1970*, London: Hamish Hamilton (1989).
2. G. Brown, *Maxton*, Edinburgh: Mainstream (1986), 241, 309, 315.
3. Ponting, op. cit., 391–3.
4. Ibid., 404.
5. Ibid., 305–6.
6. Ibid., 332–3, 217.
7. Ibid., 56.
8. Ibid., 59.
9. Ibid., 280.

10. I. Donnachie, C. Harvie and I. S. Wood (eds.), *Forward! Labour Politics in Scotland, 1888–1988*, Edinburgh: Polygon (1989).
11. Ibid., 84–98.

14. Edwin Muir

1. P. Butter (ed.), *The Complete Poems of Edwin Muir*, Aberdeen: Association for Scottish Literary Studies (1991).

15. Naomi Mitchison

1. J. Benton, *Naomi Mitchison: A Biography*, London: Pandora (1990).

16. Morganmania

1. Edwin Morgan, *Collected Poems*, Manchester: Carcanet (1990).
2. Edwin Morgan, *Crossing the Border: Essays on Scottish Literature*, Manchester: Carcanet (1990).
3. Robert Crawford and Hamish Whyte (eds.), *About Edwin Morgan*, Edinburgh: Edinburgh University Press (1990).
4. Edwin Morgan, *Nothing Not Giving Messages: Reflections on His Work and Life*, Edinburgh: Polygon (1990).

18. Karl Miller

1. K. Miller, *Authors: Studies in Literary History*, London: Oxford University Press (1989).
2. K. Miller, *Memoirs of a Modern Scotland*, London: Faber (1970).
3. K. Miller, *Cockburn's Millennium*, London: Duckworth (1975).
4. *Doubles: Studies in Literary History*, Oxford: Oxford University Press (1983).
5. I. Hamilton (ed.), *The Faber Book of Soccer*, London: Faber (1992).
6. N. Tredell, 'Karl Miller in conversation', *PN Review*, vol. 17, no. 2 (1990), 30–37.

19. Kenneth White's Orient

1. K. White, *Pilgrim of the Void: Travels in South-East Asia and the North Pacific*, Edinburgh: Mainstream (1992).

20. Alasdair Gray's *Lanark*

1. A. Gray, *Lanark*, Edinburgh: Canongate (1981); *Unlikely Stories Mostly*, Edinburgh: Canongate (1983).
2. W. Scott, 'General Preface, 1829', in *Waverley*, ed., A. Hook, Harmondsworth: Penguin (1972), 523.
3. A. Gray, *1982 Janine*, London: Cape (1984).

21. Devolving English Literature

1. R. Crawford, *Devolving English Literature*, Oxford: Oxford University Press (1992), 139.
2. R. Smith, *A Night at the Opera*, Erin (Ont.): Porcupine's Quill, (1992).

22. Jackie Kay's *Adoption Papers*

1. J. Kay, *The Adoption Papers*, Newcastle: Bloodaxe (1991).
2. In Sulter's second book *Zabat: Poetics of a Family Tree – Poems, 1986–1989*, Hebden Bridge: Urban Fox (1989), there is also just one poem voiced in Scots and no other acknowledgement of Scottish origins.

23. Losing the Traverse?

1. J. McMillan, *The Traverse Theatre Story*, London: Methuen (1988).

24. Workers' Culture – Popular Culture – Defining our Terms

1. T. Nairn, *The Break-Up of Britain: Crisis and Neo-Nationalism*, London: New Left Books (1977), 162.
2. *The DC Thomson Bumper Fun Book*, Edinburgh: Paul Harris (1977), 26–7.
3. C. McArthur (ed.), *Scotch Reels: Scotland in Cinema and Television*, London: British Film Institute (1982), 2.
4. W. Knox (ed.), *Scottish Labour Leaders, 1918–1939: A Biographical Dictionary*, Edinburgh: Mainstream (1984), 39.
5. D. Allen, 'Workers Films', in McArthur, op. cit., 93–6.
6. J. Hill, '. . . Some Notes on *The Gorbals Story*', in McArthur, op. cit., 100–111.
7. R. Bromley, *Lost Narratives*, London: Routledge (1988).
8. A. Cameron, *Scot-Free: New Scottish Plays*, London: Nick Hern (1990) ix–xi, xvii.

Index

Index

Index